The Innovation Imperative
for Developing East Asia

WORLD BANK EAST ASIA AND PACIFIC REGIONAL REPORTS

Known for their economic success and dynamism, countries in the East Asia and Pacific region must tackle an increasingly complex set of challenges to continue on a path of sustainable development. Learning from others within the region and beyond can help identify what works, what doesn't, and why, in the search for practical solutions to these challenges. This regional flagship series presents analyses of issues relevant to the region, drawing on the global knowledge and experience of the World Bank and its partners. The series aims to inform public discussion, policy formulation, and development practitioners' actions to turn challenges into opportunities.

TITLES IN THE SERIES

The Innovation Imperative for Developing East Asia

A Resurgent East Asia: Navigating a Changing World

Growing Smarter: Learning and Equitable Development in East Asia and Pacific

Riding the Wave: An East Asian Miracle for the 21st Century

Live Long and Prosper: Aging in East Asia and Pacific

East Asia Pacific at Work: Employment, Enterprise, and Well-Being

Toward Gender Equality in East Asia and the Pacific: A Companion to the World Development Report

Putting Higher Education to Work: Skills and Research for Growth in East Asia

All books in this series are available for free at https://openknowledge.worldbank.org /handle/10986/2147.

World Bank East Asia and Pacific Regional Report

The Innovation Imperative for Developing East Asia

Xavier Cirera
Andrew D. Mason
Francesca de Nicola
Smita Kuriakose
Davide S. Mare
Trang Thu Tran

ISBN (paper): 978-1-4648-1606-2
ISBN (electronic): 978-1-4648-1656-7
DOI: 10.1596/978-1-4648-1606-2

Cover and interior design: Bill Pragluski, Critical Stages, LLC.

Library of Congress Control Number: 2021931560

Contents

Boxes

Figures

Foreword

The remarkable economic rise of East Asia over the past 50 years is well known. The track records of these economies in sustaining rapid growth and poverty reduction were well documented in two preceding volumes of this regional series, *Riding the Wave: An East Asian Miracle for the 21st Century* (2018) and *A Resurgent East Asia: Navigating a Changing World* (2019).

Middle-income countries in the region aspire still higher but now face unprecedented challenges to their economic successes. Productivity growth has declined since the Global Financial Crisis. Changes in the global trade environment and technological advances are challenging the region's traditional growth engine: export-oriented manufacturing. Climate change and, more recently, the COVID-19 pandemic have increased the urgency of transitioning to new modes of production that are more environmentally friendly, more flexible, more digitally integrated, and more connected to consumers.

Can the region's past model for success continue to deliver rapid future gains? Not without the advances and rewards of innovation. To that end, this latest volume in the series—*The Innovation Imperative for Developing East Asia*—will deepen policy makers' understanding of the critical role for innovation in the region's future growth and development and will lay out a policy agenda for innovation-led growth.

For middle-income countries with widely varying institutional, technological, and firm-level capacities, "innovation" entails not only the *invention* of new products and processes at the Industry 4.0 frontier but also the *diffusion* and *adoption* of existing technologies or practices. And these more basic forms of innovation can have big payoffs. This is where *The Innovation Imperative* makes its most practical and meaningful contribution: as a guide to tailoring innovation-enabling reforms in country-specific, capacity-specific ways.

Such guidance is sorely needed. Despite the significant promise of innovation—and some high-profile success stories—most countries in developing East Asia (except China) underperform on several key indicators of innovation, including spending on research and development (R&D) and patents, as well as the adoption and use of new technologies. In fact, only a small share of the region's firms currently engage in any type of innovation activity.

Why is this? New survey evidence presented in this report reveals that the region's firms face several barriers to adopting new technologies that could transform their productivity. They lack adequate information on these technologies and face high uncertainty about the returns to their use. They often lack the capacity to innovate—due to inadequate management capabilities and workforce skills. And they frequently lack access to external financing for technology adoption or broader innovation projects. Importantly, countries' innovation policies and institutions are also often misaligned with firms' capabilities and needs.

So what will it take to spur greater innovation in developing East Asia? As this report makes clear, the region's policy makers must reorient innovation policy to focus on incentivizing a large mass of firms to simply start innovating. It is the broad *adoption* and *diffusion* of existing technologies, not only invention of new ones, that will determine the pace of economic and productivity growth in the region.

By fostering greater innovation in this way, countries in developing East Asia will be able to surmount the array of challenges they now face and reinvigorate growth and development for a better future.

Victoria Kwakwa
Regional Vice President
East Asia and Pacific Region
The World Bank

Acknowledgments

This report is a joint product of the Office of the Chief Economist, East Asia and Pacific Region, and the Finance, Competitiveness, and Innovation (FCI) Global Practice of the World Bank. It was authored by Xavier Cirera, Andrew D. Mason, Francesca de Nicola, Smita Kuriakose, Davide S. Mare, and Trang Thu Tran, under the supervision of Aaditya Mattoo, chief economist, East Asia and Pacific; and Denis Medvedev, practice manager, FCI; with the guidance of Victoria Kwakwa, regional vice president, East Asia and Pacific.

The report builds on the work of a larger team that included Pinyi Chen, Sarah Hebous, Ergys Islamaj, Sachiko Kataoka, Faruk Miguel Liriano, Fabiola Saavedra, Dea Tusha, and Pluvia Zuñiga. Valuable contributions were also made by Anna Alejo, Cha Crisostomo, Martina Ferracane, Jaime Frias, Jin Lee, Kevin Macdonald, Koji Miyamoto, Son Nguyen Hoai, Albert Park, Prerna Rakheja, Miguel Sarzosa, Haris Tiew, Erik van der Marel, and Wenshi Xuan. Cecile Wodon provided invaluable administrative and logistical assistance.

The team benefited from helpful suggestions from colleagues both within and outside the World Bank Group. Particular thanks to Asya Akhlaque, Irina Astrakhan, Mary Hallward-Driemeier, Keun Lee (Seoul National University), Toby Linden, Rajah Rasiah (University of Malaya), and Cecile Thioro Niang for serving as peer reviewers. Helpful comments and inputs were also received from Zubair Khurshid Bhatti, Alejandro Cedeno, Paulo Correa, Souleymane Coulibaly, Philippe de Meneval, Ousmane Dione, Pierre Graftieaux, Caren Grown, Birgit Hansl, Vera Kehayova, Michel Kerf, Martin Melecky, Martin Raiser, Siddharth Sharma, Sudhir Shetty, Cao Thu Anh, Georgia Wallen, and Xiaoqing Yu. The team also appreciates the feedback provided by the participants in a December 2019 Authors' Workshop.

About the Authors

Xavier Cirera is a senior economist in the Finance, Competitiveness, and Innovation (FCI) Global Practice of the World Bank. His work focuses on innovation and entrepreneurship. He has led the evaluation of innovation policies, including through the development of public expenditure reviews in science, technology, and innovation implemented in Brazil, Chile, Colombia, Ukraine, and Vietnam. He is the coauthor of *The Innovation Paradox: Developing-Country Capabilities and the Unrealized Promise of Technological Catch-Up* and *A Practitioner's Guide to Innovation Policy: Instruments to Build Firm Capabilities and Accelerate Technological Catch-Up in Developing Countries*. His most recent work focuses on the measurement and impact of technology adoption and diffusion. Before joining the World Bank, he served as a research fellow at the Institute of Development Studies at the University of Sussex. He holds a doctorate in economics from the University of Sussex.

Andrew D. Mason is lead economist in the Office of the Chief Economist, East Asia and Pacific Region, of the World Bank. He has carried out policy research on a range of issues, including poverty, social protection, labor, skills, and gender equality. He is coauthor of several World Bank flagship reports, including *A Resurgent East Asia: Navigating a Changing World; Toward Gender Equality in East Asia and the Pacific;* and *Informality: Exit and Exclusion;* as well as the World Bank Policy Research Report, *Engendering Development: Through Gender Equality in Rights, Resources, and Voice.* He has also been an affiliated professor at the Georgetown Public Policy Institute of Georgetown University. He holds a doctorate in applied economics from Stanford University and a master's degree in public policy from Harvard University.

Francesca de Nicola is a senior economist in the Office of the Chief Economist, East Asia and Pacific Region, of the World Bank. She has led operations and analytical work to support the development of the private sector and financial markets in Africa and Eastern Europe. Her research interests span various areas of development economics, including productivity, the role of political connections, and weather insurance. She has published in leading journals, including the *Journal of Development Economics, Quantitative*

Economics, and *Energy Economics.* She holds a doctorate in economics from the Johns Hopkins University.

Smita Kuriakose is a senior economist in the FCI Global Practice of the World Bank. Currently based in Kuala Lumpur, she manages the World Bank's engagement on private sector development, innovation, and entrepreneurship policy in Malaysia. Her work has covered more than 20 countries across Africa, East Asia and Pacific, and Europe and Central Asia. She has led regional and country flagship publications on innovation and entrepreneurship issues in addition to leading multisectoral operations. She holds graduate degrees in economics from the University of Maryland and from the Delhi School of Economics.

Davide S. Mare is a researcher at the World Bank and honorary lecturer at the University of Edinburgh Business School. His main research interests lie in banking, focusing on bankruptcy prediction, credit risk measurement, competition, and firm finance. His work has appeared in leading international journals, including the *European*

Journal of Operational Research and the *Journal of Financial Stability*, as well as in the World Bank's *Global Financial Development Report 2019/2020: Bank Regulation and Supervision a Decade after the Global Financial Crisis*. Before joining the World Bank, he was a lecturer (assistant professor) in business economics at the University of Edinburgh Business School and a financial consultant for large European banks. He holds a doctorate in banking and finance from the University of Rome Tor Vergata.

Trang Thu Tran is a senior economist in the FCI Global Practice of the World Bank. She is interested in research on firms, with experience working on topics spanning firm dynamics, entrepreneurship and innovation policy, international investment, and business regulations. Her most recent coauthored work includes the World Bank Group's flagship reports, *Making It Big: Why Developing Countries Need More Large Firms* and the *Global Investment Competitiveness Report 2019/2020: Rebuilding Investor Confidence in Times of Uncertainty*. She is an applied microeconomist with a doctorate from the University of Maryland.

Abbreviations

A*STAR	Agency for Science, Technology, and Research
AI	artificial intelligence
AIM	Agensi Inovasi Malaysia
ALL	Adult Literacy and Life Skills
CEES	China Employer-Employee Survey
DARPA	Defense Advanced Research Projects Agency
EISS	Epidemic Investigation Support System
ESIS	Enterprise Survey on Innovation and Skills
EU	European Union
FAT	Firm-level Adoption of Technology (survey)
FDI	foreign direct investment
fintech	financial technology
FTT	forced technology transfer
GBF	general business functions
GDP	gross domestic product
GII	Global Innovation Index
GIN	global innovation network
GPT	general purpose technology
GVC	global value chain
HEI	higher education institution
HR	human resources
IALS	International Adult Literacy and Life Skills
ICT	information and communication technology
IJV	international joint venture
IoT	internet of things
IP	intellectual property
IPO	initial public offering
IPR	intellectual property right(s)
IRAP	Industrial Research Assistance Program
IT	information technology
ITA	industrial technology adviser

M&E	monitoring and evaluation
MNE	multinational enterprise
MSMEs	micro, small, and medium enterprises
NIS	national innovation system
NIST	National Institute of Standards and Technology
NQI	national quality infrastructure
NRF	National Research Foundation
OECD	Organisation for Economic Co-operation and Development
PA	performance-based agreement
PE	performance evaluation
PER	policy effectiveness review
PIAAC	Programme for the International Assessment of Adult Competencies
PISA	Programme for International Student Assessment
PRO	public research organization
R&D	research and development
RC	research center
S&T	science and technology
SBIR	Small Business Innovation Research
SMEs	small and medium enterprises
SOE	state-owned enterprise
STEM	science, technology, engineering, and mathematics
STEP	Skills Toward Employability and Productivity
STI	science, technology, and innovation
TES	technology extension services
TFP	total factor productivity
TiVA	Trade in Value Added
TRIPs Agreement	Trade-Related Aspects of Intellectual Property Rights
TTO	technology transfer office
TVET	technical and vocational education and training
VC	venture capital(ist)
WBES	World Bank Enterprise Survey
WMS	World Management Survey
WTO	World Trade Organization

Overview

Introduction

Countries in developing East Asia have undergone significant economic transformation, but the region now faces an array of challenges in sustaining growth

East Asia's economic success over the past 50 years has been transformative. High rates of growth have propelled countries in the region from low-income to middle-income, and even in a few cases, to high-income status. An approach that has become known as the "East Asian development model"—a combination of policies that fostered outward-oriented, labor-intensive sectors growth; investments in basic human capital; and sound economic governance—has been instrumental in moving hundreds of millions of people out of poverty and into economic security.

Despite their past successes, the region's middle-income countries now face an array of challenges as they strive to continue their economic progress: First, productivity growth has declined since the 2008–09 Global Financial Crisis. This, and rapid population aging in several countries, is putting pressure on the region's growth prospects, narrowing the opportunities for reaping demographic dividends. Second, the slowing of global goods trade, uncertainty about the future of the global trading system, and rapid changes in technology are all challenging a key engine of growth in the region: export-oriented manufacturing. Third, the COVID-19 pandemic, together with ongoing climate change, are increasing economic vulnerability and highlighting a pressing need for new modes of production in the region.

These forces, alone and together, raise questions about whether the model that has driven the region's economic success in the past can continue to deliver rapid growth and development in the future.

Innovation is increasingly important to future growth

Recent studies have highlighted the critical role that innovation must play in developing East Asia if the region's countries are to maintain or increase productivity growth in a rapidly changing and highly uncertain global economic environment (Mason and Shetty 2019; World Bank and DRC 2019). Reinforcing the case for more innovation-led growth is a significant global literature showing strong links between innovation and productivity at the macro- and microeconomic levels (Cirera and Maloney 2017; Comin and Hobijn 2010; Griliches 1998; Hall 2011; Mohnen and Hall 2013; Solow 1957).

Against this background, this report seeks to deepen policy makers' understanding of the critical role for innovation in the future growth and development of developing East Asia.[1] To achieve this, the report examines the region's key innovation challenges, assesses its state of innovation, and analyzes the main constraints firms face in effectively pursuing innovation. The report then examines the policies and institutions needed to enable greater innovation and lays out an agenda for action aimed at spurring innovation-led growth in the region.

The report emphasizes the importance for the region of effectively using technologies that are already available in high-income economies as a means of raising productivity and addressing economic and societal challenges. For this reason, the report adopts a broad definition of innovation that encompasses *both* innovation as "invention" of new products and processes at the knowledge frontier *and* as "diffusion and adoption" of existing technologies and practices that enable firms to undertake new and more effective modes of production (box O.1).

BOX O.1   Defining innovation

The report adopts a broad view of innovation as the accumulation of knowledge and implementation of new ideas. Specifically, following the *Oslo Manual 2018*, a "business innovation" is defined as a "new or improved product or business process (or combination thereof) that differs significantly from the firm's previous products or business processes and that has been introduced on the market or brought into use by the firm" (OECD and Eurostat 2018, 20). The report considers innovation defined both as "invention" or "discovery" (that is, those developments that push the technological frontier) *and* as "diffusion" or "adoption" of existing technologies and practices that lead firms to novel ways of producing or acting. The latter definition is pertinent to most of the firms operating in developing East Asia.

An innovation may be either technological or nontechnological. Specifically, the *Oslo Manual 2018* defines the following two main types of innovations (OECD and Eurostat 2018, 21):

• A *product innovation* is "a new or improved good or service that differs significantly from the firm's previous goods or services and that has been introduced on the market." This includes the addition of either new functions or improvements to existing functions or user utility. "Relevant functional characteristics include quality, technical specifications, reliability, durability, economic efficiency during use, affordability, convenience, usability, and user friendliness" (OECD and Eurostat 2018, 71).

• A *business process innovation* is "a new or improved business process for one or more business functions that differs significantly from the firm's previous business processes and that has been brought into use by the firm." The *Oslo Manual 2018* lists the six functional categories to identify and distinguish between types of business process innovations (OECD and Eurostat 2018, 73):

  ▪ Innovative methods for manufacturing products or offering services
  ▪ Innovations in distribution and logistics
  ▪ Innovations in marketing and sales activities
  ▪ Innovations in the provision and maintenance of information and communication systems
  ▪ Innovations in administration and management
  ▪ Innovations in product and business process development.

Source: Adapted from OECD and Eurostat 2018.

The innovation imperative for developing East Asia

Several economic forces are driving an imperative for a more innovation-led growth model in developing East Asia.

Productivity remains relatively low in developing East Asia—and productivity growth has declined since the Global Financial Crisis

Despite their remarkable growth performance, countries in developing East Asia still face important productivity challenges. Productivity—whether measured in terms of labor productivity (output per worker) or as total factor productivity (TFP, a measure of economic efficiency)—has been rising over time, although it remains well below the productivity frontier, defined as the productivity level in the United States. Even in Malaysia, whose productivity is the highest in developing East Asia, labor productivity was only about 42 percent, and TFP about 62 percent, of levels in the United States in 2017. Although productivity generally increases as countries develop, TFP in most developing East Asian countries is below what would be predicted on the basis of their gross domestic product (GDP) per capita (figure O.1).

Productivity growth has slowed worldwide since the Global Financial Crisis, and developing East Asia has not been immune. Indeed, the region has experienced the second steepest slowdown in labor productivity growth of all emerging market and developing regions since the Global Financial Crisis (World Bank 2020). While labor productivity growth has declined across the region, the decline has been particularly pronounced in China (figure O.2). A decomposition of labor productivity growth shows that the slowdown largely reflects weaker TFP growth.

Changes in global trade and technologies are challenging the region's main engine of growth: export-oriented manufacturing

The slowing of global goods trade and ambiguity about the future of the global trading system pose risks to a development model that has effectively used trade, foreign direct investment (FDI), and integration into global value chains (GVCs) as critical channels for growth. Furthermore, a new technological revolution—Industry 4.0—poses a risk of disrupting existing production structures as it moves toward more flexible manufacturing and customization and increases the importance of proximity to customers. These technological advances could potentially shorten GVCs or result in the reshoring of production systems that have been central in fueling growth in developing East Asian countries.

The COVID-19 pandemic and other shocks, including climate change, are accelerating the need for new modes of production

The COVID-19 pandemic
The COVID-19 pandemic has underscored the importance of innovation as policy makers and private firms have rushed to adopt or develop technologies to address both the health and the economic effects of the outbreak. This effort has included, among other things, the application of digital mobile technologies to provide real-time information about the spread of the virus and support social distancing; drone technologies for such applications as aerial disinfection, contactless transportation of medical supplies, and consumer deliveries; and advanced biomedical technologies and artificial intelligence (AI) to develop testing, vaccines, and treatments for the virus.[2]

Importantly, the COVID-19 pandemic is a shock to GDP not seen for decades in the region—one that may have long-lasting

FIGURE O.1   **Total factor productivity in most developing East Asian countries is below what would be predicted based on their GDP per capita**

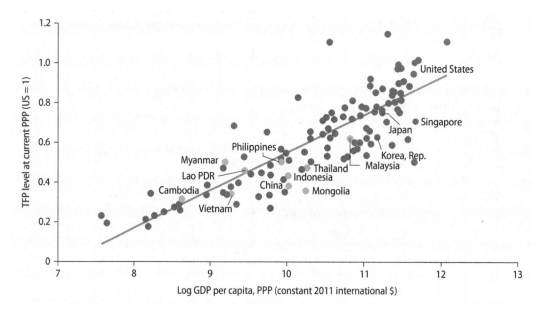

Source: World Bank elaboration, based on Penn World Table (PWT) version 9.1 and Asian Productivity Organization (APO) Database 2019, version 2 (https://www.apo-tokyo.org/wedo/productivity-measurement/).
Note: Data are from 2017. Countries in light blue designate the 10 "developing East Asia" countries studied in this report. Total factor productivity (TFP) is measured in purchasing power parity (PPP) terms relative to the United States (1.0). TFP series are calculated by the PWT team, except for Cambodia, Myanmar, and Vietnam, which are estimated through the methodology of Feenstra, Inklaar, and Timmer (2015), using data from PWT (version 9.1) and labor share estimates from the APO Database 2019 (version 2). GDP = gross domestic product; PPP = purchasing power parity; TFP = total factor productivity.

FIGURE O.2   **Labor productivity and TFP growth have declined in developing East Asia since the Global Financial Crisis**

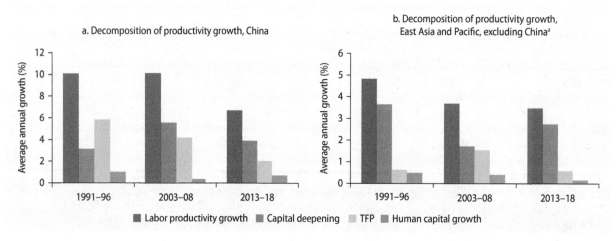

Sources: Conference Board (CB), Asian Productivity Organization (APO) Database 2019, version 2 (https://www.apo-tokyo.org/wedo/productivity-measurement/); and Penn World Table (PWT) version 9.1 data; van der Eng (2009); World Development Indicators database; and World Bank calculations.
Note: Labor productivity is defined as GDP per worker. PWT data were used as the baseline. When PWT (version 9.1) data were not available, the APO Database 2019 (version 2) was used. Conference Board data were used for 2018. GDP = gross domestic product; TFP = total factor productivity.
a. Panel b shows weighted averages calculated using GDP weights at 2010 prices. Countries included are Cambodia, Indonesia, Lao PDR, Malaysia, Mongolia, Myanmar, the Philippines, Thailand, and Vietnam. For Indonesia, TFP growth was calculated by the World Bank, extending data from van der Eng (2009).

effects. So large a shock, affecting both demand and supply, has highlighted the need for more flexible management and production processes, both to accommodate restrictions due to social-distance measures and to prepare for what may be very different economies in the post–COVID-19 era. Production processes will be more automated, digitally integrated, and connected to consumers.

One challenge for policy makers, however, is that the pandemic may have conflicting effects on each of the two dimensions of innovation: invention and diffusion. Regarding *invention*, the pandemic is boosting research and development (R&D) on tests, vaccines, and treatment to combat the disease. This is likely to have positive spillovers for broader scientific and medical research in areas such as biotechnology. At the same time, the social distancing needed to contain the disease has impeded scientific research *not* related to COVID-19, by shutting down laboratories and durably disrupting experiments.

As for *diffusion*, adapting to social distancing has boosted firms' and households' demand for technologies supporting digital communication, conveyance, and commerce that will likely be used well beyond the pandemic. However, the crisis-induced economic contraction and uncertainty are inhibiting investments in both invention and diffusion in a variety of other areas by cutting resources and dampening expected returns. Policy makers will thus need to find ways to accelerate the technological transformation of their economies while managing these tensions.

Climate change
Similarly, climate change is challenging traditional approaches to production and growth. Regarding mitigation, it is imperative to have cleaner, more energy-efficient production that reduces carbon emissions. As for adaptation, temperatures will increase significantly in developing East Asia. Warming is already causing severe weather events more frequently: heat waves, droughts, flooding, wildfires, and hurricanes. East and Southeast Asian countries are among those likely to be the hardest hit as the climate warms.

According to the Global Climate Risk Index 2020, four Southeast Asian countries—Myanmar, the Philippines, Thailand, and Vietnam—were among the 10 countries most affected by extreme weather events between 1999 and 2018 (Eckstein et al. 2019). Moreover, the continued reliance of Southeast Asian countries on agriculture and the concentration of populations in coastal regions exacerbate their vulnerability. Many major coastal cities are seriously imperiled, including Shanghai and Tianjin, China; Jakarta, Indonesia; Ho Chi Minh City, Vietnam; and Bangkok, Thailand. These changes demand urgent technological solutions, whether to ensure that agricultural production is sustainable or to enable safe and productive factory environments at higher temperatures.

To sustain high economic performance in the face of these challenges, the region's countries must move toward a more innovation-led growth model

To address all these challenges will demand that societies become more innovative. Countries in developing East Asia must find new and more effective ways to increase productivity growth as they seek to build on past economic success and move progressively from middle- to high-income status. Indeed, their high-income neighbors—Japan, the Republic of Korea, and Singapore—have all used innovation as a vehicle to improve efficiency and boost their incomes with great success.

The narrowing of productivity and technological gaps with high-income economies could help developing East Asian countries to address trade challenges, including threats of reshoring, by increasing their competitiveness and upgrading their participation in GVCs. Similarly, an effective response to the COVID-19 pandemic and the risk of other health shocks requires strong research and innovation fundamentals to address and monitor health impacts, as well as more innovative, automated, and digitally integrated business models. Finally, the risks and costs of climate change for the region's economies and societies demand more innovation and adoption of new technologies for both adaptation and mitigation.

The state of innovation in developing East Asia

Interest in innovation among the region's policy makers has peaked recently with the rise of digital technologies. Indeed, high-profile accomplishments by private sector actors—in e-commerce, digital financial technology (fintech), ridesharing, and mobile app-enabled service delivery—have captured the imaginations of policy makers, the media, and citizens alike. Enterprises in the digital space, like the Chinese multinational technology company Alibaba and the ride-hailing services Grab and Go-Jek in Southeast Asia, have become household names.

Although the achievements of high-performing "unicorns" are important and noteworthy, realizing the economic promise of innovation will require a broad swath of firms across different sectors of the region's economies to engage in innovation activities. But just how well are developing East Asian countries performing overall on innovation?

The region has experienced some important innovation-related successes

Data suggest that developing East Asia has registered some important successes with respect to innovation. Recent data on the spatial density of patents filed under the Patent Cooperation Treaty (PCT) of the World Intellectual Property Organization (WIPO) indicate a growing number of innovation clusters in the region, most notably in China (Bergquist, Fink, and Raffo 2017; Dutta, Lanvin, and Wunsch-Vincent 2019).

Looking more broadly across the region, data indicate that the region's export-oriented growth model has enabled most countries to participate in more sophisticated forms of manufacturing trade over time. Cross-country data show, for example, that most developing East Asian countries perform at or above what would be predicted from their per capita income levels with respect to both high-tech *imports* (figure O.3, panel a) and high-tech *exports* (figure O.3, panel b).

FIGURE O.3   Several developing East Asian countries are significant participants in the global value chains for high-tech products

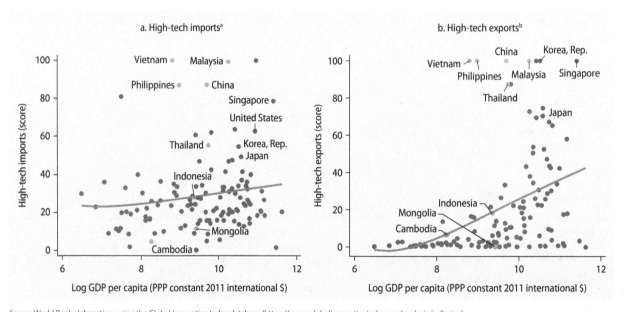

Source: World Bank elaboration, using the Global Innovation Index database (https://www.globalinnovationindex.org/analysis-indicator).
Note: High-tech export and import indicators include technical products with high research and development (R&D) intensity, as defined and classified by Eurostat, the statistical office of the European Union. "Developing East Asia" refers to the 10 middle-income countries covered in this study (designated in light blue): Cambodia, China, Indonesia, Lao PDR, Malaysia, Mongolia, Myanmar, the Philippines, Thailand, and Vietnam. The figure excludes Lao PDR and Myanmar, for which no recent data exist. GDP = gross domestic product; PPP = purchasing power parity.
a. The high-tech imports indicator measures high-tech imports as a percentage of total trade.
b. The high-tech exports indicator is defined by high-tech exports minus re-exports as a percentage of total trade.

Although much of the region's participation in this trade began with less-sophisticated components and assembly, these measures reflect the increased adoption of global technologies and production processes over time through FDI, creation of joint ventures, and participation in trade and GVCs. For example, between 2000 and 2008, the share of the domestic content of exports in electronics grew significantly in Malaysia and Thailand, as well as in industrial machinery in Indonesia and the Philippines (WTO and IDE-JETRO 2011), probably as a result of FDI to produce locally and the participation of local suppliers. Central to the region's outward-oriented manufacturing and growth strategy, these forms of international engagement have represented important opportunities for technology transfer and knowledge diffusion over the past half century.

Most countries in the region perform below predicted levels on several key indicators of innovation, however

Despite the great promise of innovation in the region—and some high-profile successes—analysis of a range of key innovation indicators suggests that countries in developing East Asia still face important challenges to fostering innovation-led growth. Most of these countries appear to underperform on several standard indicators of innovation for both *diffusion* (the adoption of existing technologies) and *discovery* (the invention of new products, processes, and technologies).

One critical input for more-basic forms of innovation, such as improving the quality of products and processes, is international certification, which gives firms access to other countries' markets. International certification has been found to contribute to firm-level productivity in several middle-income countries, including China and four Southeast Asian countries (Cirera and Maloney 2017; Escribano and Guasch 2005). However, all countries in developing East Asia except China perform below their predicted values with respect to international certification (figure O.4, panel a).

Licensing of foreign technologies—another important input for the diffusion and adoption of new technologies—is associated with higher innovation output among firms in developing East Asian countries (Iootty 2019). The region's performance regarding foreign technology licensing is more mixed: in half of the countries, a smaller share of firms obtain licenses to foreign technologies than would be expected given their countries' per capita incomes (figure O.4, panel b).

Data on the main input of *discovery* of new products and technologies, research and development (R&D), and one key proxy of *invention*, patents, show similar patterns. Most countries in the region spend less on R&D than would be expected given their per capita incomes (figure O.5, panel a). Only three countries (China, Malaysia, and Vietnam) spend at or above expected levels.

Similarly, most developing East Asian countries produce fewer patents than would be expected given their per capita incomes (figure O.5, panel b). Again, Malaysia, Vietnam, and in this case, Mongolia, perform at or near the predicted levels. China is noteworthy in that it performs significantly above expectations regarding both R&D spending and patents granted.

Similar patterns are seen with respect to the region's other innovation inputs and outputs, including several key areas related to innovation in services (despite some high-profile successes).

Developing East Asia is converging in adoption lags but diverging in intensity of technology use

Despite countries' increasing participation in high-tech value chains, new technologies do not appear to be penetrating as deeply in developing East Asia's economies as they could. Analysis of the Cross-Country Historical Adoption of Technology (CHAT) dataset on adoption and use of primarily general purpose technologies (Comin and Mestieri 2018) indicates, on the one hand, that technology

FIGURE O.4   **The share of firms with international certification is low in much of developing East Asia, and in half of the countries, fewer firms acquire licenses to foreign technology than expected given their countries' per capita incomes**

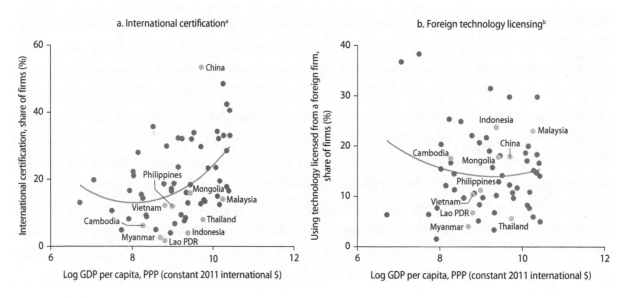

Source: World Bank elaboration, using World Bank Enterprise Survey data (most recent available years).
Note: "Developing East Asia" refers to the 10 middle-income countries covered in this study (designated in light blue): Cambodia, China, Indonesia, Lao PDR, Malaysia, Mongolia, Myanmar, the Philippines, Thailand, and Vietnam. GDP = gross domestic product; PPP = purchasing power parity.
a. International certification provides independent assurance that products or services comply with certain mutually recognized standards.
b. Foreign technology licensing includes purchase or licensing of both patented and nonpatented technologies by firms as part of their production or organizational processes.

FIGURE O.5   **Most countries in developing East Asia spend less on R&D and produce fewer patents than would be predicted by their per capita incomes**

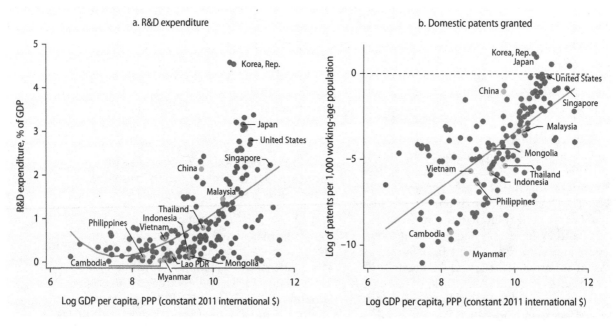

Sources: World Bank elaboration, based on 2018 data from the World Intellectual Property Organization (WIPO) Statistics Database (https://www3.wipo.int/ipstats/index.htm) and the World Development Indicators database.
Note: "Developing East Asia" refers to the 10 middle-income countries covered in this study (designated in light blue): Cambodia, China, Indonesia, Lao PDR, Malaysia, Mongolia, Myanmar, the Philippines, Thailand, and Vietnam. GDP = gross domestic product; PPP = purchasing power parity; R&D = research and development. Panel b of the figure excludes Lao PDR, for which no 2019 patent data exist.

adoption lags between developing East Asia and Organisation for Economic Co-operation and Development (OECD) countries—that is, the time between introduction of a new technology and when it is first adopted—has narrowed over time (figure O.6, panel a). On the other hand, however, differences between the region and the OECD in the "intensity of use" of new technologies—that is, how widely new technologies have been used—have increased over time (figure O.6, panel b).

Heterogeneity of innovation capabilities within countries, sectors, and firms

The aggregate performance figures presented above mask significant heterogeneity. What matters most for a country's growth and productivity performance is how rapidly technology and innovation diffuse across enterprises within a country. Without positive spillovers from sectors that perform well relative to the rest of the economy, the contribution of innovation to overall growth is limited. Within sectors, the productivity and technological divide between the leading and lagging firms in developing East Asia reflects the slow diffusion of technology. Indeed, the region shows substantial heterogeneity in the pattern of technology adoption and innovation across and within countries, sectors, and in some cases, even within firms. This heterogeneity, if persistent over time, will significantly constrain growth in the region.

Countries across the region show significant differences in innovation performance

Firm-level measures of innovation, based on World Bank Enterprise Survey data, reveal significant heterogeneity in performance across the region's countries. Firms in Indonesia, the Lao People's Democratic Republic, Myanmar, and Thailand report little innovation activity; well under half of all firms in those countries indicate that they engage in any form

of innovation-related activity (figure O.7). The data also show China as a positive outlier in the region. Close to 60 percent of Chinese firms report having a product or service innovation, and 20 percent license foreign technology. At the other end of the spectrum, less than 15 percent of firms in Myanmar and Thailand report having a product or service innovation, and a mere 5 percent have any technology licensed from foreign companies.

Innovation activity also varies widely across sectors, with less innovation in services

Although the most salient innovations portrayed in the region's popular press are examples from services sector companies (for example, Grab, Go-Jek, Alibaba, or Tencent), data from statistical sample surveys tell a different story. Measured as having implemented a product or process innovation, services sector firms in developing East Asia (and elsewhere) appear to be significantly less innovative than manufacturing firms (figure O.8). Innovation in services is key to enabling new business models and services required in the transition to Industry 4.0, but the region is lagging behind.

Most firms remain far from the technological frontier; even within firms, they vary in their use of technology across business functions

Micro evidence from the Firm-level Adoption of Technology (FAT) survey in Vietnam shows that most firms remain far from the frontier in their adoption and use of new technologies. Figure O.9 shows the most frequently used technology for different business functions, by sector, with the most sophisticated technology on top and the least sophisticated on the bottom, as follows:

- *In manufacturing*, for fabrication, most Vietnamese firms (70 percent) use operator-controlled machines, only 9 percent use computer-controlled

FIGURE O.6   **Technology adoption lags in developing East Asia are converging with those of OECD countries, but the intensity of technology use is diverging**

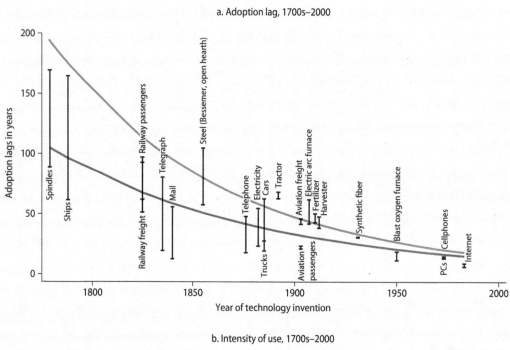

a. Adoption lag, 1700s–2000

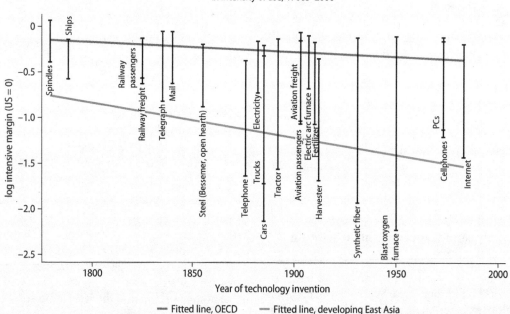

b. Intensity of use, 1700s–2000

— Fitted line, OECD   — Fitted line, developing East Asia

Source: World Bank, using country technology-level estimates from Comin and Mestieri 2018.
Note: Adoption lag (the number of years for a technology to arrive to a country after invention) and the intensive margin, or usage intensity (how widely new technologies are adopted), are both country-specific model parameters estimated structurally using the Cross-Country Historical Adoption of Technology (CHAT) database developed by Comin and Hobijn (2004). The blue and orange lines are fitted, respectively, to Organisation for Economic Co-operation and Development (OECD) and developing East Asian countries (the sample here including Cambodia, China, Indonesia, Malaysia, Mongolia, the Philippines, Thailand, and Vietnam). The bars show the median adoption lags (panel a) or intensive margins (panel b) of the two country groups for each labeled technology. PCs = personal computers.

FIGURE O.7   Developing East Asian countries vary widely in firm-level innovation activity

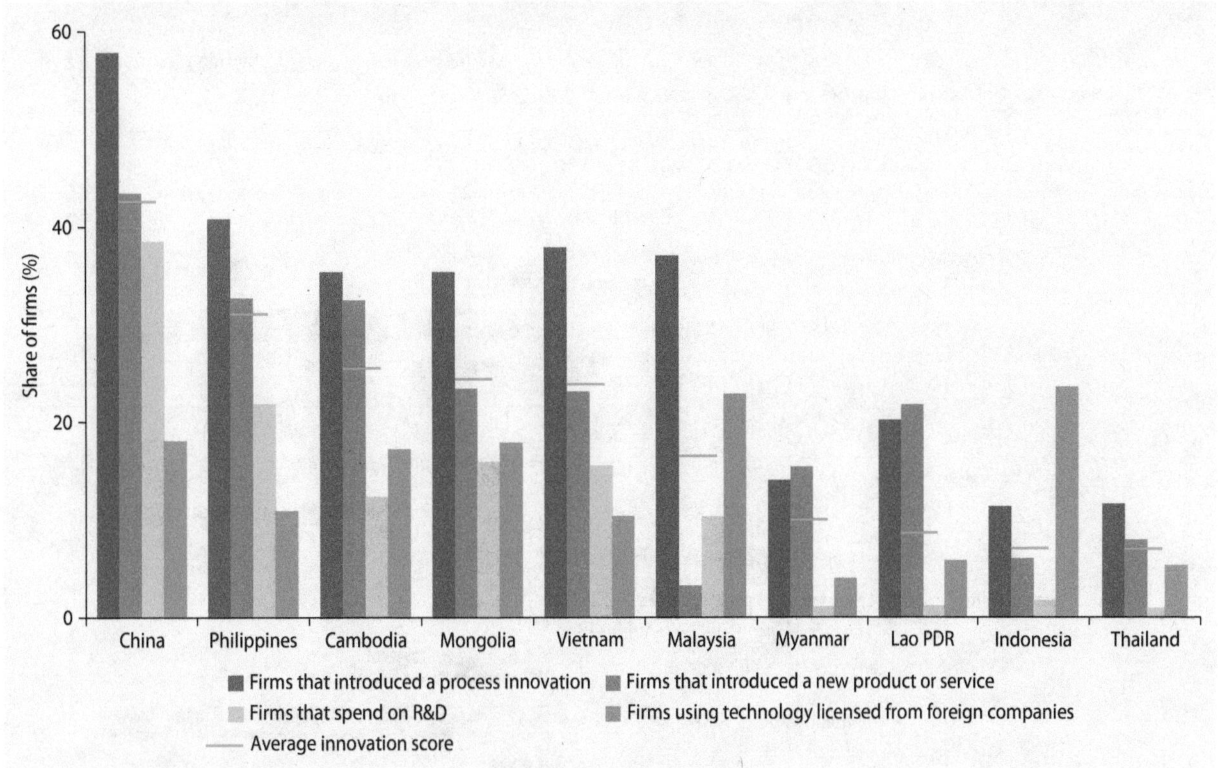

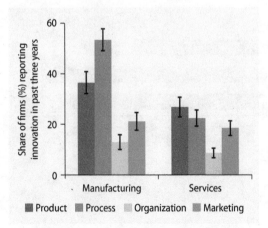

Source: World Bank calculations using latest World Bank Enterprise Survey data.
Note: The innovation score captures both innovation outputs and inputs. It is calculated as the average of the likelihood that firms have a product innovation, a process innovation, positive research and development (R&D) spending, or license technology from foreign companies.

FIGURE O.8   Manufacturing and services firms differ in rates of innovation, especially of new products or processes

Source: World Bank Enterprise Survey data, latest round.
Note: The figure shows the average share and 95 percent confidence interval in the pooled sample, accounting for country fixed effects. Data include manufacturing and services sector firms covered by the Enterprise Surveys in all 10 middle-income countries covered in this study: Cambodia, China, Indonesia, Lao PDR, Malaysia, Mongolia, Myanmar, the Philippines, Thailand, and Vietnam.

machines, and less than 1 percent use more-advanced technologies like robots, 3-D printers, or additive manufacturing (figure O.9, panel a).

- *In retail,* for inventory management, 63 percent of firms use computer databases with manual updates, 25 percent use warehouse management systems with specialized software, and only 1 percent use advanced technologies such as automated storage and retrieval systems (figure O.9, panel b).

- *In agriculture,* for weeding and pest control, almost one-third of firms still rely largely on manual techniques, and another one-third use mechanical techniques, whereas the use of automated precision agricultural techniques is almost nonexistent (figure O.9, panel c).

The radar diagrams in figure O.10 reinforce the substantial heterogeneity in the use and sophistication of technology *across* firms but also highlight the often considerable

FIGURE O.9   **The intensive use of cutting-edge technology for manufacturing, retail, and agriculture remains limited in Vietnam**

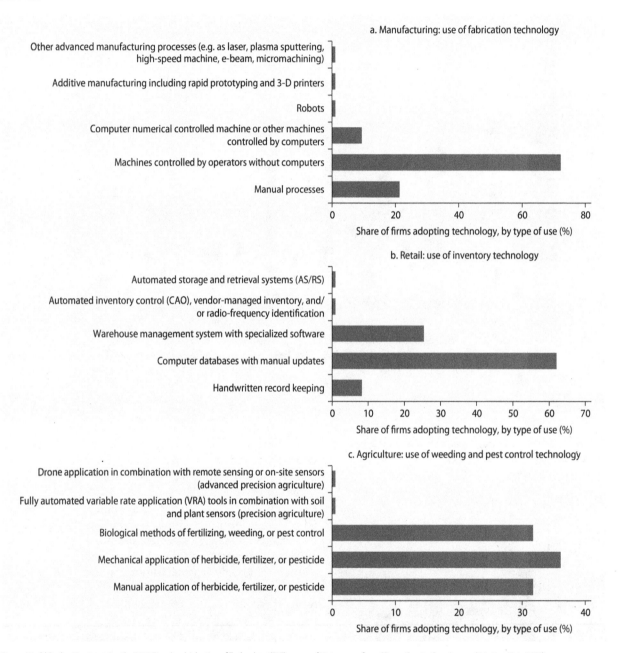

a. Manufacturing: use of fabrication technology

b. Retail: use of inventory technology

c. Agriculture: use of weeding and pest control technology

Source: World Bank estimates, using the 2020 Firm-level Adoption of Technology (FAT) survey of Vietnamese firms (Cirera, Comin, Cruz, Lee, and Martins-Neto 2020).

heterogeneity *within* firms. Using information on a typical large firm (Firm 1) and a medium-size firm (Firm 2) in the food processing sector, the figure shows that, for the same business functions, these two firms can be very different in the extensive margin of technology use (figure O.10, panel a), although the gap is smaller when use intensity (the intensive margin) is considered (figure O.10, panel b). It is noteworthy that the same firm (for example, Firm 1) can be near the technology frontier in its use of food storage technology but far from the frontier in its use of input testing technology (figure O.10, panel d).

Only a small share of firms engage in more sophisticated innovation activities such as R&D

There is similarly considerable heterogeneity between firms when it comes to the more sophisticated forms of innovation that could result in invention at the frontier, as evidenced by the high level of concentration in firms' R&D investments. Figure O.11 shows the distribution of R&D intensity (measured by R&D expenditure per full-time employee) in Cambodia, China, Malaysia, and the Philippines, using Israel as a benchmark.

FIGURE O.10 **Radar diagrams show substantial heterogeneity in technological sophistication within firms**

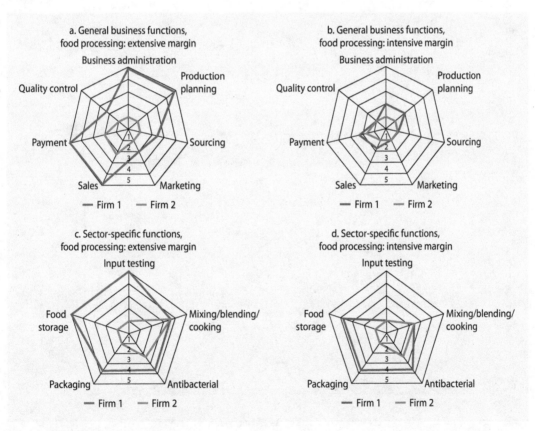

Source: Cirera, Comin, Cruz, Lee, and Martins-Neto 2020.
Note: In each radar diagram, the values 1–5 indicate relative distance from the frontier in a firm's use of technology for a given business function (1 being the most distant and 5 representing the frontier). Firm 1 and Firm 2 are Vietnamese food-processing firms that provided data for the Firm-level Adoption of Technology (FAT) survey.

In all countries shown, the vast majority of firms perform no R&D whatsoever (figure O.11, panel a). Only a relatively small share engage intensively in R&D activities. Notably, among firms that do invest in R&D, the distribution of R&D intensity differs significantly across countries (figure O.11, panel b). The distribution of R&D intensity among firms in China most closely resembles the distribution found in Israel, whereas performance among the most R&D-intensive firms in Cambodia, Malaysia, and the Philippines still falls well below Israeli levels.

FIGURE O.11   **There is significant duality in firm-level R&D investment**

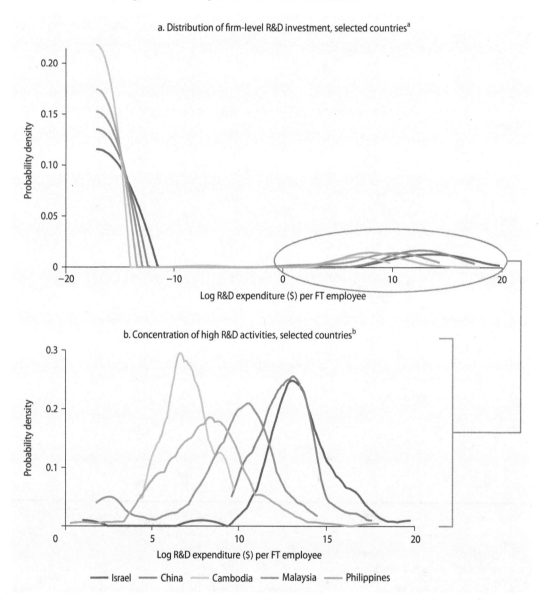

a. Distribution of firm-level R&D investment, selected countries[a]

b. Concentration of high R&D activities, selected countries[b]

Israel ⎯⎯ China ⎯⎯ Cambodia ⎯⎯ Malaysia ⎯⎯ Philippines

Source: World Bank Enterprise Survey data.
Note: In both panels, Israel (dark solid line) represents the benchmark. FT = full-time; R&D = research and development.
a. Panel a illustrates the distribution of R&D investment across all firms, by country.
b. Panel b (an enlarged portion of panel a) illustrates the distribution of R&D intensity (R&D expenditure per FT employee) among firms that *do* invest in R&D.

Why diffusion matters

Although inventions and new technologies offer the possibility for large increases in productivity, it is the diffusion of these new technologies rather than invention that ultimately determines the pace of economic and productivity growth (Hall and Khan 2003). The considerable heterogeneity observed in developing East Asia suggests that diffusion is not occurring at the pace and level that would be desirable. The approach of accelerating innovation through the acquisition of technologies embedded in imports and FDI, while an important part of the region's growth model to date, has not induced broad diffusion of new technologies and processes beyond export-linked firms. And it will be insufficient for propelling future productivity growth.

In light of the significant heterogeneity in firm innovation performance in the region, a broader innovation-based model is needed—one that still tries to maximize the absorption from FDI and participation in GVCs but that also supports a critical mass of firms in adopting new technologies and undertaking innovation. Although it remains important to enable more-sophisticated firms to undertake R&D projects and potentially to invent at the technological frontier, it is critical to support a large mass of firms to start innovating.

A large empirical literature links all types of innovation to higher firm productivity

The empirical literature that examines the relationship between innovation and productivity—focused mostly on high-income countries but also on China—indicates that innovation generally increases firm-level productivity. (For surveys of the evidence, see Hall [2011] and Mohnen and Hall [2013].) Productivity impacts tend to be strongest for product innovations, although this may partially reflect challenges associated with measuring other forms of innovation.

Recent analysis of Enterprise Survey data provides further evidence for developing East Asian countries. Consistent with the broader literature, innovation among firms in the region is associated with both higher labor productivity and higher revenue TFP (de Nicola 2019). The positive relationship between innovation and productivity holds both for firms that introduce new products and those that introduce new processes.

Although much of the literature focuses on invention, more-basic forms of innovation—increased diffusion and adoption—also pay off

Much of the literature has focused on innovation defined as invention, especially using patenting data. But it is important to emphasize that innovation in the form of imitation of products and processes, adoption of new technologies, or increased product quality is also important for productivity and growth. And policies that successfully encourage innovations that are new to the firm or new to the domestic market can have significant returns.

This advantage is clear from growth models, as in Madsen, Islam, and Ang (2010), but also from new microeconomic evidence. For example, in one of the few studies that specifically examines the impact of innovations that are only new to the firm or the local market (that is, that have been invented elsewhere), Fazlioğlu, Dalgıç, and Yereli (2019) find positive returns, based on a panel of Turkish firms. This less-sophisticated type of innovation, which helps firms to remain competitive, also pays off.

Data from the recent FAT survey in Vietnam also indicate a positive relationship between technology adoption and labor productivity at the firm level. Figure O.12 shows the results of regressing the logarithm of value added per worker on a technology index and sector dummies to control for different production functions, by sector. Firms that use more-sophisticated technologies for general business functions (GBF) such as human resource management, supply chain management, and sales (the extensive margin, shown in panel a) and that use

FIGURE O.12   **Technology adoption brings labor productivity gains to Vietnamese firms**

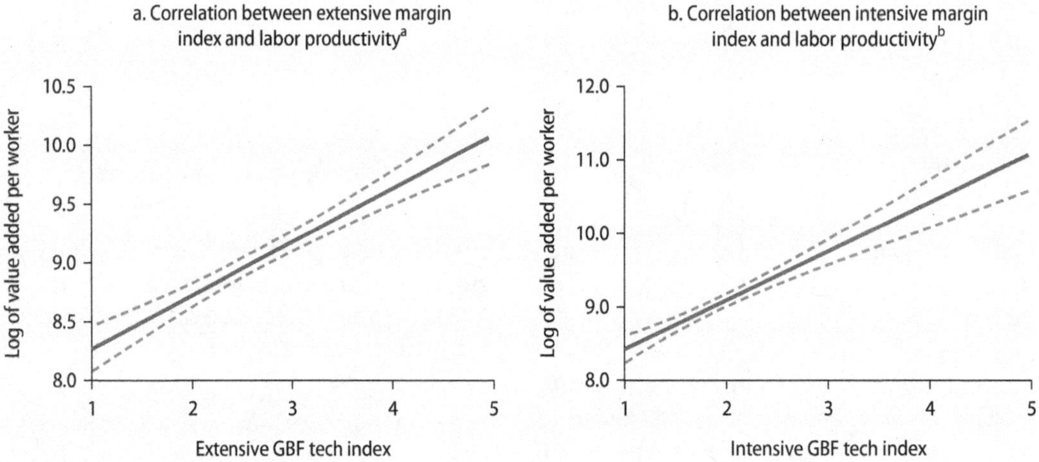

a. Correlation between extensive margin index and labor productivity[a]

b. Correlation between intensive margin index and labor productivity[b]

Source: Cirera, Comin, Cruz, and Lee 2020.
Note: The figures show the conditional predictions (solid lines) and 95 percent confidence levels (dashed lines) from regressing the log of labor value added per worker on a technology index and sector dummy variables. The index (from 1 to 5) measures the sophistication of technology—1 being the least sophisticated and 5 the most sophisticated technology for a set of general business functions (GBF) including business administration (human resources, accounting, and so on); production or service operations planning; sourcing, procurement, and supply chain management; marketing and product development; sales; payments; and quality control. The indexes were developed using data from the Firm-level Adoption of Technology (FAT) survey of Vietnamese firms in manufacturing, retail, and agriculture.
a. The "extensive" index refers to the most sophisticated use—here, as the average among all GBFs of the most sophisticated technology used in each business function, even if marginally used.
b. The "intensive" index refers to the most sophisticated use within the technologies that are used more intensively—here, as the average among all GBFs of the most sophisticated technology used more intensively for each business function (that is, the main technology used by the firm).

them more intensively (the intensive margin, shown in panel b) tend to have higher value added per worker.

Some caution is advised in interpreting these findings in terms of causality and the overall impact on TFP, because it is hard to distinguish empirically between the effects of technology adoption and capital deepening. Nonetheless, the analysis suggests that technology upgrading is likely associated with higher productivity. This is consistent with a broader micro literature that has found positive impacts from the adoption of information and communication technology (ICT) (Bloom, Sadun, and Van Reenan 2012; Brynjolfsson and Hitt 2003) and other technologies (Kwon and Stoneman 1995; Mcguckin, Streitwieser, and Doms 1998). The observed relationship is stronger for the intensive margin (the most intensively used technology), as expected.

What inhibits innovation?

Technology adoption and diffusion are determined not only by relative prices but also by factors such as differential returns to innovation, uncertainty about demand, and differences in firm-level capabilities

If returns to technology adoption, and to innovation more broadly, tend to be positive, what is constraining firm-level diffusion, adoption, and invention in the region? One prominent view of technology adoption and diffusion from a macro perspective focuses on the role of relative prices and factor abundance. The idea is that less-developed countries, because of differences in economic conditions and factor prices—including barriers to technology transfer, abundant labor, and a scarcity of skilled labor—will use different technologies than high-income countries

(Acemoglu and Zilibotti 2001). The implication is that countries in developing East Asia would be expected to use more labor-intensive and less capital-intensive technologies than do high-income countries. The extent of this will depend on how complementary technology and labor are (Acemoglu 2010) and how successful firm-level R&D is in generating new technologies.

Although it is unclear empirically how strongly some of these macro patterns of technology adoption based on factor prices affect diffusion, micro evidence suggests that other elements are at play in impeding successful technology adoption, diffusion, and invention in the region. These include uncertainty and lack of information, weak firm capabilities, inadequate workforce skills, lack of external financing, and weak or misaligned country innovation policies and institutions—each of which are discussed here, in turn.

First, firms face considerable uncertainty regarding investments in technology
Innovation is an inherently risky endeavor. Indeed, the process of technology adoption is often characterized by significant uncertainty—as to the future path of the technology and its benefits—and by limited information about the benefits, costs, and even the very existence of the technology's viability (Hall 2004).

Uncertainty about demand for new products or the efficiency of new technologies can lead to low initial adoption of new technologies among firms (as explained theoretically by Atkin et al. [2017]). Evidence of an increased investment in quality upgrading in response to new export demand provides empirical support for this argument (Atkin, Khandelwal, and Osman 2017).

Data from the FAT survey in Vietnam confirm that firms consider uncertainty to be an important factor in the decision to adopt new technology. Over 75 percent of small and medium-size firms and two-thirds of large firms surveyed indicated that uncertainty about demand and doubts about the economic benefit of investing in a new

technology are major obstacles to technology adoption (figure O.13).

In addition, more than 50 percent of firms, regardless of their size, report that lack of knowledge or related capabilities are a key barrier to investment in new technologies. Moreover, nearly half of small and medium-size firms and roughly one-third of large firms report difficulty in obtaining financing as a major barrier to technology adoption.[3] Costs of government regulations and lack of adequate infrastructure (such as electricity or internet) are also cited by firms as barriers to technology adoption, albeit to a lesser extent.

Second, firms' innovation capabilities, as reflected in management quality, is weak
Innovation requires a range of capabilities that enable firms to respond to market conditions, identify new technological opportunities, develop a plan to exploit them, and

FIGURE O.13 **Lack of demand and uncertainty is the top self-reported barrier to technology adoption among Vietnamese firms of all sizes**

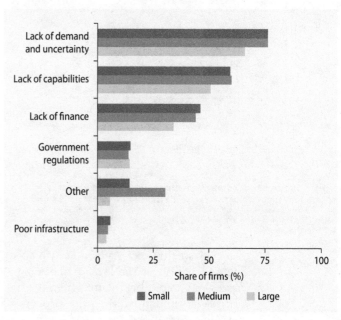

Source: Cirera, Comin, Cruz, Lee, and Martins-Neto 2020.
Note: Firm sizes small (5–19 employees), medium (20–99), and large (100+). Data were gathered from the Firm-level Adoption of Technology (FAT) survey of Vietnamese firms in manufacturing, retail, and agriculture.

FIGURE O.14   **Firms in developing East Asian countries score lower on management capabilities than firms at the global frontier**

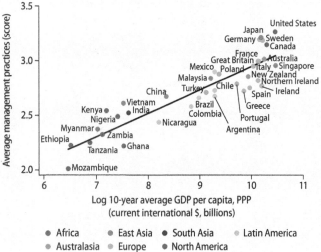

a. Average management scores in relation to per capita GDP

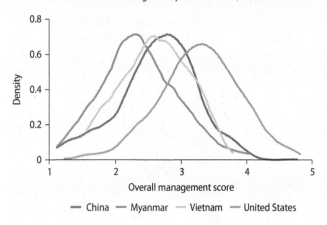

b. Distribution of management practices scores, selected countries

Source: World Management Survey (WMS), Centre for Economic Performance.
Note: The WMS scores (collected over several years) range from 1 (worst practice) to 5 (best practice) across key management practices used by organizations in different sectors. These practices are grouped into five areas: Operations Management, Performance Monitoring, Target Setting, Leadership Management, and Talent Management. GDP = gross domestic product; PPP = purchasing power parity.

having a product, process innovation, R&D project, or patent) is significantly associated with the firm's management quality (Park and Xuan 2020).

Data from the World Management Survey (WMS) indicate that firms' management quality in selected East Asian countries is roughly on par with what would be expected, given their per capita income levels.[4] However, their management quality remains far from the global frontier (proxied by the United States). Compared with US firms, firms in developing East Asia are less well-managed, on average and across the whole distribution (figure O.14).

Moreover, poor overall performance is driven by quality gaps that are generally larger for the best firms.[5] That is, the frontier firms in developing East Asia perform disproportionally worse than the frontier firms in the United States. This gap in management capabilities likely contributes to the innovation gaps between the region and the global frontier while also helping to explain some of the firm heterogeneity within countries described earlier.

Third, inadequate workforce skills impede innovation in the region
A range of advanced skills are important in enabling innovation at the firm and country levels, including advanced cognitive, socioemotional, and technical skills. Such advanced skills become increasingly important as firms move from diffusion and technology adoption toward the technological frontier.

New analysis carried out for this study highlights that employees in highly innovative firms carry out more nonroutine cognitive and interpersonal tasks and fewer manual tasks than those in less-innovative firms (figure O.15). For this reason, highly innovative firms in developing East Asia employ more (college) educated employees, with advanced technical training, greater cognitive abilities, and stronger socioemotional skills.

Firms in the region consistently report skills gaps as serious impediments to their operations. This is true of firms whether or not they innovate. Nonetheless, the

then cultivate the necessary resources to do so. The acquisition or the lack of these capabilities—and specifically, managerial capabilities—is fundamental to the process of upgrading (Sutton 2012).

New survey evidence from China supports this view. The degree of a firm's innovativeness (as measured by the firm's incidence of

FIGURE O.15 **Employees in more-innovative firms in China and Vietnam have jobs that are more intensive in nonroutine cognitive analytical and interpersonal tasks**

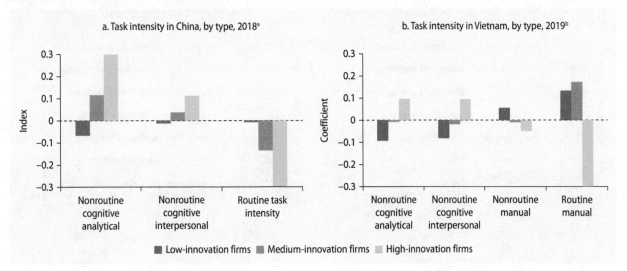

a. Task intensity in China, by type, 2018[a]

b. Task intensity in Vietnam, by type, 2019[b]

■ Low-innovation firms ■ Medium-innovation firms ■ High-innovation firms

Sources: World Bank elaboration, based on Park and Xuan 2020 and Miyamoto and Sarzosa 2020, using, respectively, the 2018 China Employer-Employee Survey (CEES) and the 2019 Enterprise Survey on Innovation and Skills (ESIS) for Vietnam.
Note: Firms are categorized by "innovation intensity," measured by the number of innovation activities undertaken, as captured in the respective surveys. Scaled from 0–5, low-, medium-, and high-innovation are defined, respectively, as those undertaking 0–1, 2–3, and 4–5 innovation activities. The Vietnam analysis does not include an aggregated measure of "routine task intensity"; therefore, panel b shows instead an individual measure of "routine manual" tasks. No information was included in either panel on routine cognitive tasks because none of the related regression coefficients was statistically significant.
a. The CEES collected responses of 2,001 manufacturing firms and 16,379 workers from five Chinese provinces: Guangdong, Jiangsu, Jilin, Hubei, and Sichuan.
b. The ESIS collected responses from 201 manufacturing and information and communication technology services firms and 849 staff in five Vietnamese provinces: Hanoi, Bac Ninh, Da Nang, Ho Chi Minh City, and Binh Duong.

challenges that innovative firms face in finding suitably skilled staff are considerable. Over 50 percent of innovating firms in Indonesia, Malaysia, Myanmar, the Philippines, Thailand, and Vietnam cite a lack of managerial and leadership skills as a challenge when hiring new workers (figure O.16). And more than half of all innovative firms in at least three of those six countries cite the scarcity of interpersonal and communication skills, foreign language skills, computer and information technology (IT) skills, or technical (non-IT) skills as critical challenges when it comes to hiring.

A fundamental challenge in this context is that most of the region's countries are still struggling to ensure that their students develop basic reading, math, and science skills. Indeed, students in several countries (Indonesia, Malaysia, the Philippines, and Thailand) score poorly on international education assessment tests given to eighth graders (the Programme for International Student

Assessment, or PISA)—considerably below what would be predicted based on their countries' income levels.

Weak development of reading, math, and science capabilities—the "foundational skills"—represents an important impediment to the development of the more advanced cognitive, technical, and socioemotional skills needed to support innovation. These skills-related constraints are relevant to the process of diffusion and adoption of existing technologies, but they are all the more severe when it comes to invention.

Fourth, a lack of diversified sources of external finance constrains firm innovation
Access to external finance—and to a suitable range of financial instruments—is critical to enabling firm innovation. How firms finance their investments and operations influences both the decision to innovate and the quality of that innovation.

FIGURE O.16   Most innovative firms in developing East Asia report difficulties in hiring workers with adequate skills

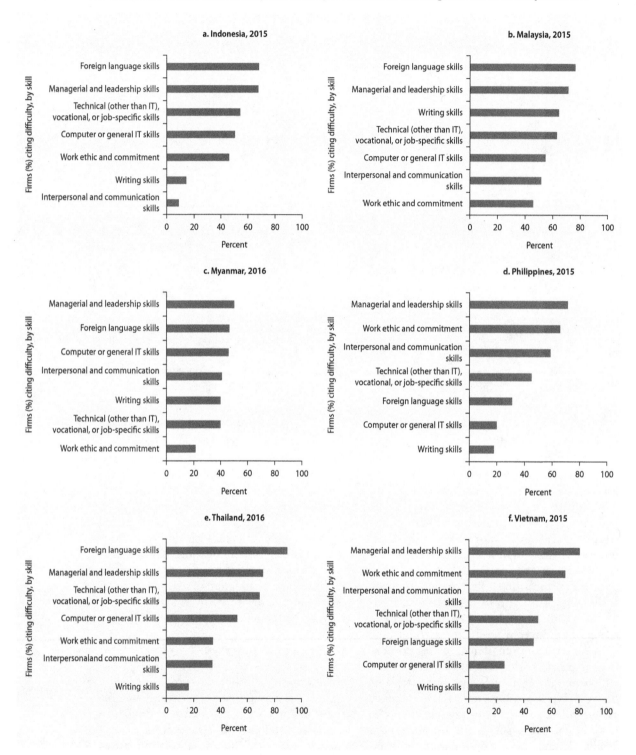

Source: World Bank calculations, based on World Bank Enterprise Surveys.
Note: "Innovative" firms are defined as those that introduced new or significantly improved products or services (product), or adopted new production methods (process), during the past three fiscal years. IT = information technology.

As noted earlier, about 16 percent of Vietnamese firms surveyed report difficulty in obtaining loans as the primary barrier to new technology adoption. More broadly, an analysis of Enterprise Survey data from developing East Asian countries shows that firms that make use of external finance, other than from banks, are more likely to innovate and to engage in more innovation activities (Mare, de Nicola, and Liriano forthcoming). A recent study of innovation in China also shows that financial constraints affect innovation quality. Firms that are financially constrained are less likely to invest in large innovation projects with the potential to transform productivity, focusing rather on making marginal improvements to existing products (Cao 2020).

Well-developed, deep financial markets allow firms to take advantage of diverse financial instruments, supporting both increased quantity and quality of innovation. A diversity of sources is important because different financial instruments have different characteristics regarding maturity, cost, and ancillary services. And these characteristics, in turn, help reduce market frictions associated with asymmetric information, cash flow uncertainty, and an extended time lag between investment and returns. Such frictions are especially serious among firms undertaking long-gestation R&D projects commonly associated with invention.

Although financial sectors in developing East Asia have become more diversified in recent years, most remain heavily banking based, having neither the depth nor the breadth to effectively support innovation-led growth (figure O.17). Moreover, financial markets remain accessible mostly to large firms (Abraham, Cortina, and Schmukler 2019). Key challenges, therefore, involve the continued deepening of countries' financial markets to ensure greater diversity of sources of finance for innovation—especially invention—and the enabling of greater access to small and medium-size enterprises.

FIGURE O.17   **Banks remain the dominant source of finance to firms in most of developing East Asia (except China)**

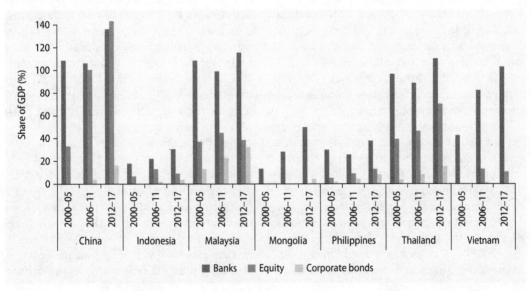

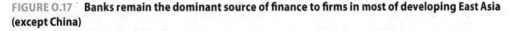

Sources: The World Bank's Global Financial Development and FinDebt databases.
Note: The graph reports averages over the three periods. "Equity" refers to stock market capitalization, "corporate bonds" to the amount outstanding of domestic bonds issued by private entities in industries other than finance, and "banks" to the outstanding amount of private credit granted by domestic banks. "Developing East Asia" refers to the 10 middle-income countries covered in this study: Cambodia, China, Indonesia, Lao PDR, Malaysia, Mongolia, Myanmar, the Philippines, Thailand, and Vietnam. The figure excludes Cambodia, Lao PDR, and Myanmar because of unavailability of data. For Mongolia, data on the corporate bond issuance are not available before 2011.

Fifth, countries' innovation policies and institutions are often not fit for purpose

Policies and agencies in developing East Asia are not well positioned to enable the process of increasing innovation and technological catch-up. Among the factors that dull the impact of policies on innovation, countries' current policy mixes are not well oriented toward building firms' capabilities for innovation or accelerating technology diffusion and adoption; nor are they set up to enable innovation in services. In addition, weak governance and institutional capacity among innovation agencies and public research organizations (PROs) often impede their ability to address countries' most pressing innovation challenges.

Innovation policies in the region neither focus on key bottlenecks nor prioritize technology adoption or building innovation capabilities

Given the lagging innovation performance of most countries in the region, it would make sense for their policies to emphasize building firms' basic capabilities and to prioritize support for technology adoption and diffusion. An in-depth review of the mix of innovation policies in Indonesia, the Philippines, and Vietnam suggests that their policies do not support these objectives, however. To different degrees across these countries, innovation policies are poorly aligned with the most pressing innovation challenges.

Two important policy gaps stand out: (a) the lack of support for technology adoption and diffusion, and (b) a virtual absence of support for innovation in services sectors. This misalignment of policies suggests, among other things, that many countries in the region have been poorly equipped to respond quickly to the technological challenges that the COVID-19 crisis has created, whether in terms of digitalization or the creation of more flexible production systems.

Most countries' capacity to implement innovation policies remains relatively weak

Detailed benchmarking exercises carried out in Indonesia, the Philippines, and Vietnam reveal numerous shortcomings in the design and implementation of innovation policies. Among the most important design shortcomings are:

- A lack of adequate economic justification for public policy;
- The absence of a logical framework to guide the design and implementation of policy interventions; and
- A lack of monitoring and evaluation (M&E) mechanisms for most policy instruments.

The outcome of this lack of good practices is that both the design and implementation of policies fall below potential. The overall quality of the policy mix was also found to be hampered by a lack of coordination across government agencies involved in innovation. Such coordination is critical because innovation needs and challenges cut across sectors, ministries, and agencies.

Innovation policy making is also hampered by weak institutions

Agencies supporting innovation in the region use outdated governance models, and together with the lack of coordination, this undermines the coherence of policies across countries' innovation systems. Some salient features of high-income countries' experience underline the importance of (a) having a clear strategy addressing market failures, (b) hiring capable staff, (c) instituting effective governance structures, and (d) instituting robust M&E frameworks.

Adopting these good practices in innovation agencies in the region would help improve both policy design and implementation and should be a top priority. Creating and empowering a dedicated innovation agency to take a high-level view of policy and to coordinate could be one way of improving and professionalizing policy making—although without due care and an appropriate mandate, there is a risk that such an agency could fail in its mission, resulting in continued lack of coordination along with additional fragmentation and competition for resources.

Inadequate governance structures and a lack of mission orientation constrain the contribution of public research to innovation

A new survey of PROs and research centers in Malaysia, the Philippines, and Vietnam shows that those governments have strengthened their national research capacity, increasing their investments in supporting PROs to create opportunities for new knowledge generation and innovation-based competencies. In Malaysia and to a lesser extent in the Philippines and Vietnam, the number of researchers in the public sector has grown rapidly during the past decade. This has been accompanied by a significant increase in publication activity, especially in Malaysia, and an upsurge in patenting by universities and PROs.

However, the results of these efforts and the impact of PROs on innovation and the economy are still far from clear. The surveys showed that, with a few noteworthy exceptions, PROs and university research departments develop few industry-science links (including knowledge links and human capital interactions). Indeed, technology transfer activities are still embryonic and mainly concentrated among a few organizations.

The impact of PROs and research centers could be leveraged by addressing governance and funding issues, along with inconsistencies in national regulatory frameworks governing public research systems. Specifically, inadequate governance is related to:

- Low levels of autonomy;
- A lack of links between institutional funding policies and performance measurements; and
- Inadequacy of academic incentives, which deters technology transfer activities, with often unclear mechanisms for sharing intellectual property.

The main factor that dissuades researchers from engaging in technology transfer and entrepreneurial activities, however, is the heavy weight that scientific publication (that is, the number of published articles) still receives among the criteria for researchers' career advancement and salary enhancement.

Spurring innovation in developing East Asia: Directions for policy

To spur innovation more effectively in developing East Asia—both diffusion of existing technologies and invention at the frontier—and to better keep pace with the wave of new technologies, policy makers in the region need to invest in building firms' innovation capabilities. This approach was effectively used by now high-income countries in East Asia, such as Japan, Korea, and Singapore, which accomplished rapid technological convergence by focusing on policies that addressed their innovation capabilities gaps (Cirera and Maloney 2017).

But what does such an approach look like in practice? How should policy makers deal with the substantial heterogeneity in their countries' innovation capabilities? To strengthen innovation policies and spur innovation-led growth by addressing the innovation inhibitors described above, countries can take several key steps:

- *Reorient policy objectives* in a graduated manner (the "capabilities escalator") to reduce uncertainty and information problems by removing current biases against diffusion; building management and innovation capabilities; and including a focus on services sector innovation
- *Strengthen complementary factors*—skills and finance—for innovation
- *Reform innovation institutions* and agencies and strengthen their capacity.

Reorient policy objectives and remove policy biases against adoption and services sector innovation

Effectively fostering innovation, both diffusion and invention, requires a graduated approach of moving firms toward the frontier—one that recognizes heterogeneity in the capacity to innovate

Cirera and Maloney (2017) propose assessing the adequacy of policies and institutions through the lens of the "capabilities escalator"—to reflect the capacity of firms and country systems to absorb and use knowledge (figure O.18).

Production capabilities. On the lowest step of the escalator, firms have productive, but few technological, capabilities. Policies should focus on building technological capabilities by addressing the uncertainty and critical information required for adoption (for example, through management extension and national quality infrastructure), improving skills, and supporting improvements in management quality. Where the business climate and competition are weak, policies should focus on creating an environment conducive to investment and knowledge diffusion, where firms compete, have access to competitive inputs, and can maximize knowledge spillovers through FDI and trade.

Technology adoption capabilities. In countries where some firms have technological capabilities, but few have R&D and invention capabilities—the next step on the escalator—policies should focus on expanding and strengthening technological capabilities while also supporting more firms in implementing R&D projects oriented toward invention.

Invention capabilities. In countries where firms have more sophisticated capabilities,

the goal of policy should be to enable invention by supporting more-complex, long-term R&D projects. At this stage, countries also require adequate intellectual property protection and will benefit from significant collaboration between industry and universities or other knowledge providers.

Figure O.18 illustrates several sets of policy instruments, each corresponding to a different level of the capabilities escalator.

Addressing heterogeneity in innovation capabilities requires that governments support diffusion and adoption as well as invention, prioritizing policies and allocating resources consistent with capabilities

The framework presented here does not imply that only one type of policy applies to each country. It does mean, however, that the policies and public resources for innovation should be well aligned with the capacities and needs of the private sector. Thus, countries with relatively low innovation capabilities—typically the region's lower-middle-income countries—are best advised to prioritize the adoption and diffusion of existing technologies. As innovation capabilities rise, the mix of policies can

FIGURE O.18   **Appropriate policy instruments to foster innovation differ depending on the level of innovation capabilities**

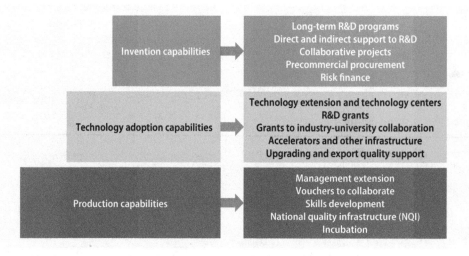

Source: Adapted from Cirera and Maloney 2017. ©World Bank. Further permission required for reuse.
Note: R&D = research and development.

shift, progressively focusing on the more technically advanced needs of leading firms.

Notably, even East Asia's high-income, high-capacity countries such as Japan, Korea, and Singapore—as well as Canada and the United States—offer support for technology adoption as well as invention, with different sets of policies to encourage both dimensions of innovation. At any level of capabilities, the point is not to focus policies only on either adoption or invention but rather to allocate more resources in a way commensurate with innovation capabilities.

Figure O.19 provides an approximation of where the countries of developing East Asia may be in terms of innovation capabilities. The scatterplot uses Global Innovation Index data on innovation *inputs* (measuring infrastructure, institutions, R&D, research, and human capital quality) and an innovation

outputs index that captures the quality of knowledge, technology, and creative outputs of the economy.

As expected, the relationship is positive. Most countries in the upper-right portion of the figure, with the exception of China, are high-income countries, whereas the countries in the lower-left portion of the figure are low- and middle-income countries. The figure shows three clusters that, with a few exceptions, correspond to the levels of capabilities depicted in the "capabilities escalator" (figure O.18).

Policy priorities require adjustment over time as innovation capabilities are developed

Climbing the capabilities escalator is a dynamic process and hence requires adjusting priorities over time. High-innovation

FIGURE O.19 **Developing East Asian countries occupy three distinct clusters with respect to innovation capabilities**

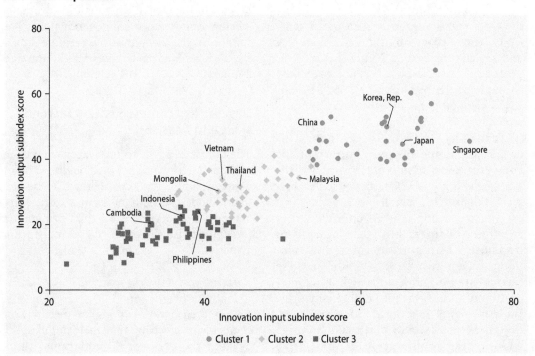

Source: World Bank elaboration from Global Innovation Index (GII) data (https://www.globalinnovationindex.org/).
Note: The "innovation input" subindex scores aspects such as infrastructure, institutions, research and development (R&D), and human capital quality. The "innovation output" subindex scores the quality of knowledge, technology, and creative outputs of the economy. Among the 10 developing East Asia countries in this study (Cambodia, China, Indonesia, Lao PDR, Malaysia, Mongolia, Myanmar, the Philippines, Thailand, and Vietnam), Lao PDR and Myanmar are excluded for lack of data.

countries in East Asia, such as Korea and Singapore, periodically adjusted their policy mixes over time to achieve convergence to the technological frontier.

Korea's journey has two important lessons for developing East Asia: First, the country has pursued an overarching objective and focus throughout the period on the importance of developing technological capabilities. Second, it has had an evolving prioritization of policies grounded in its evolving innovation and technological capabilities. Policy priorities were updated over time, reflecting changing challenges—from prioritizing the building of basic innovation capabilities in the 1960s and 1970s; to maximizing links to GVCs, FDI, and entry into export markets in the 1980s; to a significant focus on R&D and patenting in the 2000s; and to technological leadership in selected sectors in the 2000s.

A current priority includes removing policy biases against services

Traditionally, innovation and technology development have been seen as primarily processes driven by the manufacturing and agriculture sectors. Networks of PROs performing R&D have been established throughout the region and globally in narrowly defined areas of manufacturing and agriculture.

The reality, however, is that innovation in services is increasingly important for competitiveness in manufacturing, for the strengthening of GVCs, and also for services themselves, which employ the largest share of people in all countries. For example, business internationalization depends on transport, logistics, and communication networks. Innovations in these services are thus critical to facilitating integration of local firms into global networks. Improvements in digital infrastructure, digital networks, and platforms are also enabling the proliferation of innovative services firms in the region. Yet, innovation policy rarely supports innovation in services.

Removing this bias requires action on two fronts. First, it is important to go beyond instruments that traditionally support services firms, such as accelerators, and to reach out to services and retail firms with other innovation instruments such as matching grants for innovation projects or digitalization. Second, it is necessary to expand the scope of innovation activities to include design—a significant component of R&D (Kox and Rubalcaba 2007) in manufacturing but also in services—and to strengthen firms' digital capabilities. Services sectors are extremely diverse, and innovation takes different forms with different priorities across subsectors. For example, digital and AI elements are more important in routine services, whereas design, business models, and delivery are more important in knowledge-intensive services (Salter and Tether 2006).

Recognizing these differences and designing adequate policies will thus be critical to enabling innovation in this increasingly important sector of the economy. This can be seen in the United Kingdom, for example, where the government's innovation policy has supported the growth of the creative industry, a sector that contributes £90 billion and 2 million jobs to the UK economy.

Develop key complementary factors: skills and finance

The ability of firms to innovate depends on multiple factors that fall outside the realm of innovation policy, strictly defined. These factors include the availability of a sufficiently skilled workforce and adequate financing to support firms'—often risky—innovation activities.

Building strong workforce skills is critical to fostering innovation

As noted earlier, policy makers face a *dual challenge* of ensuring that their populations develop the necessary foundational skills while also building the types of advanced skills needed to enable innovation. To meet this dual challenge, it will be important for policy makers to act on several fronts, as described below.

Strengthen students' foundational skills by improving basic education. Lessons from high-performing education systems in East Asia and beyond suggest that building stronger basic skills will require strengthening the conditions for learning; improving teacher preparation and the quality of teaching; ensuring adequate public spending for basic education; increasing children's readiness to learn, including through early childhood education and development services; and undertaking regular learning assessments to diagnose challenges and inform improvements (World Bank 2018).

Lay the foundation for advanced cognitive and socioemotional skills early in the education life cycle. Even where countries have recognized the importance of cultivating more critical thinking, creativity, problem solving, and the ability to work effectively in teams, there remains a need to institutionalize the development of advanced cognitive and socioemotional skills into standard school curricula and extracurricular programs. Strong innovation performers in the region—Japan, Korea, and Singapore—have all revised their curricula to include an emphasis on higher-order cognitive and socioemotional skills development (Kataoka and Alejo 2019). Recent studies of skills formation emphasize that building strong cognitive and socioemotional skills is best begun early in the learning life cycle (Arias, Evans, and Santos 2019; Cunningham and Villaseñor 2016).

Strengthen technical skills through improved access to and quality of science, technology, engineering, and mathematics (STEM) education. The demand for technical skills to innovate is quite diverse across firms. For firms focused on diffusion and adoption of existing technologies, basic digital literacy and the capacity to use general purpose technologies and existing software applications may be sufficient. As firms move toward the technical frontier, more sophisticated technical skills are required. Efforts are needed to improve access to and the quality of technical

education in much of the region. Establishing opportunities for continuous skills development will support skills upgrading in the current workforce.

Continuous skills development—or lifelong learning—systems for adult workers are necessary to support skills upgrading in the face of rapid technological change. There may be scope for incentivizing on-the-job training, which, evidence suggests, contributes to firm-level innovation activity. Singapore, for example, has instituted a promising system of individual training accounts to promote upgrading of people's workforce skills (Kataoka and Alejo 2019). Technical and vocational education and training (TVET) programs can also play a role—although, to be effective, such programs must closely reflect private sector demand to ensure their market relevance.

Strengthening finance can enable innovation

As discussed above, access to both external finance and a suitable range of financial instruments are critical to enabling innovation at the firm level. To strengthen finance for innovation, the region's countries should implement policies in three different areas: (a) developing well-functioning capital markets, (b) promoting venture capital markets, and (c) broadening the range of financial instruments available to innovating firms through the banking sector.

Developing deep, well-functioning capital markets. The development of deep capital markets is critical to ensuring alternative sources of external capital to innovative firms at different stages of a firm's life cycle. Some countries in the region have already moved in this direction by introducing capital market reforms targeted to increasing the investor base; improving financial market infrastructure (for example, introducing a capital market data warehouse system); and enhancing investor protection (Abraham, Cortina, and Schmukler 2019). Where countries have made progress in deepening capital markets, the main beneficiaries to date have been relatively larger firms. Innovative instruments are still required to improve capital market access to small and medium-size firms, however (Mason and Shetty 2019).

Promoting the development of venture capital markets. Three broad, complementary sets of measures are important for the development of successful venture capital markets: First, the supply side of the market can be enhanced by enabling domestic investment and attracting foreign capital, such as through clear bankruptcy rules and transparent accounting standards. Second, the demand for risk finance can be stimulated by fostering an active entrepreneurial and innovation ecosystem. And third, governments can provide support for all market players by strengthening the institutional and regulatory framework for venture capital, as well as by investing directly or through public-private partnerships (for example, the successful Yozma program in Israel). Careful design of public intervention is important to ensure that programs are effectively addressing market failures and do not crowd out investment from the private sector.

Leveraging existing bank-firm relationships. Governments in the region could also channel financing to firms through the banking sector, exploiting existing bank-firm relationships. Well-designed government lending programs can help to align debtors' and creditors' incentives, lessening moral hazard problems (Cirera, Frias, Hill, and Li 2020; SQW 2019). This approach is not without risk, however, because identifying, targeting, and monitoring potential innovation projects may be difficult and costly for government agencies. Credit guarantee schemes may be more efficient because they make use of existing lending products, allowing banks to select projects and maintain the incentives to monitor borrowers' behavior. An example of such a scheme is the Korea Technology Finance Corporation (KOTEC), which has been successfully providing loan guarantees to small and young firms in high-tech sectors.

Reform innovation institutions and agencies and strengthen their capacity

Investing in institutional capacity is critical for more effective innovation policies

To date, discussions of innovation and technology policies have commonly ignored countries' capacities to effectively design and implement innovation policy, but these capacities are critical for the effectiveness of interventions. An initial review of innovation agencies indicates that some developing East Asian countries lag in the use of best practices in public management for innovation policy.

Going forward, it will be critical to invest more in policy-making capacity. Countries need to recruit capable staff and provide adequate training on innovation policy and public management, and to ensure that managers have adequate digital infrastructure to monitor beneficiaries and register innovation project outcomes.

More professionalized innovation agencies and increased interagency coordination are essential

Agencies supporting innovation policy in the region use outdated governance models and lack coordination across entities, which undermines policy alignment. Innovation policy requires coordination among agencies or ministries because of its cross-cutting nature. The current lack of coordination results in significant fragmentation in effort, along with policies that are poorly designed and executed.

In addition to improving the innovation agencies' public management capabilities, governments in the region need to (a) ensure better coordination of the different ministries and institutions in charge of innovation policy, and (b) adopt new agency models that enable recruitment of sufficient talent and professionalized services. There is no single model for coordination, and each country needs to find its own approach. Nonetheless, coordination is needed to ensure more integrated, focused, and effective innovation policy.

Strengthening the governance and incentive structures of PROs and research centers would help to maximize their contribution to innovation and technology diffusion

The impacts of government efforts to strengthen the national research capacity and of investments in science and technology in public research institutions are still unclear. Public institutions and university research departments engage little in industry-science collaboration (including knowledge links and personnel exchanges). Moreover, technology transfer activities remain embryonic and concentrated among a small number of organizations. Maximizing the contributions of these research institutions to innovation will require reforms in four key areas:

- *Improving governance,* for example, increasing autonomy, clarifying legal mandates for technology transfer, and strengthening links between institutional funding and performance; and disseminating good public management practices and strategic planning
- *Improving academic incentives* for research-industry collaboration and technology transfer
- *Adopting mission-oriented policies* to address specific innovation challenges facing the region (such as COVID-19 and climate change)
- *Incentivizing PROs* to enhance their impact on firm innovation and productivity through technology extension; upgrading of support services (including for new technology-based entrepreneurship); licensing of new technologies to small and medium enterprises (SMEs); and support to start-ups.

Final remarks

Developing East Asia has achieved unprecedented growth in the past several decades that has raised incomes broadly and lifted hundreds of millions of people out of poverty.

This report has argued that the region's growth performance is under threat if countries do not transform their development model to one in which innovation is at the forefront. The impacts of the COVID-19 pandemic have been severe, and as the region focuses on the recovery, it is an opportune moment to accelerate pending reforms to accelerate the process of technological catch-up.

Although this transformation would be important under all circumstances, the COVID-19 pandemic has served to highlight the urgency of reform. The pandemic is likely to tighten the constraints on innovation identified in this report: limited capabilities of firms, scarcity of human capital and finance, and uncertainty about demand and returns to innovation. Moreover, the pandemic is raising uncertainty and may deepen the international divisions that were already simmering before the outbreak. Restrictions on trade, investment, and the mobility of people can hurt not just the flow of existing knowledge but also the creation of new knowledge through international collaboration. Similarly, mutual suspicion can divide the digital infrastructure and curb the digital flows that are vital for all creative activity today.

To accelerate progress in the face of challenges, countries in developing East Asia must update their objectives and give greater priority to better innovation policies. It is critical to focus on technological diffusion and to incentivize more firms to undertake innovation. This process requires stronger regulatory frameworks as well as policies that are aligned with the technological capabilities of the private sector in each country. Beyond domestic policy, East Asia must continue to deepen its tradition of international openness, which could also induce openness in other parts of the world, and help sustain the flows of ideas, trade, investment, and people that facilitate the creation and diffusion of knowledge. The time for action is now.

Notes

1. The terms "East Asia" and "developing East Asia" will be used throughout the report. For convenience, unless otherwise specified, these terms refer to the 10 middle-income countries covered in this study: Cambodia, China, Indonesia, the Lao People's Democratic Republic, Malaysia, Mongolia, Myanmar, the Philippines, Thailand, and Vietnam.
2. For more information on innovative responses to COVID-19, see the Coronavirus Innovation Map (https://coronavirus.startupblink.com/); the World Economic Forum COVID Action Platform (for example, Chandran [2020], at https://www.weforum.org/agenda/2020/03/asia-technology-coronavirus-covid19-solutions/); and Huang, Sun, and Sui (2020).
3. Challenges associated with obtaining external finance for innovation are discussed in more detail later in this Overview.
4. The WMS (https://worldmanagementsurvey.org/), operated by the Centre for Economic Performance of the London School of Economics and Political Science, is conducted through in-depth interviews of over 20,000 firms in 35 countries. Management practices, as measured in the WMS, capture several dimensions, including firms' practices in target setting, monitoring, and human resource management. The WMS is not specific to innovation, but it is a proxy for firms' overall capabilities.
5. These differences are statistically significant at 95% confidence level and hold true for different quantiles of the overall WMS management score distribution.

References

Abraham, Facundo, Juan J. Cortina, and Sergio L. Schmukler. 2019. "The Rise of Domestic Capital Markets for Corporate Financing." Policy Research Working Paper 8844, World Bank, Washington, DC.

Acemoglu, Daron. 2010. "When Does Labor Scarcity Encourage Innovation?" *Journal of Political Economy* 118 (6): 1037–78.

Acemoglu, Daron, and Fabrizio Zilibotti. 2001. "Productivity Differences." *Quarterly Journal of Economics* 116 (2): 563–606.

Arias, Omar, David Evans, and Indhira Santos. 2019. *The Skills Balancing Act in Sub-Saharan Africa: Investing in Skills for Productivity, Inclusivity, and Adaptability*. Africa Development Forum series. Washington, DC: World Bank.

Atkin, David, Azam Chaudhry, Shamyla Chaudry, Amit K. Khandelwal, and Eric Verhoogen. 2017. "Organizational Barriers to Technology Adoption: Evidence from Soccer-Ball Producers in Pakistan." *Quarterly Journal of Economics* 132 (3): 1101–64.

Atkin, David, Amit K. Khandelwal, and Adam Osman. 2017. "Exporting and Firm Performance: Evidence from a Randomized Experiment." *Quarterly Journal of Economics* 132 (2): 551–615.

Bergquist, Kyle, Carsten Fink, and Julio Raffo. 2017. "Identifying and Ranking the World's Largest Clusters of Inventive Activity." Economic Research Working Paper No. 34, World Intellectual Property Organization (WIPO), Geneva.

Bloom, Nicholas, Raffaella Sadun, and John Van Reenen. 2012. "Americans Do IT Better: US Multinationals and the Productivity Miracle." *American Economic Review* 102 (1): 167–201.

Brynjolfsson, Erik, and Lorin M. Hitt. 2003 "Computing Productivity: Firm-Level Evidence." *Review of Economics and Statistics* 85 (4): 793–808.

Cao, Yu. 2020. "Financial Constraints, Innovation Quality, and Growth." Doctoral dissertation, University of Southern California, Los Angeles.

Chandran, Rina. 2020. "Here's How Asia Is Using Tech to Tackle COVID-19." Reuters article on the World Economic Forum COVID Action Platform, March 18. https://www.weforum.org/agenda/2020/03/asia-technology-coronavirus-covid19-solutions/.

Cirera, Xavier, Diego A. Comin, Marcio Cruz, and Kyung Min Lee. 2020. "Technology Within and Across Firms." NBER Working Paper No. 28080, National Bureau of Economic Research, Cambridge, MA.

Cirera, Xavier, Diego A. Comin, Marcio Cruz, Kyung Min Lee, and Antonio Soares Martins-Neto. 2020. "Firm-Level Technology Adoption in Vietnam." Unpublished manuscript, World Bank, Washington, DC.

Cirera, Xavier, Jaime Frias, Justin Hill, and Yanchao Li. 2020. A *Practitioner's Guide to Innovation Policy: Instruments to Build Firm Capabilities and Accelerate Technological Catch-Up in Developing Countries*. Washington, DC: World Bank.

Cirera, Xavier, and William F. Maloney. 2017. *The Innovation Paradox: Developing-Country*

Capabilities and the Unrealized Promise of Technological Catch-Up. Washington, DC: World Bank.

Comin, Diego, and Bart Hobijn. 2004. "Cross-Country Technology Adoption: Making the Theories Face the Facts." *Journal of Monetary Economics*, 51 (1): 39–83.

Comin, Diego, and Bart Hobijn. 2010. "An Exploration of Technology Diffusion." *American Economic Review* 100 (5): 2031–59.

Comin, Diego, and Martí Mestieri. 2018. "If Technology Has Arrived Everywhere, Why Has Income Diverged?" *American Economic Journal: Macroeconomics* 10 (3): 137–78.

Cunningham, Wendy V., and Paula Villaseñor. 2016. "Employer Voices, Employer Demands, and Implications for Public Skills Development Policy Connecting the Labor and Education Sectors." *World Bank Research Observer* 31 (1):102–34.

de Nicola, Francesca. 2019. "Assessing How Returns to Innovation Vary Depending on the Business Environment and Firms' Characteristics." Background paper for this study, World Bank, Washington, DC.

Dutta, Soumitra, Bruno Lanvin, and Sacha Wunsch-Vincent, eds. 2019. *Global Innovation Index 2019: Creating Healthy Lives—The Future of Medical Innovation*. 12th ed. Ithaca, NY: Cornell University; Fontainebleau, France: INSEAD; and Geneva: World Intellectual Property Organization (WIPO).

Eckstein, David, Vera Künzel, Laura Schäfer, and Maik Winges. 2019. *Global Climate Risk Index 2020: Who Suffers Most from Extreme Weather Events? Weather-Related Loss Events in 2018 and 1999 to 2018*. Berlin: Germanwatch eV.

Escribano, Alvaro, and J. Luis Guasch. 2005. "Assessing the Impact of the Investment Climate on Productivity Using Firm-Level Data: Methodology and the Cases of Guatemala, Honduras, and Nicaragua." Policy Research Working Paper 3621, World Bank, Washington, DC.

Fazlıoğlu, Burcu, Başak Dalgıç, Ahmet Burçin Yereli. 2019. "The Effect of Innovation on Productivity: Evidence from Turkish Manufacturing Firms." *Industry and Innovation* 26 (4): 439–60.

Feenstra, Robert C., Robert Inklaar, and Marcel P. Timmer. 2015. "The Next Generation of the Penn World Table." *American Economic Review* 105 (10): 3150–82.

Griliches, Zvi. 1998. *R&D and Productivity: The Econometric Evidence*. Chicago: Chicago University Press.

Hall, Bronwyn H. 2004. "Innovation and Diffusion." NBER Working Paper No. 10212, National Bureau of Economic Research, Cambridge, MA.

Hall, Bronwyn H. 2011. "Innovation and Productivity." NBER Working Paper No. 17178, National Bureau of Economic Research, Cambridge, MA.

Hall, Bronwyn H., and Beethika Khan. 2003. "Adoption of New Technology." NBER Working Paper No. 9730, National Bureau of Economic Research, Cambridge, MA.

Huang, Yasheng, Meicen Sun, and Yuze Sui. 2020. "How Digital Contact Tracing Slowed Covid-19 in East Asia." *Harvard Business Review*, April 15. https://hbr.org/2020/04/how-digital-contact-tracing-slowed-covid-19-in-east-asia.

Iootty, Mariana. 2019. "Assessing Innovation Patterns and Constraints in Developing East Asia: An Introductory Analysis." Policy Research Working Paper 8706, World Bank, Washington, DC.

Kataoka, Sachiko, and Ana Alejo. 2019. "Skills for Innovation." Background paper for this report, World Bank, Manila, Philippines.

Kox, Henk, and Luis Rubalcaba. 2007. "The Contribution of Business Services to European Economic Growth." In *Business Services in European Economic Growth*, edited by Luis Rubalcaba and Henk Kox, 74–94. London: MacMillan/Palgrave.

Kwon, Myung Joong, and Paul Stoneman. 1995. "The Impact of Technology Adoption on Firm Productivity." *Economics of Innovation and New Technology* 3 (3–4): 219–34.

Madsen, Jakob B., Md. Rabiul Islam, and James B. Ang. 2010. "Catching Up to the Technology Frontier: The Dichotomy between Innovation and Imitation." *Canadian Journal of Economics* 43 (4): 1389–411.

Mare, Davide S., Francesca de Nicola, and Faruk Miguel Liriano. Forthcoming. "Financial Structure and Firm Innovation: Cross-Country Evidence," Background paper for this report, World Bank, Washington, DC.

Mason, Andrew D., and Sudhir Shetty. 2019. *A Resurgent East Asia: Navigating a Changing World*. East Asia and Pacific Regional Report. Washington, DC: World Bank.

Mcguckin, Robert H., Mary L. Streitwieser, and Mark Doms. 1998. "The Effect of Technology

Use on Productivity Growth." *Economics of Innovation and New Technology* 7 (1): 1–26.

Miyamoto, Koji, and Miguel Sarzosa. 2020. "Workforce Skills and Firm Innovation: Evidence from an Employer-Employee Linked Survey Data in Vietnam." Unpublished manuscript, World Bank, Washington, D.C.

Mohnen, Pierre, and Bronwyn H. Hall. 2013. "Innovation and Productivity: An Update." *Eurasian Business Review* 3 (1): 47–65.

OECD and Eurostat (Organisation for Economic Co-operation and Development and the Statistical Office of the European Union). 2018. *Oslo Manual 2018: Guidelines for Collecting, Reporting and Using Data on Innovation.* 4th ed. Paris: OECD; Luxembourg: Eurostat.

Park, Albert, and Wenshi Xuan. 2020. "Skills for Innovation in China." Background paper for this report, Hong Kong University of Science and Technology, Hong Kong SAR, China.

Salter, Ammon J., and Bruce S. Tether. 2006. "Innovation in Services: Through the Looking Glass of Innovation Studies." Background paper for the Advanced Institute of Management (AIM) Grand Challenge on Service Science, April 7, Oxford University.

Solow, Robert M. 1957. "Technical Change and the Aggregate Production Function." *Review of Economics and Statistics* 39 (3): 312–20.

SQW. 2019. "Evaluation of Innovation Loans: Final Interim Report to Innovate UK." Evaluation report, SQW, Oxford, UK.

Sutton, John. 2012. *Competing in Capabilities: The Globalization Process.* Oxford: Oxford University Press.

van der Eng, Pierre. 2009. "Capital Formation and Capital Stock in Indonesia, 1950–2008." *Bulletin of Indonesian Economic Studies* 45 (3): 345–71. doi:10.1080/00074910903301662.

World Bank. 2018. *Growing Smarter: Learning and Equitable Development in East Asia and Pacific.* East Asia and Pacific Regional Report. Washington, DC: World Bank.

World Bank. 2020. *Global Economic Prospects, January 2020: Slow Growth, Policy Challenges.* Washington, DC: World Bank.

World Bank and DRC (Development Research Center of the State Council, The People's Republic of China). 2019. *Innovative China: New Drivers of Growth.* Washington, DC: World Bank.

WTO and IDE-JETRO (World Trade Organization and the Institute of Developing Economies). 2011. *Trade Patterns and Global Value Chains in East Asia: From Trade in Goods to Trade in Tasks.* Geneva: WTO.

The State of Innovation in Developing East Asia | 1

Introduction

East Asia has undergone a significant economic transformation over the past half century. High rates of growth have propelled countries in the region from low- to middle-income, and even in a few cases, to high-income status. An approach that has become known as the "East Asian development model"—a combination of policies that fostered outward-oriented, labor-intensive growth; investments in basic human capital; and sound economic governance—has been instrumental in moving hundreds of millions of people out of poverty and into economic security.

Despite their past economic successes, the region's middle-income countries face an array of challenges as they strive to continue their economic progress. First, productivity growth has declined since the 2008–09 Global Financial Crisis. This, coupled with rapid population aging in several countries, is putting pressure on the region's growth prospects, narrowing the opportunities for reaping demographic dividends. Second, the slowing of global goods trade, uncertainty about the future of the global trading system, and rapid changes in technology are all challenging a key engine of growth in the region: export-oriented manufacturing. Third, the COVID-19 pandemic, together with ongoing climate change, is increasing economic vulnerability and highlighting the need for new modes of production in the region.

Such forces, alone and together, raise questions about whether the model that has driven the region's economic success in the past can continue to deliver rapid growth and development in the future.

Innovation will be essential to overcoming these challenges. In fact, it has already played a critical role in the economic transformation of developing East Asian countries over the past half century, beginning with the diffusion and adoption of high-yielding rice varieties, modern fertilizers, and other agricultural technologies (for example, pesticides and machinery)—a set of advances in agricultural production commonly known as the Green Revolution. High-yielding rice varieties developed initially by international agricultural research centers (such as the International Rice Research Institute in the Philippines) in partnership with national agricultural research systems were not only instrumental in raising agricultural productivity across the region but also helped lay the foundation for the structural transformation that fueled development in the region.

Innovation will play a central role in enabling the countries of developing East Asia to move from lower-middle-income to upper-middle-income and, ultimately, to high-income levels.

Interest in innovation among the region's policy makers has peaked recently with the rise of digital technologies. Indeed, high-profile accomplishments by private sector actors—in e-commerce, digital financial technology (fintech), ridesharing, and mobile app-enabled service delivery—have captured the imaginations of policy makers, the media, and citizens alike. Enterprises in the digital space, like the Chinese multinational technology company Alibaba and the ride-hailing services Grab and Go-Jek in Southeast Asia, have become household names. In addition, most countries are developing strategies to prepare for the next wave of advanced technologies. These technologies (including advanced robotics, artificial intelligence, 3-D printing, and the internet of things) are often referred to collectively as the "fourth industrial revolution" (or "Industry 4.0") technologies.[1]

Despite the great promise of innovation—and some high-profile successes—analysis of a range of key innovation indicators suggests that countries in developing East Asia still face important challenges to fostering innovation-led growth. They are not unique in this regard. Recent global research on innovation shows that despite potentially high returns to investment in innovation, low- and middle-income countries around the world commonly underinvest and underperform in innovation for several reasons: weak capacity of firms to adopt, use, or invent new technologies; misalignment between public innovation policies and institutions and countries' needs; unconducive economic policy environments; and missing complementary factors, such as the necessary skills to innovate or inadequate instruments to finance innovation (Cirera and Maloney 2017).

The objective of this report is to deepen policy makers' understanding of innovation and its critical role in the future growth and development of East Asia as well as to provide guidance on the types of policy and institutional reforms needed to enable more innovation-led growth in the region.[2] To achieve this, the report examines the region's key innovation challenges, assesses its state of innovation, and analyzes the main constraints firms face in effectively pursuing innovation. The report then analyzes the policies and institutions currently in place to support innovation in developing East Asia and lays out an agenda for action aimed at spurring innovation-led growth.

This chapter provides an overview of the state of innovation in the region. It begins by providing the broad definition of innovation that will be used throughout the report. The chapter then examines the productivity and related challenges facing developing East Asian countries as they seek to sustain their high economic performance. To help contextualize the analysis presented in the remainder of the report, the chapter then reviews the region's innovation accomplishments and challenges, placing developing East Asian countries in a global context. The chapter concludes with a road map for the remainder of the report.

Defining innovation

It is useful to begin by defining innovation explicitly because innovation means different things to different people. This report adopts a broad definition of innovation based on the *Oslo Manual* (OECD and Eurostat 2018), which uses the term to refer to a new or improved product or business process that differs significantly from the firm's previous products or business processes and that has been introduced to the firm and on the market (box 1.1). This definition relates to various functions of the firm (not only its products) and, more importantly, requires only that the "innovation" represent a significant improvement to the firm, which may include upgrading of processes and imitation of other existing products in the market.

BOX 1.1   Defining firm-level innovation

The report adopts a broad view of innovation as the accumulation of knowledge and implementation of new ideas. Specifically, the *Oslo Manual 2018* defines "business innovation" as a "new or improved product or business process (or combination thereof) that differs significantly from the firm's previous products or business processes and that has been introduced on the market or brought into use by the firm" (OECD and Eurostat 2018, 20). This report considers innovation defined both as "invention" or "discovery" (that is, those developments that push the technological frontier) *and* as "diffusion" or "adoption" of existing technologies and practices that lead firms to novel ways of producing or acting. The latter definition is pertinent to most of the firms operating in developing East Asia.

Several observations can be made regarding this definition:

• "An innovation must be *novel* or a *significant improvement*, at least to the firm and possibly to the market (or other higher levels)" and must be *implemented* (that is, introduced inside the firm or commercialized). There is no requirement for the innovation to be *successful*, however.
• The general definition does not mention *intention* or *objective*, but implicit is the idea that innovation aims at improving the firm's competitive position and is associated with uncertainty.
• The broad definition makes no reference to technology, and the current definition (based on the fourth edition of the *Oslo Manual* [OECD and Eurostat 2018]) considers nontechnological forms of innovation, thereby encompassing a broader range of knowledge types than strictly scientific or technical ones.

The *Oslo Manual 2018* defines the following two main subtypes of innovations (OECD and Eurostat 2018, 21):

• A *product innovation* is "a new or improved good or service that differs significantly from the firm's previous goods or services and that has been introduced on the market." This includes the addition of new functions or improvements to existing functions or user utility. "Relevant functional characteristics include quality, technical specifications, reliability, durability, economic efficiency during use, affordability, convenience, usability, and user friendliness" (OECD and Eurostat 2018, 71). In this context, traditional surveys have used three metrics to capture the complexity or novelty of the innovation:
  ▪ New products to the firm
  ▪ New products to the market
  ▪ New products to the international market.
• A *business process innovation* is "a new or improved business process for one or more business functions that differs significantly from the firm's previous business processes and that has been brought into use by the firm." The *Oslo Manual 2018* lists six functional categories to identify and distinguish between types of business process innovations, based on contemporary management research, that capture innovations in both core and supporting business functions of the firm (OECD and Eurostat 2018, 73):
  ▪ Innovative methods for manufacturing products or offering services
  ▪ Innovations in distribution and logistics, including transportation and delivery of inputs, products, or services; warehousing; and order processing
  ▪ Innovations in marketing and sales activities, which cover innovative marketing methods, pricing strategies, and sales and after-sales activities (including help desks and customer support)
  ▪ Innovations in the provision and maintenance of information and communication systems, including hardware, software, databases, repairs, web hosting, and so on
  ▪ Innovations in administration and management, including strategic and general business management; corporate governance; accounting, auditing, and other financial activities; management of human resources; procurement; and management of external relations with suppliers, alliances, and so on
  ▪ Innovations in product and business process development, which covers activities to scope, identify, develop, or adapt products or a firm's business processes.

box continues next page

BOX 1.1   Defining firm-level innovation *(continued)*

It is important to note that although this report adopts a broad and multifaceted definition of innovation, existing data do not always enable analysis across all the dimensions identified here. For example, data on firm-level innovation in the World Bank Enterprise Surveys are based on the definition used in the third edition of the *Oslo Manual* (OECD and Eurostat 2005) because the surveys were designed before the fourth edition was released in 2018. The Enterprise Surveys thus include two additional categories of innovation: organizational and marketing. These categories have been subsumed under business process innovations in the 2018 edition and are captured by the six newly introduced functional categories.

To highlight as clearly as possible the multiple dimensions across which firms innovate, the analysis of Enterprise Survey data presented in this report will occasionally distinguish between four different types of innovation defined in the 2005 *Oslo Manual*. A complete mapping of the differences and correspondence of activities between the 2005 and 2018 definitions can be found in the *Oslo Manual 2018* (OECD and Eurostat 2018, 75). Hence, although data availability makes it impossible to examine all dimensions empirically, the analysis will be cognizant of the full range of innovation activities defined here.

Source: Adapted from OECD and Eurostat 2018.

The term "significantly improved"—and the fact that some advances are new to the firm or to the local market while others are new to the world—reflects the broad literature on innovation, which often uses different terms to convey similar concepts. Improvements in products or processes that are new to the *firm* or to the domestic *market* are alternatively referred to as "imitation" or "incremental innovation." Improvements that are new to the *world* are alternatively referred to as "invention," "discovery," or "radical innovation," terms intended to indicate the newness or uniqueness of the innovation.

Another important distinction is between innovation and technology. Innovation often involves the adoption of a new technology because implementation of a product or process innovation may require the introduction and use of a specific technology. Thus "diffusion" involves the process through which both past innovations (of some firms) and new technologies are spread, adopted, and used by other firms. The diffusion process can occur across or within countries, sectors, firms, and locations—and it is mirrored by the process of "adoption" of new technologies by firms.

The innovation imperative for developing East Asia

Several economic forces are driving the imperative for a more innovation-led growth model in developing East Asia.

Productivity remains relatively low in developing East Asia—and productivity growth has declined since the Global Financial Crisis

Despite their remarkable growth performance over time, countries in developing East Asia still face important productivity challenges. Although labor productivity has grown rapidly in recent years (averaging 6.3 percent per year between 2013 and 2018), the region's output per worker remains well below the productivity frontier, defined as the productivity level in the United States (figure 1.1, panel a). Even in Malaysia, whose output per worker is the highest in the region, labor productivity was only about 42 percent of the US level in 2017. In the region's next tier of countries (China, Indonesia, the Philippines, and Thailand), labor productivity only ranged between 18 percent and 24 percent of the US level in 2017.

FIGURE 1.1   Although productivity in the major economies of developing East Asia has been rising, it remains well below the frontier

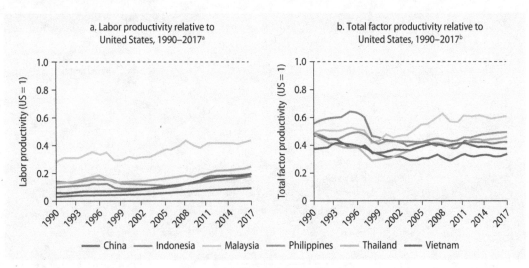

a. Labor productivity relative to United States, 1990–2017[a]

b. Total factor productivity relative to United States, 1990–2017[b]

China — Indonesia — Malaysia — Philippines — Thailand — Vietnam

Sources: World Bank elaboration, based on Asian Productivity Organization (APO) Database 2019, version 2 (https://www.apo-tokyo.org/wedo/productivity-measurement/); and Penn World Table version 9.1 data.

Note: The developing East Asian countries included in these figures—China and the five largest emerging economies of the Association of Southeast Asian Nations (ASEAN)—are those for which the most reliable data series are available.

a. Labor productivity is measured as gross domestic product (GDP) per worker.

b. Total factor productivity (TFP) is measured in purchasing power parity (PPP) terms. TFP series are calculated by the Penn World Table (PWT) team, except for Vietnam. For Vietnam, TFP is estimated using the methodology in Feenstra, Inklaar, and Timmer (2015), capital stock data from PWT (version 9.1) and labor share estimates from the APO Productivity Database 2019 (version 2).

Similarly, total factor productivity (TFP) levels in most of developing East Asia remain far below the frontier (figure 1.1, panel b). Again, Malaysia's TFP, while higher than elsewhere in the region, was still only about 62 percent of US TFP in 2017. Although productivity generally increases as countries develop, TFP in most developing East Asian countries is below what would be predicted on the basis of their gross domestic product (GDP) per capita (figure 1.2).

Productivity growth has slowed worldwide since the Global Financial Crisis, and developing East Asia has not been immune. Indeed, the region experienced the second steepest slowdown in labor productivity growth of all emerging market and developing regions since the Global Financial Crisis (World Bank 2020b). Although labor productivity growth declined across the region, the decline has been particularly pronounced in China (figure 1.3). A decomposition of labor productivity growth shows that the slowdown largely reflects weaker TFP growth.

Recent studies have highlighted the key role that innovation must play in developing East Asia if its countries are to maintain or increase productivity growth in a rapidly changing and highly uncertain global economic environment (Mason and Shetty 2019; World Bank and DRC 2019). Reinforcing the case for innovation-led growth is empirical evidence from high-income economies as well as the region, showing strong links between technology adoption, innovation, and higher productivity (Cirera and Maloney 2017; Comin and Hobijn 2010; de Nicola 2019; Hall 2011; Mohnen and Hall 2013). Andrews, Criscuolo, and Gal (2016) further suggest that a critical component of the global productivity slowdown since the late 1990s is the technological divergence between leading and lagging firms. For that reason, promoting broad-based innovation—oriented not only to leading firms capable of invention but also to other firms with the potential to adopt existing technologies—is warranted.

FIGURE 1.2   **Total factor productivity in most developing East Asian countries is below what would be predicted based on their GDP per capita**

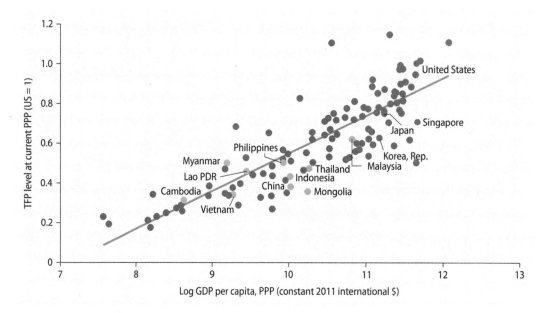

Sources: World Bank elaboration, based on Penn World Table (PWT) version 9.1 and Asian Productivity Organization (APO) Database 2019, version 2 (https://www.apo-tokyo.org/wedo/productivity-measurement/).
Note: Data are from 2017. Countries in light blue designate the 10 "developing East Asia" countries studied in this report. Total factor productivity (TFP) is measured in purchasing power parity (PPP) terms relative to the United States (1.0). TFP series are calculated by the PWT team, except for Cambodia, Myanmar, and Vietnam, which are estimated through the methodology of Feenstra, Inklaar, and Timmer (2015), using data from PWT (version 9.1) and labor share estimates from the APO Database 2019 (version 2). GDP = gross domestic product; PPP = purchasing power parity; TFP = total factor productivity.

FIGURE 1.3   **Labor productivity and TFP growth have declined in developing East Asia since the Global Financial Crisis**

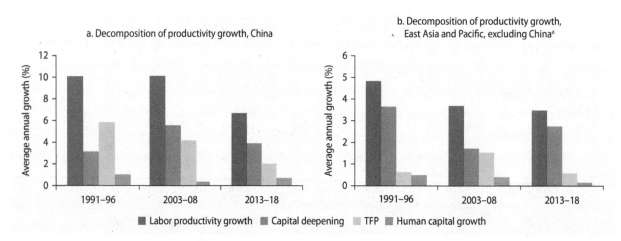

Sources: Conference Board; Asian Productivity Organization (APO) Database 2019, version 2 (https://www.apo-tokyo.org/wedo/productivity-measurement/); and Penn World Table (PWT) version 9.1 data; van der Eng 2009; World Bank calculations.
Note: Labor productivity is measured as GDP per worker. PWT data were used as the baseline. When PWT (version 9.1) data were not available, the APO Database 2019 (version 2) was used. Conference Board data were used for 2018. GDP = gross domestic product; TFP = total factor productivity.
a. Panel b shows weighted averages calculated using GDP weights at 2010 prices. Countries included are Cambodia, Indonesia, Lao PDR, Malaysia, Mongolia, Myanmar, the Philippines, Thailand, and Vietnam. For Indonesia, capital stock was calculated by World Bank staff, extending data from van der Eng (2009).

Spurring productivity growth through greater innovation will thus be important to the economic fortunes of developing East Asia in the medium term. Innovation can enable the production of new and better goods and services as well as increase productivity through organizational or marketing improvements. Innovation can enhance productivity growth largely by raising TFP—that is, enabling higher levels of output with the same quantity of resources. Indeed, innovation has been an important element in the rise of the region's high-income countries. Japan, the Republic of Korea, and Singapore have all used innovation to improve efficiency and boost their incomes, with great success (Hobday 1995).

Changes in global trade and rapid technological advances are challenging the region's main engine of growth: export-oriented manufacturing

The slowing of the global goods trade and ambiguity about the future of the global trading system in general pose risks to a development model that has effectively used trade, foreign direct investment (FDI), and integration into global value chains (GVCs) as critical channels for growth. Furthermore, a new technological revolution—Industry 4.0—poses a risk of disrupting existing production structures as it moves toward more flexible manufacturing and customization and increases the importance of proximity to customers. These technological advances, discussed further in chapter 2, could result in the shortening of GVCs or the reshoring of production systems that have helped fuel growth in developing East Asian countries.

Although the extent to which these changes will occur is still uncertain, new technology-driven production processes could put pressure on the region's labor-intensive, export-oriented production model, potentially unwinding gains associated with countries' participation in the global trading system. Meeting these challenges will require innovation to narrow the productivity and technological gaps with high-income economies and preserve countries' competitiveness in the global economy.

The COVID-19 pandemic and climate change are accelerating the need for digitalization and new production methods

The COVID-19 pandemic

The COVID-19 pandemic has underscored the importance of innovation as policy makers and private firms have rushed to adopt or develop technologies to address both the health and the economic effects of the outbreak. This effort has included, among other things, the application of digital technologies to provide real-time information about the spread of the virus; the use of drone technologies for such applications as aerial disinfection, noncontact transport of medical supplies, and consumer deliveries; and the use of advanced biomedical technologies and artificial intelligence to develop testing, vaccines, and an eventual treatment for the virus.[3] Firms in the region have made greater use of digital platforms and invested in digital solutions to maintain their businesses in the face of mobility restrictions and social distancing (figure 1.4).

As importantly, the COVID-19 pandemic has been a shock to GDP not seen for decades in the region—one that can have long-lasting effects. So large a shock, affecting both demand and supply, has highlighted the need for more flexible management, more automated and digitally integrated production processes, and more digitally enabled delivery of services to offset some of the costs imposed by social-distance measures (see, for example, Hatayama, Viollaz, and Winkler 2020).

This shift has already begun in the region, although the shock is also altering research and innovation priorities, with potentially important trade-offs (box 1.2). Policy makers will need to find ways to accelerate the technological transformation of their economies, while managing these trade-offs, to pave the

FIGURE 1.4   **COVID-19 has induced greater use of and investment in digital solutions in developing East Asia since the beginning of the pandemic**

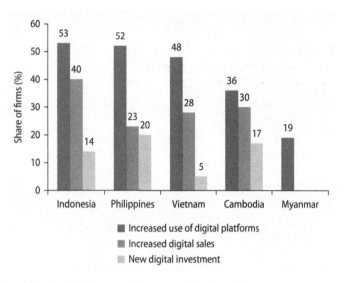

Legend:
- Increased use of digital platforms
- Increased digital sales
- New digital investment

Source: World Bank 2020a, based on COVID-19 Business Pulse Survey (BPS) data.
Note: Data on increased digital sales and new digital investment since the pandemic are not available for Myanmar. The survey was conducted in May 2020 for Myanmar; in June 2020 for Cambodia, Indonesia, and Vietnam; and in July 2020 for the Philippines. The BPS is a telephone survey implemented in 51 countries in six regions of the world using the same questionnaire. The figure shows results for the countries included in the BPS from developing East Asia. Sample size varies by country but is representative for small, medium, and large firms.

way for what will likely be very different economies in the post–COVID-19 era.

Indeed, many of the changes induced by the pandemic are likely to be long lasting, with changes in consumer preference requiring many traditional brick-and-mortar companies to adopt business models that increase their presence on digital platforms. The closure of physical retail stores dictated by COVID-19 containment measures already appears to have encouraged the diffusion of e-commerce across the region (box 1.2). And the growth of e-commerce provides a potential avenue for new business and job creation by generating opportunities for start-ups offering value-added services.

Accelerating this digital transformation in firms is imperative to recovery given continuing unknowns about the trajectory of COVID-19 and the high likelihood of other, future pandemics. Firms' digital transformation in the region will thus determine not only their ability to survive this crisis but also their competitiveness and resilience in the face of unforeseen crises.[4]

BOX 1.2   COVID-19: Changing the innovation landscape

The spread of COVID-19 and the policy response may have conflicting effects on each of the two dimensions of innovation: (a) invention, and (b) diffusion and adoption. Regarding *invention*, the pandemic has boosted research and development (R&D) on tests, vaccines, and treatment to combat the disease. This will likely have positive spillovers for broader scientific and medical research in areas such as biotechnology. At the same time, the social distancing needed to contain the disease has hurt scientific research *not* related to COVID-19, by shutting down laboratories and durably disrupting experiments.

As for *diffusion*, adapting to social distancing has boosted firms' and households' adoption of technologies for digital communication, conveyance, and commerce that will likely be used beyond the pandemic. Apedo-Amah et al. (2020), using a sample of 51 countries (mainly low- and middle-income countries, including 5 developing East Asia countries),[a] find that 49 percent of firms made greater use

of technology or improved their product mix in response to the pandemic.

However, the crisis-induced economic contraction and uncertainty are inhibiting investments in both invention and adoption in a variety of other areas by cutting resources and dampening expected returns. To mitigate COVID-19's pernicious impact, significant funds and resources have been allocated toward medical and pharmaceutical R&D to develop diagnostics, treatment, and vaccines. But research on other topics and in other fields faces a different reality. Containment measures have resulted in the closure of research labs that are not working on COVID-19, thus delaying, if not compromising, the realization of technological improvements. For example, bacterial colonies were slid into freezers for an indefinite rest, clinical trial participants were told to stay home, and populations of lab mice were reduced to the bare minimum, while researchers shifted their focus to writing grant proposals

box continues next page

---

and drafting manuscripts, being unable to continue hands-on research (Servick et al. 2020).

Even when labs and firms remain operative, heightened uncertainty due to the pandemic shock is hampering economic activity. Focusing on the US economy, Baker et al. (2020) show that about 60 percent of output contraction is because of COVID-induced uncertainty. Moreover, Apedo-Amah et al. (2020) find that firms in low- and middle-income countries are three times more pessimistic and four times more uncertain than firms in the United States—and these more-pessimistic firms tend to fire more workers.

Furthermore, beyond these current effects, the uncertainty likely will have longer-term negative consequences because of the postponing and downscaling of irreversible expenses, such as investments in intangible capital and R&D expenditures (Barrero, Bloom, and Wright 2017). These cuts to innovation inputs may happen in firms of all sizes: recent surveys underscore that pandemic-induced uncertainty is a key concern for firms both small (Apedo-Amah et al. 2020; Bloom et al. 2020) and large (Hassan et al. 2020).

COVID-19 is inducing diffusion of technologies in several ways that may permanently change the economic landscape in the region. First, the use of digital platforms has increased everywhere. Apedo-Amah et al. (2020) estimate that 34 percent of firms have increased or started using digital platforms and social media. E-commerce grew substantially in China, in response to the restrictions put in place because of the 2003 severe acute respiratory syndrome (SARS) outbreak, and COVID-19 is having a similar effect (*Economist* 2020). The closure of physical retail stores dictated by COVID-19 containment measures has encouraged the diffusion of e-commerce as well. Shopee, one of Southeast Asia's largest e-commerce platforms by web traffic, doubled its year-on-year orders during the first quarter of 2020 (Loh 2020).

Moreover, the growth in e-commerce in the region corresponded to a change in the composition of goods sold online. Before the pandemic, e-commerce marketplaces focused on fashion; cosmetics; and computer, communication, and consumer electronics. The pandemic has prompted an increase in online sales of grocery and fresh produce. Brick-and-mortar supermarkets and fresh produce specialty stores have striven to increase their presence on platforms such as Shopee, Lazada, and Tokopedia when COVID-19 containment measures forced them to close their physical stores.

Finally, the pandemic is also catalyzing greater use of fintech. Digital financial services have become key to (a) facilitating the disbursement of emergency liquidity to businesses and cash transfers to households, as well as (b) keeping people safe by promoting contactless payment systems during this time of social distancing (Pazarbasioglu and Mora 2020). This diffusion of fintech may, in turn, yield productivity gains, by (a) promoting competition in the financial sector (Ruehl and Kynge 2019), and (b) increasing financial inclusion, because information gathered via fintech enables people and enterprises to build credit scores, which in turn strengthens their access to finance.

a. The countries are Cambodia, Indonesia, Mongolia, the Philippines, and Vietnam.

Climate change

Climate change is also challenging traditional approaches to production and growth. Temperatures will increase significantly in developing East Asia, and warming is already causing severe weather events more frequently: heat waves, droughts, flooding, wildfires, and hurricanes. East and Southeast Asian countries are among those likely to be hardest hit as the climate warms further (map 1.1).

According to the Global Climate Risk Index 2020, 4 Southeast Asian countries— Myanmar, the Philippines, Thailand, and Vietnam—were among the 10 countries most affected between 1999 and 2018 (Eckstein et al. 2019). Moreover, the continued reliance of Southeast Asian countries on agriculture and the concentration of populations in coastal regions exacerbates their vulnerability. Many major coastal cities are seriously imperiled, including Shanghai and Tianjin,

MAP 1.1   **East Asian countries are among those most at risk from climate change**

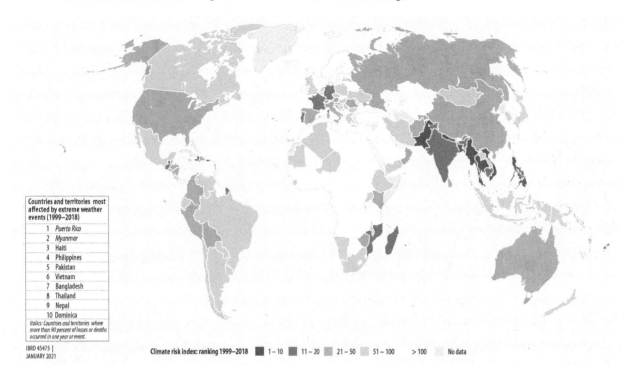

Countries and territories most affected by extreme weather events (1999–2018)	
1	*Puerto Rico*
2	*Myanmar*
3	Haiti
4	Philippines
5	Pakistan
6	Vietnam
7	Bangladesh
8	Thailand
9	Nepal
10	Dominica

Italics: Countries and territories where more than 90 percent of losses or deaths occurred in one year or event.

IBRD 45475 |
JANUARY 2021

Climate risk index: ranking 1999–2018   ■ 1 – 10   ■ 11 – 20   ■ 21 – 50   ■ 51 – 100   > 100   No data

Source: Adapted from Eckstein et al. 2019. ©Germanwatch. Reproduced, with permission, from Germanwatch; further permission required for reuse.

China; Jakarta, Indonesia; Ho Chi Minh City, Vietnam; and Bangkok, Thailand.

Significant technological changes are required to address climate change effectively (box 1.3). From the perspective of mitigation, it is imperative to have "cleaner" and more energy-efficient production that reduces carbon emissions. From the perspective of adaptation, new and sustainable technological solutions are necessary to ensure that agricultural production is sustainable and to enable safe and productive factory environments at higher temperatures. These responses can only be carried out if policy objectives shift toward prioritizing more innovation and the adoption of new technologies.

Innovation performance in developing East Asia

Much attention has been paid in the popular press recently to a growing number of high-profile, high-tech firms operating and innovating in the region, particularly those in the digital space. Although the achievements of high-performing "unicorns" are important and noteworthy, realizing the economic promise of innovation will require a broad swath of firms across different sectors of the region's economies to engage in innovation activities. But how well are developing East Asian countries performing overall on innovation? And how do the region's economies measure up to others at similar levels of development?

The region has experienced some important innovation-related successes

There are several examples of strong innovation performance in developing East Asia (map 1.2). Beijing; Shanghai; and the region of Shenzhen and Hong Kong SAR, China, are all among the top 20 global innovation clusters

BOX 1.3   Mitigating effects of climate change through effective technology adoption

Low- and middle-income economies' long-term growth is dependent on technology advancement that drives productivity and economic performance (Jones 2016). New technologies that are embodied in capital equipment and that generate a stream of innovations are among the principal drivers of productivity and arbiters of economic performance. However, research and development (R&D) investment is below 1 percent of gross domestic product (GDP) in most Southeast Asian countries. Increasing global temperatures stand to hit East and Southeast Asian countries hard, affecting food security, water availability, mortality, labor productivity, student learning, migration patterns, physical infrastructures, conflict incidence, and localized violence. Hence, technology must be borrowed and adapted while domestic innovation capabilities are being built through R&D and investments in science, technology, engineering, and mathematics (STEM) fields.

Buttressing labor productivity

Labor productivity, export and industrial value added, service output, and GDP decrease as the temperature rises (Flouris et al. 2018). The poor are most affected because their activities are often concentrated in heat-prone areas. Air conditioning on a broad scale is one solution, but it is costly and energy intensive.

Technological advances in three areas could bring climate control within reach of low- and middle-income countries while curtailing carbon emissions: (a) development of low-carbon, cost-effective cooling technologies;[a] (b) electrification using renewable energy technologies; and (c) use of distributed generation, smart grid technology, and utility-scale storage devices.

Minimizing exposure to extreme heat in farming, manufacturing, and construction calls for greater mechanization and automation. So, countries need to increase R&D and innovation to ensure user-friendly, cost-effective technology including customized fabrics for extreme heat.

Maintaining agricultural yields

Feeding the world's population will be an increasing challenge in a warming environment. Four commonly consumed crops (wheat, rice, maize, and soybean) decrease in yield as the global temperatures rise.

Crops are also affected by disease and pests, disappearance of pollinators, water stress, reduction in food quality, increased risk of spoilage, and infestation by mycotoxins (Mbow et al. 2019). Agricultural output losses due to warming in Asia could contribute to greater malnutrition and stunting.

Mitigation remedies include biogenetic, nanochemical, mechanical, and digital technologies to improve crop variety and resistance-maximizing yields. Countries that lack the physical and human capital for frontier technologies can use adaptive innovations to minimize output loss and avoid acute food crisis. In fact, a number of existing technologies, if adopted, hold considerable promise for raising productivity and improving sustainability of agriculture in developing East Asia (Rajalahti 2021).

Ensuring water availability

Freshwater resources underpin agricultural processes and determine the survival, growth, and quality of life. Domestic and industrial demands intensify as warming causes renewable water availability to decline and people's exposures to floods to rise. For each degree of warming, roughly 7 percent of the world's population is projected to experience a decrease in renewable water resources of at least 20 percent; whereas by the end of the century, the number of people exposed annually to 100-year river floods could triple (Jiménez Cisneros et al. 2014). Water scarcity in Asian countries is the result of drought and water politics, water pollution, and excessive groundwater extraction. These forces, combined with warming, could mean that 40 percent of Asia's population lack access to drinking water by 2030.

Technology must complement efficient use of water resources to reduce the energy and costs of recycling and desalinating water. Because 70 percent of water globally is used for agriculture,[b] research in low- and middle-income countries (publicly or privately financed) must support development of cost-effective technologies for the desalination of brackish water and seawater. However, current technologies of reverse osmosis and flash distillation are capital and energy intensive. Although researchers are developing new techniques to reduce and recapture energy, technologies for contaminant removal remain costly.

box continues next page

BOX 1.3   Mitigating effects of climate change through effective technology adoption *(continued)*

A range of technologies can support countries in controlling carbon emissions and coping with the threats to labor productivity, food and water availability, and human welfare posed by climate change. Countries in developing East Asia will need to increase spending on systems of innovation to create or adapt the technologies needed to address their current and emerging needs, however. Indeed, innovations to support greener growth in the region is an increasingly urgent priority.

Source: Adapted from Yusuf 2020.

a. Recent technology competitions, such as the Global Cooling Prize, have spotlighted several promising cooling solutions. These include "smart hybrid technology to optimize on efficiency and handle temperature and humidity separately; no or low-GWP [global warming potential] climate-friendly refrigerants; reusing system-generated waste heat and water; smart controls, sensors, and automation to optimize hybrid operation based on outdoor and indoor conditions; or integration of a small solar panel on the outdoor unit to significantly reduce the overall climate impact" (Lalit 2020).

b. A higher percentage of water is needed for agriculture in low-income countries (over 80 percent in Africa and Asia) and significantly lower percentages are needed in high-income countries (41 percent on average, 21 percent in Europe, and 51 percent in North America).

MAP 1.2   **Developing East Asia is home to several of the world's top 100 innovation clusters**

Source: Bergquist, Fink, and Raffo 2017. ©World Intellectual Property Organization (WIPO). Reproduced, with permission, from WIPO; further permission required for reuse.

Note: The innovation clusters are identified based on the density of patent filings in a city or set of neighboring cities, using the geocoded addresses of inventors listed in patents published between 2010 and 2015 under WIPO's Patent Cooperation Treaty (PCT). Cluster size is determined by the number of PCT applications associated with the inventors present in a given cluster. "Developing East Asia" refers to the 10 middle-income countries covered in this study: Cambodia, China, Indonesia, Lao PDR, Malaysia, Mongolia, Myanmar, the Philippines, Thailand, and Vietnam.

according to data on the spatial density of patents filed under the World Intellectual Property Organization's Patent Cooperation Treaty (Bergquist, Fink, and Raffo 2017). All of these clusters specialize in innovation in digital communication. In addition, the top 100 global innovation clusters include two Chinese cities (Guangzhou and Hangzhou) as well as Kuala Lumpur, Malaysia—all three of which specialize in computer technology.

Other evidence indicates that the region's export-oriented growth model has enabled countries to participate in more sophisticated forms of manufacturing trade over time. Cross-country data show, for example, that most of the region's countries perform at or above what would be predicted based on their per capita income levels with respect to high-tech *imports*, high-tech and medium-high-tech *outputs*, and high-tech *exports* (figure 1.5).

Although much of the region's participation in this trade began with less-sophisticated components and assembly, these measures reflect the increased adoption of global technologies and production processes over time through

FIGURE 1.5 **Several developing East Asian countries are significant participants in the global value chains for high-tech products**

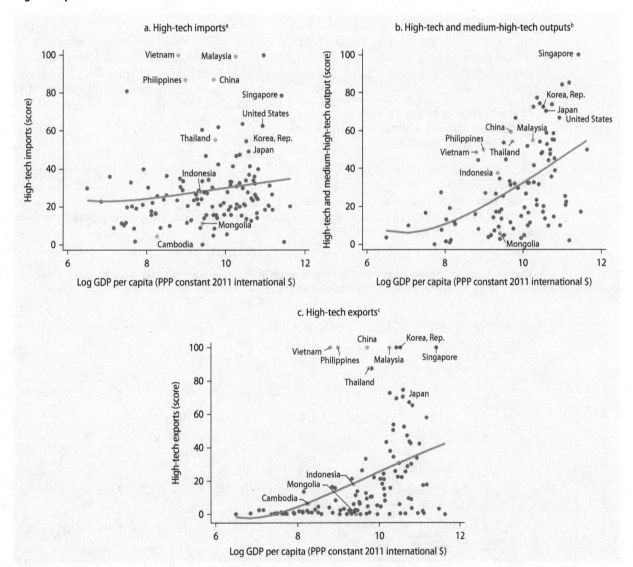

Source: World Bank elaboration, using data reported in *Global Innovation Index 2019* (Dutta, Lanvin, and Wunsch-Vincent 2019).
Note: High-tech export and import indicators include technical products with high research and development (R&D) intensity, as defined and classified by Eurostat, the statistical office of the European Union. "Developing East Asia" refers to the 10 middle-income countries covered in this study (designated in light blue): Cambodia, China, Indonesia, Lao PDR, Malaysia, Mongolia, Myanmar, the Philippines, Thailand, and Vietnam. The figure excludes Lao PDR and Myanmar, for which no recent data exist. GDP = gross domestic product; PPP = purchasing power parity.
a. The high-tech imports indicator measures high-tech imports as a percentage of total trade.
b. The high-tech and medium-high-tech output indicators measure high-tech and medium-high-tech output as a percentage of total manufacturing output, based on the classification of technology intensity defined by the Organisation for Economic Co-operation and Development (OECD). High-tech and medium-high-tech output indicators are missing for Cambodia.
c. The high-tech exports indicator is defined as high-tech exports minus re-exports as a percentage of total trade.

FDI, creation of joint ventures, and participation in trade and GVCs. For example, between 2000 and 2008, the share of the domestic content of exports in electronics grew significantly in Malaysia and Thailand as well as in industrial machinery in Indonesia and the Philippines (WTO and IDE-JETRO 2011), probably as a result of FDI to produce locally and increased participation of local suppliers. Central to the region's outward-oriented manufacturing and growth strategy, these forms of international engagement have represented important opportunities for technology transfer and knowledge diffusion over the past half century.[5]

Most countries in the region underperform on several key indicators of innovation, however

Despite the great promise of innovation in the region, analysis of a range of key innovation indicators reveals that countries in developing East Asia still face important challenges to fostering innovation-led growth. Most of these countries appear to underperform on several standard indicators of innovation for both *diffusion* (the adoption of existing technologies) and *discovery* (the invention of new products, processes, and technologies, as discussed in box 1.1).[6]

One critical input for more-basic forms of innovation, such as improving the quality of products and processes, is international certification, which gives firms access to other countries' markets. International certification has contributed to firm-level productivity in several middle-income countries, including China and four Southeast Asian countries (Cirera and Maloney 2017; Escribano and Guasch 2005). However, all countries in developing East Asia except China perform below their predicted values regarding international certification (figure 1.6, panel a).

Licensing of foreign technologies—another important input for the diffusion and adoption of new technologies—is also associated with higher innovation output among firms in developing East Asia (Iootty 2019). Across

FIGURE 1.6 The share of firms with international certification is low in much of developing East Asia, and in half of the countries, fewer firms acquire licenses to foreign technology than expected given their countries' per capita incomes

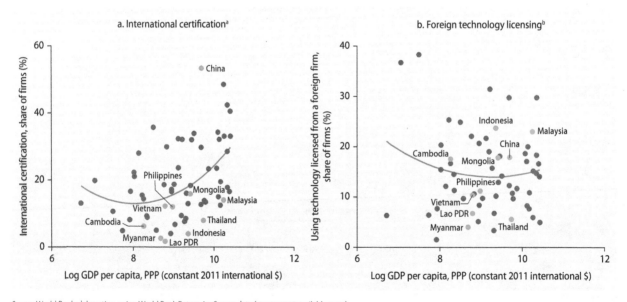

a. International certification[a]

b. Foreign technology licensing[b]

Source: World Bank elaboration, using World Bank Enterprise Survey data (most recent available years).
Note: "Developing East Asia" refers to the 10 middle-income countries covered in this study (designated in light blue): Cambodia, China, Indonesia, Lao PDR, Malaysia, Mongolia, Myanmar, the Philippines, Thailand, and Vietnam. GDP = gross domestic product; PPP = purchasing power parity.
a. International certification provides independent assurance that products or services comply with certain mutually recognized standards.
b. Foreign technology licensing includes purchase or licensing of both patented and nonpatented technologies by firms as part of their production or organizational processes.

the region, performance regarding foreign technology licensing is more mixed: in half of the countries, a smaller share of firms obtain licenses to foreign technologies than would be expected given their countries' per capita incomes (figure 1.6, panel b).

Data on the main input of *discovery* of new products and technologies (R&D) and one key proxy of *invention* (patents) highlight similar challenges. Most countries in the region spend less on R&D, a key innovation input, than would be expected given their per capita incomes (figure 1.7, panel a). Only three countries (China, Malaysia, and Vietnam) spend at or above expected levels.

Similarly, most developing East Asian countries produce fewer patents—a commonly used measure of innovation output that can result in invention—than would be expected given their per capita incomes (figure 1.7, panel b). Again, Malaysia, Vietnam, and in in this case, Mongolia, perform at or near the predicted levels.

China is noteworthy in that it performs significantly above expectations regarding both R&D spending and patents granted. Similar patterns are seen in China's other innovation inputs and outputs.

Despite some high-profile successes, countries face ongoing challenges with services sector innovations, including in the digital space

Services are playing an increasingly important role in the region's economies—in manufacturing, trade, and in their own right—as the demand for services grows. Nonetheless, developing East Asian countries still face challenges concerning innovation in services, including in the digital space. As figure 1.8 shows, most of the region's countries perform below expectations, given per capita GDP, in mobile app creation, information and communication technology (ICT) services exports, and the export of "cultural and creative

FIGURE 1.7   **Most countries in developing East Asia spend less on R&D and produce fewer patents than would be predicted by their per capita incomes**

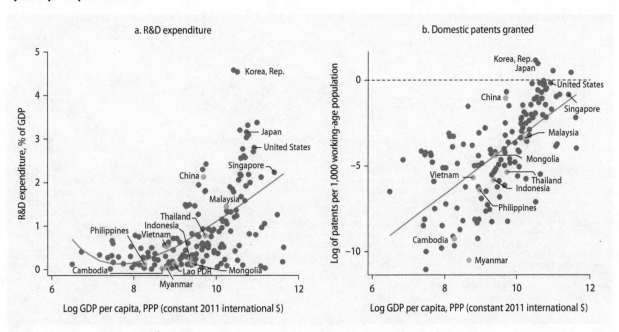

Source: World Bank elaboration, based on 2018 data from the World Intellectual Property Organization (WIPO) Statistics Database (https://www3.wipo.int/ipstats/index.htm) and the World Development Indicators database.
Note: "Developing East Asia" refers to the 10 middle-income countries covered in this study (designated in light blue): Cambodia, China, Indonesia, Lao PDR, Malaysia, Mongolia, Myanmar, the Philippines, Thailand, and Vietnam. GDP = gross domestic product; PPP = purchasing power parity; R&D = research and development.

FIGURE 1.8   **With some noteworthy exceptions, developing East Asian countries still face challenges concerning innovation in services, including in the digital space**

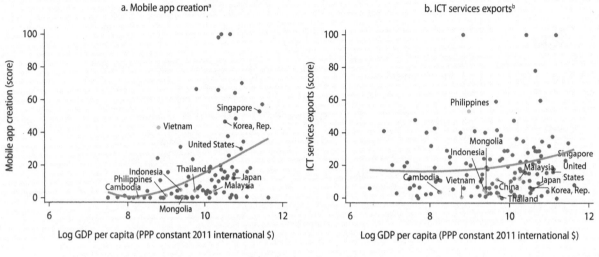

a. Mobile app creation[a]

b. ICT services exports[b]

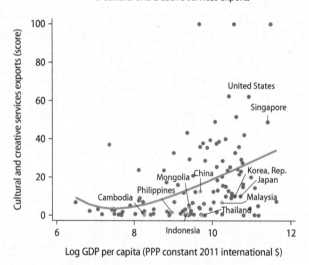

c. Cultural and creative services exports[c]

Source: World Bank elaboration, using data reported in *Global Innovation Index 2019* (Dutta, Lanvin, and Wunsch-Vincent 2019).

Note: "Developing East Asia" refers to the 10 middle-income countries covered in this study (labeled in light blue): Cambodia, China, Indonesia, Lao PDR, Malaysia, Mongolia, Myanmar, the Philippines, Thailand, and Vietnam. The figure excludes Lao PDR and Myanmar, for which no recent data exist. GDP = gross domestic product; ICT = information and communication technology; PPP = purchasing power parity.

a. The mobile app creation indicator measures global downloads of mobile apps, by origin of the headquarters of the developer or firm, scaled by GDP (in PPP international $, billions). Global downloads are compiled by App Annie Intelligence, public data sources, and the company's proprietary forecast model based on data from the Google Play store and iOS App store in each country between January 1, 2018, and December 31, 2018. Since data for China are not available for Google Play store and only for iOS App store, data from China are treated as missing and considered "n/a" (Dutta, Lanvin, and Wunsch-Vincent 2019, 365).

b. The information and communication technology (ICT) services exports indicator represents telecommunications, computer, and information services exports (percentage of total trade), based on the 2010 Extended Balance of Payments Services (EBOPS 2010) classification (UNSD 2012).

c. The cultural and creative services exports indicator measures creative services exports (percentage of total exports), covering information services; advertising, market research, and public opinion polling services; audiovisual and related services; and other personal cultural and recreational services, based on EBOPS 2010 (UNSD 2012). The cultural and creative services exports indicator is missing for Vietnam.

services"—defined to include information services; advertising, market research, and public opinion polling services; audiovisual and related services; and other personal cultural and recreational services (Dutta, Lanvin, and Wunsch-Vincent 2019).

However, the data show a few clear examples of better-than-expected performance. Vietnam stands out as a high performer in mobile app creation (figure 1.8, panel a) and the Philippines as a high performer in ICT services exports (figure 1.8, panel b), most likely reflecting that country's global role in providing business process outsourcing (BPO) services (World Bank 2019).[7]

Firms in the region engage in product, process, marketing, and organizational innovation—although the extent varies considerably across countries

Data from the World Bank's Enterprise Surveys provide a more granular view of countries' innovation outputs. Consistent with the *Oslo Manual* definitions (discussed in box 1.1), the surveyed firms report whether they have introduced new or significantly improved (a) products (goods or services), (b) processes, (c) marketing methods, and (d) organizational practices. Figure 1.9 presents the share of firms in developing East Asia that reported innovations in each of those four domains.

Despite considerable variability across countries in the share of firms that report innovations, a few patterns emerge:

- In 7 out of 10 countries in the region, a higher share of firms report undertaking process innovations than other forms of innovation.
- In all but one country (Lao PDR), a higher share of firms report undertaking process innovations than product innovations.
- A relatively large share of firms (20 percent or more in 6 out of 10 countries) also report undertaking marketing innovations.

Although not shown in figure 1.9, the Enterprise Survey data indicate that when firms in developing East Asia innovate, they are likely to engage in multiple innovation activities across the four innovation domains.

Consistent with the cross-country indicators discussed above, a substantially larger share of firms in China report undertaking

FIGURE 1.9 **Countries in developing East Asia show considerable variation in the incidence and type of firm-level innovation**

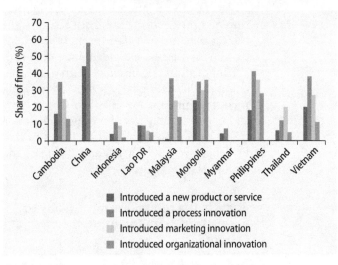

Source: World Bank estimates from Enterprise Survey data (latest available year).
Note: No data on marketing or organizational innovations are reported in the China or Myanmar surveys.

innovation than in any other country in the region. For example, nearly 60 percent of Chinese firms report introducing a process innovation, while around 45 percent report introducing a product innovation.

Also noteworthy is the relatively high share of firms reporting innovation activities in several fast-growing lower-middle-income countries. Around one-third of firms in Cambodia and Mongolia report undertaking process innovations, while in Vietnam, the share is close to 40 percent. These outcomes likely reflect the adoption and diffusion of new production and business processes among firms integrated into the international economy through trade and GVCs. As figure 1.9 also shows, a much lower share of firms in several other countries—Indonesia, Lao PDR, Myanmar, and to a lesser extent, Thailand—report engaging in innovation.

Deeper analysis of the same Enterprise Survey data indicates that firm innovation in developing East Asia is positively associated with firm productivity—whether measured as labor productivity or as revenue TFP. Specifically, firms that innovate generate 20 percent more output per worker than those that do not, and TFP can be up to 35 percent higher among innovative firms than non-innovative firms (de Nicola 2019).

The positive relationship between innovation and productivity holds for firms in the region that introduce either new products or new processes. This evidence on product innovation is consistent with a broader empirical literature, largely focused on high-income countries but also on China, that shows positive impacts of product innovation on revenue productivity. For surveys of that evidence, see Hall (2011) and Mohnen and Hall (2013).

Firms in the region are more likely to innovate in manufacturing than in services

Enterprise Survey data also indicate that higher shares of firms undertake innovation in manufacturing than in services (figure 1.10). Only in Cambodia are the shares of firms reporting innovation in manufacturing and in services roughly equivalent. In China and Malaysia, the differences in the shares of firms reporting innovations in manufacturing and in services are particularly large.

As chapter 2 will discuss further, innovation in services is important not only in its own right but also to ensure that firms in the region can maintain their competitiveness in manufacturing and global trade. This, in turn, has implications for innovation policy.[8]

While many firms in the region still do not innovate, innovating firms commonly engage in the adoption of existing technologies and practices

Innovating firms in the region also report whether the innovations they introduce are new to the firm (only) or new to their main market. Innovations that are new only to the firm can be interpreted as resulting from the diffusion, adoption, and use of already existing technologies and practices, whereas some share of innovations that are new to the market are likely to be the result of invention. In the Enterprise Surveys for developing East Asia, it is not possible to distinguish between new-to-market innovations that are new only to the local market and those that are new to international markets. In reality, many of those innovations reported as new to the market likely represent diffusion and adoption applied to the local market, especially in the lower-middle-income countries.

Innovating firms in developing East Asia report both new-to-firm and new-to-market innovations (figure 1.11). The visible exception is China, for which no data on new-to-market innovations are available. But separate firm-level data from five Chinese provinces reinforce the finding that firms introduce both new-to-firm and new-to-market innovations, depending on their capabilities (Park and Xuan 2020).

This distinction between innovation defined as *diffusion and adoption* of existing technologies and innovation defined as *invention* is important in the context of developing East Asia. As the subsequent chapters will discuss in greater detail, there is tremendous heterogeneity in countries' and firms' capacities to innovate across the region. Especially among the lower-middle-income countries in the region (such as Cambodia, Lao PDR, and Myanmar) and among most small and medium enterprises (SMEs), adoption and diffusion of existing but new-to-firm technologies and practices may be the only feasible route to innovation in the short term and thus of critical importance to increasing firms' productivity and aggregate productivity growth.

FIGURE 1.10   In developing East Asia, a higher share of firms reports innovating in manufacturing than in services

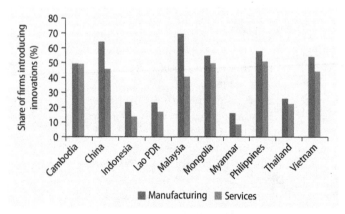

Source: World Bank estimates, based on Enterprise Survey data (latest available year).

FIGURE 1.11 Firms in developing East Asia report a mix of innovations that are new to the firm and new to the domestic market

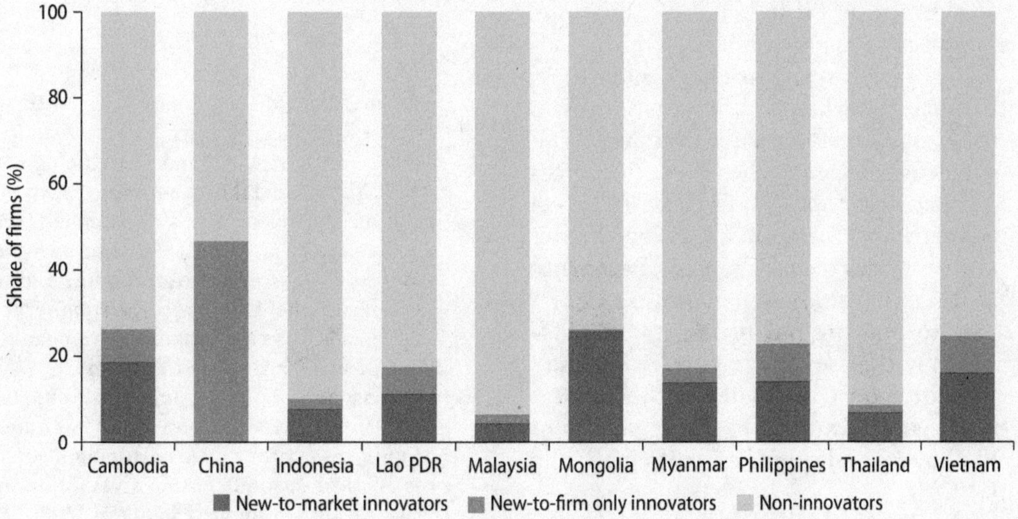

Source: World Bank calculations, using Enterprise Survey data (latest available year).
Note: Enterprise Survey data from developing East Asia distinguish between innovations that are new to the firm and new to the market, but do not distinguish between innovations that are new to the local versus international market. The Enterprise Survey for China did not collect data on new-to-market innovation.

In fact, historical evidence suggests that the development accomplishments of Japan and then the Four Asian Tigers (Hong Kong SAR, China; Korea; Singapore; and Taiwan, China) all involved substantial reduction in technology adoption lags relative to the Organisation for Economic Co-operation and Development (OECD) country average (Comin and Hobijn 2010). Comin and Hobijn (2011) estimate that the post–World War II growth experience of Western Europe and Japan can be explained, in large part, by the rapid adoption of existing foreign technologies. Moreover, US economic aid and technical assistance (for example, through the Marshall Plan) is significantly associated with reduction in adoption lags across these countries.

More-recent estimates by Santacreu (2015), using imports of intermediate goods, suggest that technology diffusion is an especially important source of growth for less-developed countries. The author estimates that between 1996 and 2007, 65 percent of labor productivity growth can

be explained by foreign innovations embodied in imports; in OECD countries, this figure is only 35.5 percent.

Road map for this report

So, what will it take for developing East Asian countries to successfully transition to an innovation-led growth model, one in which non-innovating firms begin to adopt new technologies and undertake innovation activities, while more-advanced firms progressively engage in R&D and innovation at the technological frontier? In seeking to answer this question, the chapters of this report are organized as follows:

• Chapter 2, *Conceptual Framework and Stylized Facts,* begins by describing some key concepts for thinking about innovation and the adoption and diffusion of technology. It presents a framework for thinking about a graduated set of policies through which countries with different levels of innovation capability can more effectively promote diffusion and adoption as well as invention.

- Chapter 3, *Technology Adoption and Diffusion: A Firm-Level Perspective,* then focuses more specifically on the diffusion of innovation and technology. It describes where the region stands in terms of technology adoption and documents its tremendous heterogeneity across countries, sectors, and firms with respect to innovation performance. The chapter also examines the factors that affect firms' abilities to innovate, including access to information and management quality, as well as several important channels for diffusion of knowledge for innovation that are external to the firm, such as FDI, trade, and countries' participation in GVCs.

- Chapter 4, *Skills and Finance for Innovation,* examines two key complementary factors associated with innovation in developing East Asia: skills and finance for innovation. Specifically, the chapter discusses the roles of workforce skills and different sources of finance in enabling innovation, the status of skills development and innovation finance in the region, and the challenges that developing East Asian countries face in ensuring adequate supplies of skills and risk-capital finance to support innovation.

- Chapter 5, *Policies and Institutions in the Region: An Assessment,* analyzes the adequacy of the region's current policies and institutions in addressing the barriers that firms face concerning innovation. To that end, it assesses the mix of policies designed to promote innovation. It also examines the effectiveness of institutions and polices designed to facilitate the transfer of knowledge essential to innovation. Special attention is paid to the role and efficacy of country research institutions that aim to facilitate innovation and knowledge transfer.

- Chapter 6, *Action for Innovation: A Policy Agenda,* builds on the analysis presented in the first five chapters by outlining several directions for policy to help countries

in developing East Asia effectively foster innovation-led growth.

Notes

1. For further discussion of Industry 4.0, see chapter 2 (particularly box 2.1).
2. The terms "East Asia" and "developing East Asia" will be used throughout the report. For convenience, unless otherwise specified, these terms refer to the 10 middle-income countries covered in this study: Cambodia, China, Indonesia, the Lao People's Democratic Republic, Malaysia, Mongolia, Myanmar, the Philippines, Thailand, and Vietnam.
3. For more information on innovative responses to COVID-19, see the Coronavirus Innovation Map (https://coronavirus.startupblink.com/); the World Economic Forum COVID Action Platform (for example, Chandran [2020], at https://www.weforum.org/agenda/2020/03/asia-technology-coronavirus-covid19-solutions/); and Huang, Sun, and Sui (2020).
4. As part of its economic response to the pandemic, the government of Korea has announced the "K-New Deal," which has two pillars—a digital new deal and a green economy new deal—to accelerate recovery from the pandemic and to address climate shocks. These are considered key priorities to increase employment in the country (MOEF 2020). To support firms' digital adoption, the government has undertaken special measures to ensure that micro, small, and medium enterprises (MSMEs), not only large firms, can implement the digital transition.
5. The roles of FDI, joint ventures, trade, and GVC participation in enabling innovation in developing East Asian countries are discussed at greater length in chapter 3.
6. For a more detailed discussion of key innovation concepts, see chapter 2.
7. No data are available for China on mobile app creation. However, given China's role as a global innovation cluster leader on digital communications, it is possible that it performs above predicted levels in this area as well.
8. See the chapter 2 discussion of "servicification," the increasing importance of service inputs into manufactures. Chapter 5 examines existing biases against services in innovation policy, while chapter 6 examines the implications for innovation policy.

References

Andrews, Dan, Chiara Criscuolo, and Peter N. Gal. 2016. "The Best versus the Rest: The Global Productivity Slowdown, Divergence across Firms and the Role of Public Policy." OECD Productivity Working Papers No. 5, Organisation for Economic Co-operation and Development, Paris.

Apedo-Amah, Marie Christine, Besart Avdiu, Xavier Cirera, Marcio Cruz, Elwin Davies, Arti Grover, Leonardo Iacavone, et al. 2020. "Unmasking the Impact of COVID-19 on Businesses: Firm Level Evidence from Across the World." Policy Research Working Paper 9434, World Bank, Washington, DC.

Baker, Scott, Nicholas Bloom, Steven Davis, and Stephen Terry. 2020. "COVID-Induced Economic Uncertainty and Its Consequences." NBER Working Paper No. 26983, National Bureau of Economic Research, Cambridge, MA.

Barrero, Jose Maria, Nicholas Bloom, and Ian Wright. 2017. "Short and Long Run Uncertainty." NBER Working Paper No. 23676, National Bureau of Economic Research, Cambridge, MA.

Bergquist, Kyle, Carsten Fink, and Julio Raffo. 2017. "Identifying and Ranking the World's Largest Clusters of Inventive Activity." Economic Research Working Paper No. 34, World Intellectual Property Organization (WIPO), Geneva.

Bloom, Nicholas, Philip Bunn, Scarlet Chen, Paul Mizen, and Pawel Smietanka. 2020. "The Economic Impact of Coronavirus on UK Businesses: Early Evidence from the Decision Maker Panel." VoxEU/CEPR Policy Portal, March 27, https://voxeu.org/article/economic-impact-coronavirus-uk-businesses.

Chandran, Rina. 2020. "Here's How Asia Is Using Tech to Tackle COVID-19." Reuters article on the World Economic Forum COVID Action Platform, March 18. https://www.weforum.org/agenda/2020/03/asia-technology-coronavirus-covid19-solutions/.

Cirera, Xavier, and William F. Maloney. 2017. *The Innovation Paradox: Developing-Country Capabilities and the Unrealized Promise of Technological Catch-Up*. Washington, DC: World Bank.

Comin, Diego, and Bart Hobijn. 2010. "An Exploration of Technology Diffusion." *American Economic Review* 100 (5): 2031–59.

Comin, Diego, and Bart Hobijn. 2011. "Technology Diffusion and Postwar Growth." *NBER Macroeconomics Annual* 25 (1): 209–46.

de Nicola, Francesca. 2019. "Assessing How Returns to Innovation Vary Depending on the Business Environment and Firms' Characteristics." Background paper for this study, World Bank, Washington, DC.

Dutta, Soumitra, Bruno Lanvin, and Sacha Wunsch-Vincent, eds. 2019. *Global Innovation Index 2019: Creating Healthy Lives—The Future of Medical Innovation*. 12th ed. Ithaca, NY: Cornell University; Fontainebleau, France: INSEAD; and Geneva: World Intellectual Property Organization (WIPO).

Eckstein, David, Vera Künzel, Laura Schäfer, and Maik Winges. 2019. *Global Climate Risk Index 2020: Who Suffers Most from Extreme Weather Events? Weather-Related Loss Events in 2018 and 1999 to 2018*. Berlin: Germanwatch eV.

Economist. 2020. "Less Globalisation, More Tech: The Changes Covid-19 Is Forcing on to Business." *Economist*, April 11. https://www.economist.com/briefing/2020/04/11/the-changes-covid-19-is-forcing-on-to-business.

Escribano, Alvaro, and J. Luis Guasch. 2005. "Assessing the Impact of the Investment Climate on Productivity Using Firm-Level Data: Methodology and the Cases of Guatemala, Honduras, and Nicaragua." Policy Research Working Paper 3621, World Bank, Washington, DC.

Feenstra, Robert C., Robert Inklaar, and Marcel P. Timmer. 2015. "The Next Generation of the Penn World Table." *American Economic Review* 105 (10): 3150–82.

Flouris, Andreas D., Petros C. Dinas, Leonidas G. Ioannou, Lars Nybo, George Havenith, Glen P. Kenny, and Tord Kjellstrom. 2018. "Workers' Health and Productivity under Occupational Heat Strain: A Systematic Review and Meta-Analysis." *The Lancet Planetary Health* 2 (12): e521–e531.

Hall, Bronwyn H. 2011. "Innovation and Productivity." NBER Working Paper No. 17178, National Bureau of Economic Research, Cambridge, MA.

Hassan, Tarek Alexander, Stephan Hollander, Laurence van Lent, Markus Schwedeler, and Ahmed Tahoun. 2020. "Firm-Level Exposure to Epidemic Diseases: COVID-19, SARS, and H1N1." Working Paper No. 26971, National

Bureau of Economic Research, Cambridge, MA.

Hatayama, Maho, Mariana Viollaz, and Hernan Winkler. 2020. "Jobs' Amenability to Working from Home: Evidence from Skills Surveys for 53 Countries." Policy Research Working Paper 9241, World Bank, Washington, DC.

Hobday, Michael. 1995. *Innovation in East Asia: The Challenge to Japan.* Cheltenham, UK: Edward Elgar.

Huang, Yasheng, Meicen Sun, and Yuze Sui. 2020. "How Digital Contact Tracing Slowed Covid-19 in East Asia." *Harvard Business Review,* April 15. https://hbr.org/2020/04/how-digital -contact-tracing-slowed-covid-19-in-east-asia.

Iootty, Mariana. 2019. "Assessing Innovation Patterns and Constraints in Developing East Asia: An Introductory Analysis." Policy Research Working Paper 8706, World Bank, Washington, DC.

Jiménez Cisneros, Blanca E., Taikan Oki, Nigel W. Arnell, Gerardo Benito, J. Graham Cogley, Petra Döll, Tong Jiang, and Shadrack S. Mwakalila. 2014. "Freshwater Resources." In *Climate Change 2014: Impacts, Adaptation, and Vulnerability. Part A: Global and Sectoral Aspects. Working Group II Contribution to the Fifth Assessment Report of the Intergovernmental Panel on Climate Change,* edited by Christopher B. Field, Vicente R. Barros, David Jon Dokken, Katharine J. Mach, Michael D. Mastrandrea, et al., 229–69. Cambridge and New York: Cambridge University Press.

Jones, Charles I. 2016. "The Facts of Economic Growth." *Handbook of Macroeconomics,* Vol. 2A, edited by John B. Taylor and Harald Uhlig, 3–69. Amsterdam: Elsevier.

Lalit, Radhika. 2020. "These Innovations Could Keep Us Cool without Warming the Planet." Article for the World Economic Forum Annual Meeting, January 21–24, Davos, Switzerland. https://www.weforum.org/agenda/2020/01 /these-innovations-could-keep-us-cool -without-heating-us-up/.

Loh, Dylan. 2020. "Coronavirus Pandemic Fuels Asia E-Commerce Boom." Nikkei Asia, May 31. https://asia.nikkei.com/Business /Retail/Coronavirus-pandemic-fuels-Asia-e -commerce-boom.

Mason, Andrew D., and Sudhir Shetty. 2019. *A Resurgent East Asia: Navigating a Changing World.* East Asia and Pacific Regional Report. Washington, DC: World Bank.

Mbow, Cheikh, Cynthia Rosenzweig, Luis G. Barioni, Tim G. Benton, Mario Herrero, Murukesan Krishnapillai, Emma Liwenga, et al. 2019. "Food Security." In *Climate Change and Land: An IPCC Special Report,* Supplementary Material, 5SM-1–17. https://www.ipcc.ch/site /assets/uploads/sites/4/2020/06/IPCCJ7230 -Land_SM5_200226.pdf.

MOEF (Ministry of Economy and Finance, Republic of Korea). 2020. "Korean New Deal: National Strategy for a Great Transformation." National strategic plan, MOEF, Seoul.

Mohnen, Pierre, and Bronwyn H. Hall. 2013. "Innovation and Productivity: An Update." *Eurasian Business Review* 3 (1): 47–65.

OECD and Eurostat (Organisation for Economic Co-operation and Development and the statistical office of the European Union). 2005. *Oslo Manual: Guidelines for Collecting and Interpreting Innovation.* 3rd ed. Paris: OECD; Luxembourg: Eurostat.

OECD and Eurostat. 2018. *Oslo Manual 2018: Guidelines for Collecting, Reporting and Using Data on Innovation.* 4th ed. Paris: OECD; Luxembourg: Eurostat.

Park, Albert, and Wenshi Xuan. 2020. "Skills for Innovation in China." Background paper for this report, Hong Kong University of Science and Technology, Hong Kong SAR, China.

Pazarbasioglu, Ceyla, and Alfonso Garcia Mora. 2020. "Expanding Digital Financial Services Can Help Developing Economies Cope with Crisis Now and Boost Growth Later." *Voices* (blog), World Bank, April 29. https://blogs. worldbank.org/voices/expanding-digital -financial-services-can-help-developing -economies-cope-crisis-now-and-boost-growth -later.

Rajalahti, Riikka. 2021. "Agricultural Innovation in Developing East Asia: Productivity, Safety, and Sustainability." Background paper for this study, World Bank, Washington, DC.

Ruehl, Mercedes, and James Kynge. 2019. "Fintech: The Rise of the Asian 'Super App.'" *Financial Times,* December 12. https://on.ft .com/36F7wd5.

Santacreu, Ana Maria. 2015. "Innovation, Diffusion, and Trade: Theory and Measurement." *Journal of Monetary Economics* 75: 1–20.

Servick, Kelly, Adrian Cho, Jennifer Couzin-Frankel, and Giorgia Guglielmi. 2020. "Coronavirus Disruptions Reverberate through Research." *Science* 367 (6484): 1289–90.

UNSD (United Nations Statistics Division). 2012. *Manual on Statistics of International Trade in Services 2010.* New York: United Nations.

van der Eng, Pierre. 2009. "Capital Formation and Capital Stock in Indonesia, 1950–2008." *Bulletin of Indonesian Economic Studies* 45 (3): 345–71. doi:10.1080/00074910903301662.

World Bank. 2019. "Systematic Country Diagnostic of the Philippines: Realizing the Filipino Dream for 2040." Report No. 143419-PH, World Bank, Washington, DC.

World Bank. 2020a. *From Containment to Recovery. World Bank East Asia and Pacific Economic Update, October 2020.* Washington, DC: World Bank.

World Bank. 2020b. *Global Economic Prospects, January 2020: Slow Growth, Policy Challenges.* Washington, DC: World Bank.

World Bank and DRC (Development Research Center of the State Council, The People's Republic of China). 2019. *Innovative China: New Drivers of Growth.* Washington, DC: World Bank.

WTO and IDE-JETRO (World Trade Organization and the Institute of Developing Economies). 2011. *Trade Patterns and Global Value Chains in East Asia: From Trade in Goods to Trade in Tasks.* Geneva: WTO.

Yusuf, Shahid. 2020. "Technological Priorities for Developing Countries in a Warming World." Unpublished manuscript, World Bank, Washington, DC.

Conceptual Framework and Stylized Facts | 2

Introduction

Developing East Asia faces a set of challenges that is putting a strain on the region's economic development model, as discussed in chapter 1. The transition to an innovation-led growth model is even more urgent in the current context of rapid technological change, further accelerated by the COVID-19 pandemic. The questions for policy makers are how to speed up this transition and what policies and institutions are required to facilitate it.

Successful responses to these questions require identifying key actors, institutions, and policies that facilitate innovation and address the bottlenecks that impede progress. To that end, this chapter starts by defining some key concepts. It then examines the rising importance of supporting technology adoption by firms in light of rapid technological advances around the world. The chapter then presents a framework linking innovation performance with (1) a set of policies and institutions that can facilitate the *diffusion* and *adoption* of technologies, and (2) policies that can

support greater *invention* among frontier firms.

Key concepts

Innovation is a broad concept that includes many types of knowledge activities and levels of complexity

As discussed in chapter 1, this report adopts a broad definition of "innovation" based on the *Oslo Manual* (OECD and Eurostat 2018). The term refers to a product, process, technology, business model, organizational structure, or marketing strategy that is "new or significantly improved" and that is effectively introduced in the firm or the market. It relates to different functions of the firm, not just products, and more importantly requires only that the "innovation" represent a significant improvement to the firm, which may include upgrading of processes or the imitation of other products already in the market. The concepts related to innovation and the diffusion of innovation and technology are broad, comprising activities of very different levels of sophistication and complexity.

Innovation is a process of accumulating and using knowledge

All types of innovation require significant investment in what are called "innovation inputs," which vary according to the type and complexity of the innovation implemented. Figure 2.1 introduces the concept of the "innovation knowledge function." The idea is that firms invest in and accumulate knowledge (inputs) that are transformed into innovation outputs (products, services, or processes) or outcomes, such as patents. These investments vary in type—from knowledge embedded in technology and technology licenses, use of intellectual property, investment in human capital and training, and development of managerial and organizational quality, to the most commonly known innovation input: research and development (R&D).

In interpreting the knowledge function, three dimensions are critical:

- Different combinations of knowledge activities are possible, depending on the *type* of innovation introduced. A stylized fact drawn from the knowledge function literature is that "invention" and other more-complex types of innovation, often proxied by patents, require more-intensive R&D investments.[1] Other forms of innovation may require other inputs more intensively. For example, adopting lean manufacturing processes may require training, organizational changes, and investments in software and technology.

- Different firms have different "productivity" or ability to transform knowledge activities or inputs into innovation outputs. A burgeoning literature has identified the heterogeneous capacity of firms to innovate as central to explaining persistent productivity differences across firms (Acemoglu et al. 2018).

- Knowledge activities are not always developed in-house but often implemented in collaboration with other firms and knowledge providers—for example, from partner firms in joint innovation projects, through contracting of public research organizations (PROs) and universities for R&D projects, or through transfer of knowledge from buyers and suppliers.

FIGURE 2.1   The innovation knowledge function begins with investments and inputs that, once transformed into innovation outputs and outcomes, can yield improved firm performance

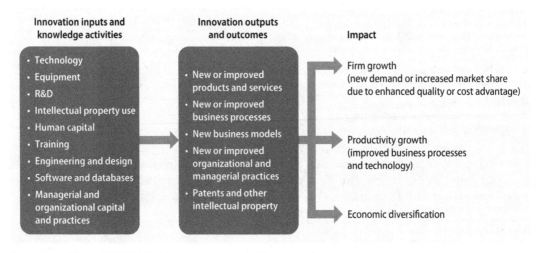

Source: Cirera and Maloney 2017. ©World Bank. Further permission required for reuse.
Note: R&D = research and development.

Imitation and adoption are more prevalent than invention—especially in low- and middle-income countries

The reality in most low- and middle-income economies is that innovation consists primarily of (a) imitating existing products and processes, and (b) facilitating the diffusion and adoption of existing technologies. Science and R&D are important, but the capabilities of firms to successfully implement R&D projects, patenting, and invention are commonly limited. The ability to undertake more-complex forms of innovation increase as firms build their innovation capabilities.

In more-advanced economies, sophisticated firms able to patent and invent new products and technology coexist with many less sophisticated firms, for which innovation is still about imitating and improving existing products and processes. Figure 2.2 shows that the extent of imitation—new products that are new only to the firm or the local market—is greater in lower-income countries, while more "radical" or sophisticated forms of innovation that are new to the international market are more prevalent in higher-income countries.[2] This mix of new-to-firm and new-to-market innovations is also seen specifically in developing East Asia (chapter 1, figure 1.11).

A linear view of innovation—from science and R&D to innovation—is not aligned with the reality of most low- and middle-income countries and can harm policy effectiveness

Innovation has traditionally been associated in popular media outlets and policy circles with the discovery and invention of new products, processes, and technologies. As such, innovation processes have generally been characterized as the result of science and R&D efforts, and this conceptualization of innovation has significantly biased innovation policies. In many countries, the responsibility for innovation policies lies with ministries of science and technology or sometimes even with ministries of education (the latter being more concerned with addressing the problems

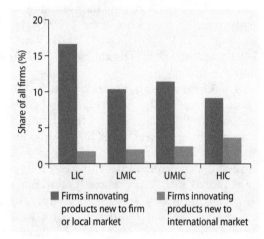

FIGURE 2.2   Sophistication of firm-level innovation correlates strongly with countries' economic development

Source: World Bank calculations, using Enterprise Survey data (latest available years).
Note: Enterprise Survey data used are from 44 selected countries outside of developing East Asia (whose data do not distinguish between innovations that are new to the local market versus the international market). HIC = high-income countries; LIC = low-income countries; LMIC = lower-middle-income countries; UMIC = upper-middle-income countries. Country income classifications are calculated using the World Bank Atlas method (https://datahelpdesk.worldbank.org/).

of higher education and academia than those of industry).

Following this linear view of innovation—from science to R&D to innovation—has often translated into misdirected and inefficient use of public resources to support R&D and PROs. Specifically, it has led to a focus on generating new technologies rather than on firm adoption and diffusion of existing technologies and undertaking the basic upgrading that better suits firms' capabilities. As firms increase their capacity to innovate over time, technological upgrading can become progressively more sophisticated and unique.

The process of technological catch-up requires moving more firms from imitation to discovery

The process of technological catch-up to the frontier requires accelerating technological diffusion and adoption and, ultimately, transitioning more firms from imitation to increased R&D investments and invention (Madsen, Islam, and Ang 2010). This process is captured visually in figure 2.3, which shows the relationship between countries' proximity to the technological frontier (proxied by their income per capita) and innovation quality (proxied by their score in the 2019 Global Innovation Index [GII], issued by the World Intellectual Property Organization [WIPO] and its partners).

The GII is a composite index that incorporates data on the quality of innovation outputs (such as patents) and the quality of innovation inputs (such as R&D). Although the GII is a crude indicator of innovation, it includes multiple dimensions of innovation and, as such, captures the level of innovation complexity across countries. The figure shows a clear and positive correlation between per capita income and the GII, with higher-income countries demonstrating more sophisticated innovation capacity.

Within the East Asia region, there are clear differences in overall innovation performance

between high-income countries (right of the orange line in figure 2.3), which are relatively strong performers on innovation, and most countries in developing East Asia (left of the orange line). Policies in developing East Asia must therefore focus on narrowing technological and innovation gaps, helping more firms to become more innovative and to use more sophisticated technologies.

It is difficult to define precisely how this process of technological catch-up occurs and when countries have successfully transitioned to an innovation-led growth model. However, East Asia has examples of such transitions in countries like Japan, the Republic of Korea, and Singapore, and a large literature has described their experiences (see, for example, Hobday 1995), highlighting the importance of outward orientation and learning. However, as chapter 1 discussed and chapter 3 will further elaborate, technology embedded in foreign direct investment (FDI) and trade

FIGURE 2.3 Innovation quality correlates closely with countries' per capita income

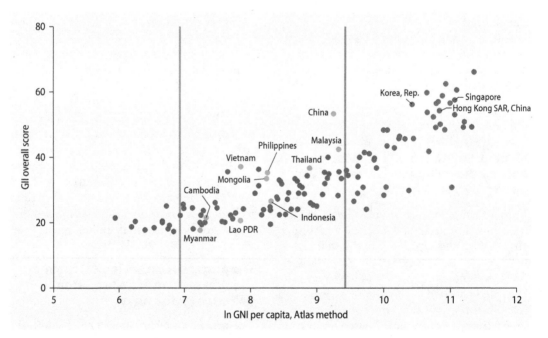

Sources: World Bank elaboration, using Global Innovation Index (GII) 2019 data (https://www.globalinnovationindex.org/) and the World Development Indicators database.
Note: The teal vertical line separates low- from middle-income countries, and the orange vertical line, middle- from high-income countries. No data are available for Lao PDR and Myanmar. The World Bank Atlas method estimates of the size of economies based on GNI converted to current US dollars, smoothing exchange rate fluctuations by using a three-year moving average, price-adjusted conversion factor. GNI = gross national income; ln = natural logarithm.

in developing East Asia has not diffused widely beyond the sectors directly affected. Broadening and accelerating the diffusion of technologies and innovation is thus critical to developing an innovation-led growth model. Indeed, the evidence suggests that without adequate diffusion, innovation and new technologies have little impact on productivity and growth (Hall and Khan 2003).

Several complementary factors are critical to enabling innovation

If innovation is likely to boost productivity growth, the question becomes why lagging firms and countries fail to invest more in innovation inputs and knowledge activities (as listed in figure 2.1). Chapter 3 explores this issue in more detail for developing East Asia, but, in general, the incentives to invest in innovation depend on the benefits (returns) that innovation brings to firms in terms of increased productivity or profitability.

At the same time, the extent to which innovation increases productivity depends not only on the firm's knowledge investments but also on other (complementary) factors, such as management capabilities, availability of technical skills and finance, and on having an enabling business environment and competitive framework that incentivizes and facilitates innovation and diffusion (Cirera and Maloney 2017). Without adequate workers' skills, firms cannot effectively use new technologies. Without adequate finance, it is difficult for firms to purchase new machinery or finance R&D for innovation projects. And without good management, it is difficult for firms to identify and effectively implement innovation projects.

Using country-level panel data, Goñi and Maloney (2017) find that the relationship between returns to R&D and country gross domestic product (GDP) per capita follows an inverted-U shape (figure 2.4). A likely explanation of this inverted-U shape is that the

FIGURE 2.4   **The relationship between returns to innovation and distance to the frontier follows an inverted U-shape**

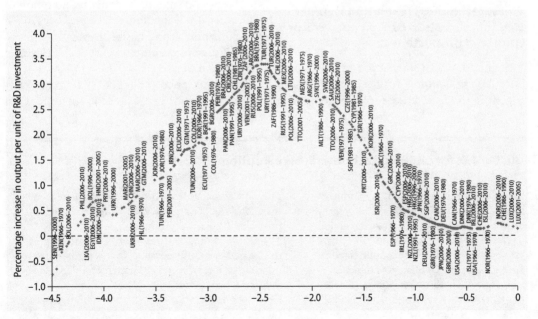

Source: Goñi and Maloney 2017.
Note: "Distance from the technological frontier" is measured as the difference from the highest percentile of income per capita, with a 0 value when the country is, during that period (shown within parentheses), at the higher income-per-capita level. Countries are designated by ISO alpha-3 code. R&D = research and development.

potential gains from technological catch-up increase as the distance to the technological frontier increases (as denoted by higher negative values on the x-axis of the figure). At some point, however, these returns are reduced by the lack of complementary factors. Below a certain level of development, firms lack these necessary factors, such as capital markets that would enable them to buy the necessary machinery, managers who know how to take new ideas to market, and skilled workers to manage innovation projects, all leading to a decrease in returns to innovation activity.

Two of these key complementary factors, finance and skills for innovation, are analyzed in more detail in chapter 4. More broadly, however, identifying these missing complementary factors is essential to designing and implementing policies to increase returns to innovation—the expectation of which is the main incentive for firms to decide to innovate.[3]

Importance of innovation and diffusion of technology in addressing the region's challenges

A new technology revolution is under way that threatens current patterns of trade and production

The importance of innovation to developing East Asia's economic future is all the more urgent in the face of the rapid technological changes affecting the global economy. This ongoing wave of change, sometimes referred to as the fourth industrial revolution (Schwab 2016) or "Industry 4.0," comprises several interrelated strands—physical, biological, and digital—each of which benefits from the others as new discoveries are made and progress achieved (box 2.1).

Changes in *physical* technologies emerge from advances in molecular-level engineering and high-tech manufacturing, and they include advanced materials, advanced manufacturing (including advanced robotics), and additive manufacturing (or 3-D printing). New *biological* technologies are enabling the manipulation of genes and deoxyribonucleic acid (DNA) sequences to influence medical outcomes and correct genetic defects. And *digital* technological change includes transformations in such fields as financial technology (fintech), the internet of things (IoT), and artificial intelligence (AI).

These technological advances have the potential to lower costs but, even more fundamentally, to change patterns of comparative advantage by altering the relative importance of labor and capital. In doing so, adoption of Industry 4.0 technologies by companies in the high-income economies—or even in China—could disrupt developing East Asia's low-cost labor advantage.

For instance, cheaper and more user-friendly robots offer the prospect of

---

BOX 2.1   Industry 4.0: An ongoing technological revolution

The term "fourth industrial revolution," or Industry 4.0, refers to a current wave of rapid technological advances that stand to dramatically change the global economy. The term, popularized around 2011, first arose from a project promoting the computerization of manufacturing, led by the German government.

Industry 4.0 follows three earlier phases of technological change that have revolutionized production since the late 1700s (figure B2.1.1):

- *The first industrial revolution,* which began at the end of the 18th century, used water and steam power to mechanize production.
- *The second industrial revolution,* beginning at the start of the 20th century, followed the introduction of electric power, which enabled mass industrial production.
- *The third industrial revolution,* which began in the latter part of the 20th century, used

box continues next page

BOX 2.1   Industry 4.0: An ongoing technological revolution *(continued)*

electronics and information technology (IT) to further automate manufacturing.
* *The fourth industrial revolution,* which builds on the third, is characterized by a fusion of technologies based on cyber-physical systems.

The transition between the third and the fourth industrial revolutions has many analogies to the transition from the first to the second. While electricity networks and the railroad established the networks for the second industrial revolution, advanced electronics and digital systems are providing a critical foundation for Industry 4.0.

Industry 4.0 is characterized by the adoption of cyber-physical systems, including advanced robotics and drones, 3-D printing, artificial intelligence (AI), and machine learning, whose effects are being felt across all economic sectors. These technologies are reshaping not only how manufacturing is done or services are provided but also where they are located.

The fourth industrial revolution goes beyond the use of technology per se, going hand in hand with novel production and management processes, including user-centered design or flexible production, customization, and data management.

Industry 4.0 is also significant because of its potential impacts on employment and income distribution (Autor and Dorn 2013; Frey and Osborne 2017). This is already becoming apparent, with advanced robotics and AI enabling the reshoring of some manufacturing and services to high-income economies, often with fewer jobs that require more-sophisticated skill sets (Acemoglu and Restrepo 2018; Ford 2015). This raises important challenges for developing East Asia because traditional labor cost advantages become less relevant with advanced automation and manufacturing that could potentially be reshored to more advanced economies.

Source: DFKI 2011.

FIGURE B2.1.1   The four stages of industrial revolution have repeatedly transformed manufacturing

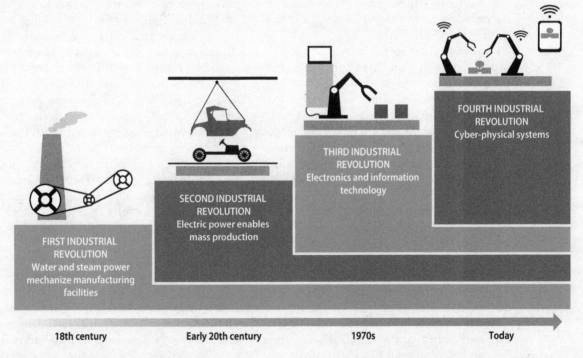

Source: Adapted from DFKI 2011.

productivity increases while substituting for low-skilled labor. This prospect, in turn, could encourage labor-scarce high-income and upper-middle-income economies to consider "reshoring" their production, marking a move away from the offshoring and the fragmentation of production that has characterized much of the export-oriented manufacturing in the region.

Similarly, 3-D printing allows for the customization of production closer to consumers, which could reduce the importance of scale economies in production and disrupt existing supply networks. Advances in AI and machine learning will also drastically change the way knowledge tasks are organized and reinforce the incentives to automate.

As Industry 4.0 technologies continue to develop, there are concerns that reshoring of production to high-income economies will disrupt existing production structures and value chains in the region. Indeed, a rapid reshoring of production to Europe or North America could put pressure on the region's export-oriented production model and unwind many of the gains associated with countries' participation in global value chains (GVCs).

Evidence regarding the impacts of Industry 4.0 technologies on investment, production, and exports in developing East Asia is still relatively scarce. And, to the extent that such evidence exists, the findings are mixed.[4] Nevertheless, as the costs of new technologies continue to fall, there is a risk that investments in such technologies could erode much of the region's comparative advance and shorten the value chains that have been so important to developing East Asia's development. Moreover, other external forces (discussed in chapter 1), including slowing global trade, increased protectionist sentiment in some economies, and the COVID-19 pandemic, are accelerating the adoption of advanced technologies.

In short, rapidly advancing technologies, especially when viewed together with other key global economic forces, reinforce the importance of policies to spur innovation in developing East Asia. Together, these technologies have three important implications for innovation policy. Specifically, there is a need to

- *Accelerate innovation and technology adoption,* based on a better understanding of the factors that constrain adoption and diffusion;
- *Adopt new organizational and business models* that are better aligned with more-advanced technologies; and
- *Eliminate policy biases* against innovation in services sectors, which are becoming increasingly important to the region's economies.

These three implications are now discussed in turn.

The policy imperative is to accelerate technology adoption and diffusion

Rapid technological change, along with changing global economic forces, is likely to transform the structure of production, and developing East Asia must accelerate its technological catch-up. To do so, the region must first recognize that reshoring decisions will depend on a set of factors that can be summarized by productivity differentials, costs and customization, and closeness to customers and supply chains. In this regard, the region must try to minimize these productivity differentials by accelerating its own path toward the technological frontier. In addition, the increasing demand for customized products will occur in the countries with an increasingly demanding middle class, implying that firms need technologies to supply goods and services with greater agility to meet rising local demand.

Both these factors—minimizing the differentials and meeting rising demand—require that the region accelerate the diffusion of new technologies. As discussed in chapter 1, global challenges arising from pandemics or climate change also demand rapid adoption of advanced technologies. But what determines technology diffusion?

Supply and demand factors are more important than relative prices in determining technology adoption and diffusion

A widespread view of technology adoption and diffusion at a more macro level focuses on relative prices and factor abundance. The idea is that poor countries typically have barriers to technology transfer, abundant low-skilled labor, and a scarcity of skilled labor, and thus they will use different technologies than wealthy countries (Acemoglu and Zilibotti 2001). Factor prices and context play a critical role in selecting technologies, and there is an appropriate set of technologies for each country (Caselli and Coleman 2006). Ultimately, however, the choice depends on how complementary technology and labor are (Acemoglu 2010) and also how forcefully R&D in the country can generate new technologies.

Although it is unclear exactly how factor prices affect diffusion, micro evidence suggests that other elements may be at play in explaining differences in technology adoption and innovation outcomes. A rich microeconomic literature has explained the diffusion of technology as depending on a series of supply and demand factors (Stoneman and Battisti 2010). Supply factors determine the complexity and price of the technology, which affect the firms' decision to adopt it. Demand factors determine the firms' ability and willingness to either adopt a given technology now or wait for later. Hall (2006) summarizes some of these key demand factors: (a) benefits that users can obtain from technology, (b) network effects from several users in a cluster, (c) costs of implementing the technology, (d) information available and the uncertainty associated with implementing technology, and (e) market structure.

All these factors influence the adoption of technology and explain some of the stylized facts that arise from the empirical work on diffusion, specifically (a) the S-shape diffusion curve (box 2.2), and (b) the faster diffusion of technologies across countries (the extensive margin) than within countries (the intensive margin).

BOX 2.2   Understanding adoption and diffusion: S-shaped diffusion curves

A common pattern observed throughout the technology diffusion literature is that the process of diffusion across regions fits an S-shaped curve (that is, a logistic function). Evidence on this began with the seminal work of Griliches (1957), who analyzed the technological gap across regions of the United States in the use of hybrid seed corn (figure B2.2.1). According to the author, hybrid corn was a new method of breeding superior corn for specific locations. But it was not immediately adopted everywhere.

The differences in S-shaped curves[a] across certain states in the United States reflected two different problems associated with technology adoption: (a) the acceptance problem, which refers to differences in the rate of farmers' adoption of hybrids in states for which the technology was already available; and (b) the availability problem, which refers to the lag in the development of hybrid corn technologies that were suitable for specific areas.

Following Griliches's work, several other studies supported S-shaped curves as a good fit for traditional measures of technology diffusion. Mansfield (1961) analyzes the factors determining the speed of technology diffusion across firms.[b] In addition to observing heterogeneity across industries, his findings suggest that the growth over time of firms having introduced an innovation conforms to a logistic function (S-shaped). The author finds that

box continues next page

BOX 2.2   **Understanding adoption and diffusion: S-shaped diffusion curves** *(continued)*

FIGURE B2.2.1   **S-shaped diffusion curves in the adoption of hybrid seed corn in selected US states, 1933–56**

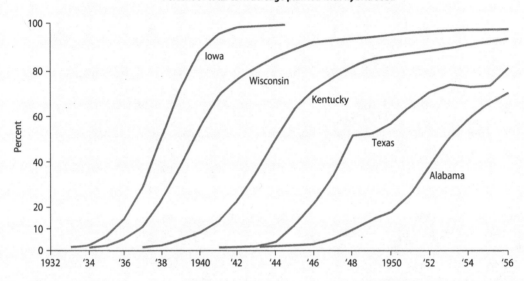

Source: Griliches 1957.

the probability of a firm introducing a new technique is an increasing function of the proportion of firms already using it and the profitability of doing so and, conversely, a decreasing function of the size of the investment required. Other studies supporting this pattern include Skinner and Staiger (2007), Alm and Cox (1996), and Gort and Klepper (1982), among others.

Most of the studies supporting S-shaped diffusion curves do not take into consideration the intensity in the use of technologies, however.

a. The S-curve is partially the result of the metric of analysis, which is bounded between 0 and 1.
b. Mansfield (1961) focuses on 12 innovations across four industries in the United States.

Evidence suggests that technological catch-up is not accelerating in low- and middle-income countries

Although the diffusion of technology between countries (extensive margin) may be accelerating, the speed of internal diffusion (intensive margin) and intensity of its use in low- and middle-income countries is lagging behind that of high-income countries. Comin, Hobijn, and Rovito (2006) find that the speed of convergence is three times faster

in technologies invented after 1925 than in technologies invented earlier.[5] Indeed, using data from the Cross-Country Historical Adoption of Technology (CHAT) dataset,[6] Comin and Mestieri (2018), show that the adoption lag (defined as the time for the technology to arrive to a country following its invention) between "Western countries" and the rest of the world has narrowed considerably over time (figure 2.5). However, the authors also show that the gap in the intensity

FIGURE 2.5 **Lags in the adoption of new technologies are now similar between Western countries and the rest of the world, but gaps in the intensity of technology use have widened**

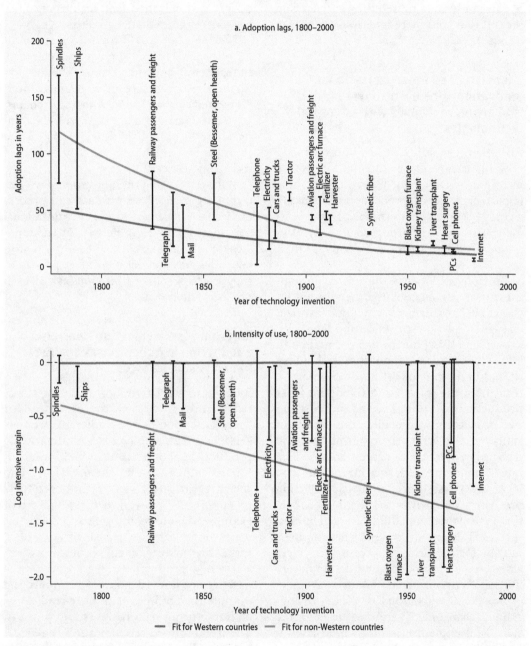

Source: Comin and Mestieri 2018.

Note: Bars show the median margins of adoption of various technologies for Western versus non-Western countries. The adoption lag (the number of years it takes for a technology to arrive to a country since invention) and the intensive margin (the intensity of use in a country) are estimated structurally using country-specific model parameters derived from the Cross-Country Historical Adoption of Technology (CHAT) database. The lines are fitted lines for "Western countries" and the rest of the world. The bars show the median adoption lags or intensive margins of the two country groups for each technology. "Western countries" are defined to include Australia, Austria, Belgium, Canada, Denmark, Finland, France, Germany, Italy, Japan, the Netherlands, New Zealand, Norway, Sweden, Switzerland, United Kingdom, and United States. The technologies are coded numerically as follows (here listed in order of invention): 1. spindles; 2. ships; 34. railway passengers and freight; 5. telegraph; 6. mail; 7. steel (Bessemer, open hearth); 8. telephone; 9. electricity; 101. cars and trucks; 12. tractors; 134. aviation passengers and freight; 15. electric arc furnaces; 16. fertilizer; 17. harvester; 18. synthetic fiber; 19. blast oxygen furnaces; 20. kidney transplant; 21. liver transplant; 22. heart surgery; 23. personal computers (PCs); 24. cell phones; and 25. internet.

of technology use is widening. Facilitating technological convergence when the frontier is constantly moving requires accelerating the diffusion and more-intensive use of new technologies.

There is a need for organizational innovation and new business models that are more aligned with advanced technologies

Although it is still early to know exactly how the nature of production will evolve in response to the new technologies, some important changes in production methods are already occurring. For example, all the leading sports footwear producers already offer the possibility of customizing some of their products.

Previous experience during technological transitions suggests that new technologies come hand in hand with organizational changes and new business models. (See Bresnahan [2010] for the implementation of information and communication technology [ICT].) In the case of the new technological transition, the move from fixed and mass production to more flexible and customized production will require different sets of skills but also stronger organizational and managerial practices to process and use data integration, manage leaner inventories and logistics systems, and coordinate production processes. Similarly, more-flexible production systems require additional capabilities, such as IT engineers, as well as new business models for the firm, to offer new services associated with products and develop more integrated customer relationships.

Box 2.3 describes some of the key organizational changes likely to be required for the successful implementation of Industry 4.0 technologies. As chapter 1 discussed, these will be further accelerated given the increase in digitalization and automation in response to the COVID-19 pandemic. These new technologies will require firms to adapt and create new business models that are often very different from those associated with more traditional modes of production. Value addition is likely to shift from production to design, customization, and maintenance services associated with the products sold.

Weking et al. (2019) studied 32 case studies of organizational innovation related to Industry 4.0 implementation. The authors identify two types of new business models related to integration with value chains: (a) "servicification" associated with the combined production of goods with services, and (b) expertise, which includes the provision of consulting services.

Policies focusing on innovation have traditionally focused on product and process innovation, not innovation in organizational structures or business models. As technologies rapidly advance, it will be important to take a broader view of innovation policies to support changes in organizations as well as in products and processes.

Emerging "servicification" warrants a reduction in policy biases against innovation in services

As suggested earlier, one characteristic of Industry 4.0 is the potential for "servicification"—the ability to produce services that complement manufacturing production. For example, Weking et al. (2019) emphasize that the use of IoT and the integration of sensors into products to enable the provision of services (for example, remote monitoring and predictive maintenance services) transforms manufacturing firms into de facto service providers. These new production structures require a new set of knowledge-intensive inputs and outputs that complement more-traditional manufacturing sector inputs and outputs. The trend toward servicification challenges policy makers' longstanding focus on innovation in manufacturing, which has biased public policy against services (as discussed in chapter 5).

Innovation has been seen traditionally in terms of *product* and *process* inventions and improvements, especially in manufacturing.

BOX 2.3   Organizational changes associated with Industry 4.0

Key to understanding the impact of Industry 4.0 is understanding the types of organizational changes needed to adapt to these technologies. Industry 4.0 will lead to the emergence of dynamic, real-time optimized, self-organizing value chains. This will likely have a profound impact on firms' organizational structures and processes, which will need to be redesigned to enable adoption of these technologies. These changes will offer new opportunities but also several challenges, particularly for countries that are lagging behind in terms of digital infrastructure and human capital. Here are some examples of organizational changes that are likely to become more prevalent as firms adopt Industry 4.0 technologies.

Evolving business models. Mass production will likely yield to greater customization, leading to customer-specific products integrated with new service offerings. Manufacturers will increasingly shift their revenue from products to services, creating new value-added services embedded in products. Borders between companies within industries are already becoming blurred. Companies can create value within business networks, for example, by offering unused production capacity in a marketplace to companies that temporarily need more capacity.

End-to-end digital engineering. Rigid preplanning processes will likely disappear. Smart

IoT (Internet of Things) machines will enable more active, autonomous, and self-organizing production based on small units. An increasing number of products will belong to a global digital chain.

Top-floor to shop-floor integration. Factories will adapt automatically to changes because of more autonomous decision making. Autonomous manufacturing units—coupling robotics with highly skilled workers—will adapt to continuous customer-driven product changes, enabling a single production line to create different product types without reengineering the production process.

Real-time, value-added networks. Digitalization and pervasive connectivity will enable real-time analysis of all business activities. Cost structures can be simulated to support decision making. Market changes can be anticipated and business ideas implemented more quickly.

Enhanced work environments. As customized production becomes the norm, workers can be assigned as needed to coordinate automated production processes and intervene when machines call for action. Workers will have new demands in managing complexity, problem solving, and self-organization.

Source: Cirera et al. 2017.

This is partly explained by the nature of services, which makes service innovation more difficult to define. As Tether (2003, 483) describes, "Because services tend not to have an independent physical existence, service innovations can be invisible, and because services are interactive, often being coproduced by the provider and user acting together (with simultaneous production and consumption), the authorship of any innovation is often unclear. Furthermore, because service events are often unique, it is often difficult to differentiate between service variations and innovations."

This difficulty in defining innovation in services, and a manufacturing-centric view

of productive development, have translated into a large innovation policy bias against the services sector. Even though services account for the largest share of GDP and employment in many economies, services innovation has been neglected in innovation policy mixes in both high-income and low- and middle-income economies. As chapter 5 will discuss, most policies and PROs focus on manufacturing or agriculture, and public programs to support innovation tend to have fewer services firms as beneficiaries. Eliminating this policy bias against services will be important to facilitating faster diffusion and adoption of technologies and enabling greater innovation-led growth.

Core elements for designing policies that accelerate technology adoption and diffusion

Given the technological imperative that the region faces, a key question for innovation policy is *how* to accelerate diffusion of new technologies. Central to this process is building firms' innovation capabilities and removing barriers to firms' accumulation of the knowledge needed to adopt and productively use new technologies. This section outlines several key principles for designing policies to enable greater technology adoption and diffusion.

Innovation depends on a constellation of actors, policies, and frameworks

A first entry point to understanding which actors, policies, and institutions matter for innovation and technology diffusion can be found in a country's national innovation system (NIS). Although different authors characterize such systems in different ways,[7] for practical purposes a country's NIS can be thought of as comprising firms; a country's science and technology institutions, including PROs, universities, and private research centers; government ministries and agencies whose actions can either enable or impede innovation; the broader business and regulatory environment; industry associations; and other institutions that build a country's skills base and support finance for innovation.

Operationalizing this framework requires defining the boundaries of actors and institutions that affect innovation. There are different ways of doing this conceptualization and setting these boundaries. A key common element across these NIS frameworks is the dependence of firm-level innovation on a large set of factors and institutions and their systemic interactions. Acting upon one pillar only—for example, skills for innovation—does not guarantee that innovation activity will be increased or technology diffusion facilitated. *Policies need to be systemic,* affecting incentives and mobilizing the range of relevant actors.[8]

Innovation also depends on building absorptive capacity and removing barriers to knowledge accumulation

Several issues must be considered as policy makers seek to encourage innovation in developing East Asia.

Matching of knowledge supply and demand. Knowledge-supply capabilities (the research, knowledge, and technologies created by research institutions, universities, and other firms) must be matched by firms' demand for that knowledge (that is, adequate absorptive capacity). This matching of supply and demand for knowledge is often overlooked, with policies and institutions traditionally focused on encouraging public R&D that may be disconnected from firms' capabilities and demand. It is impotant that policies focus on the accumulation of capabilities in both the supply and demand for knowledge.

In cases where the quality of knowledge created—whether by firms, PROs, or other domestic knowledge providers—does not suit firms' capabilities and needs, obtaining knowledge generated from abroad is critical. This can be done by incentivizing knowledge spillovers from multinational enterprises (MNEs), diffusing existing technologies via imports, and in some cases by working with international research organizations or private sector consortia.

Legal and financial barriers. When encouraging innovation, one must be mindful of a range of barriers that impede knowledge accumulation. For example, labor laws that discourage the recruitment of skills needed for innovation or barriers to the financing of innovation projects and ventures directly undermine innovation. By affecting the broader economic environment, factors such as regulatory distortions, barriers to firm entry, and weak rule of law raise the cost of doing business and thus affect investment, including investment in knowledge for innovation. Such impediments include regulatory bottlenecks that affect the deployment and use of new technologies. The IoT, for example, largely depends not only on infrastructure but also on regulations on its use and access to the internet network.

These more-general barriers have received relatively little attention in the innovation literature because, among other reasons, they often lie outside the policy space occupied by innovation agencies and ministries. Nevertheless, these are critical elements affecting innovation decisions.

Factors affecting firm incentives and capabilities. Another important set of issues relate to factors that directly affect firms' demand for innovation. These factors may be either external or internal to the firm. External factors affect the incentives and use of inputs for innovation, including trade regimes that can encourage or discourage the import of technology; competition and market structure; and macroeconomic policies. A critical set of internal factors relate to firms' own capabilities. This includes employees' skills and management quality, as well as the decisions and processes firms use to accumulate, use, and create knowledge and bring it to market.

An enabling environment for innovation. Finally, a critical consideration relates to complementary factors that affect all the interactions needed for innovation. When creating an enabling environment for innovation, it is important for policy makers to ensure the flow of knowledge from its creators to the firms absorbing it; an adequate supply of skills, finance, and good management practices that can support the implementation of innovative projects; and the appropriate regulatory and policy frameworks that enable innovation. These are key characteristics of a well-developed NIS and are needed to accelerate the adoption of new technologies.

Innovation requires knowledge accumulation—with the firm at the center of the process

These considerations surrounding the NIS can be summarized from the firm's perspective (figure 2.6). The ability to patent inventions, introduce new products, and invent and generate new technologies often entails initially investing in imitation of existing products and processes, adopting existing technologies, and eventually investing in formal and more sophisticated forms of R&D.

This knowledge accumulation and learning process depends on a firm's internal efforts but also on its ability to learn and partner with external sources of learning—for example, knowledge acquired from other firms or MNEs, knowledge embedded in imports, research produced in universities or PROs, and knowledge services purchased from public or private sources. This learning process is affected by several types of policies, ranging from regulatory frameworks that affect the cost of doing business or market competition to regulations on trade and investment. The intellectual property regime, policies to incentivize scientific enterprise and university-industry collaboration, as well as incentives to carry out R&D activities, also affect this learning process.

Policy makers must prioritize the policies that build innovation capabilities

Policy makers need to prioritize certain policies over others based on the level of technological capabilities of the country's private sector, which itself tends to be heterogenous, differing tremendously between large, internationally linked firms and small domestic enterprises. The question is how to make such a prioritization.

Figure 2.7 approximates where the countries in developing East Asia are in terms of innovation capabilities. The scatterplot uses GII data on innovation inputs (measuring infrastructure, institutions, R&D, and human capital quality) and an innovation outputs index that captures the quality of knowledge, technology, and creative outputs of the economy.

As expected, the relationship is positive and linear: except for China, most of the countries on the right of the graph—the highest scorers on both inputs and outputs—are high-income countries, whereas the countries on the left side of the graph are low- and

FIGURE 2.6 **Accumulating knowledge to reach the innovation frontier: A firm-centered process**

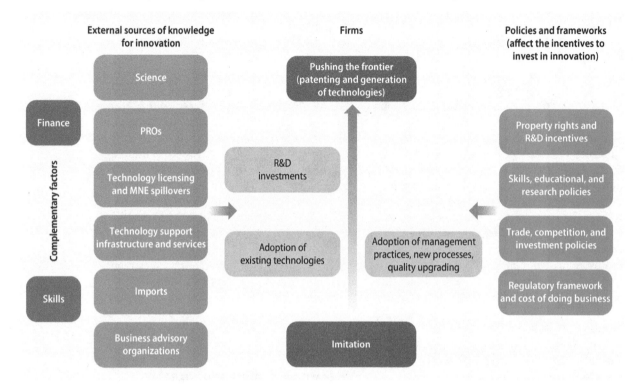

Source: Original table for this publication.
Note: MNE = multinational enterprise; PROs = public research organizations; R&D = research and development.

middle-income countries. The figure shows three clusters that, with some few exceptions, resemble the levels of capabilities depicted earlier in figure 2.3:

- *Cluster 1* includes the high-income countries in the region, such as Japan, Korea, and Singapore, which are clustered at the frontier. Driven primarily by a large increase in the number of patents and scientific production, China has also joined this first group with more-advanced technological capabilities.
- *Cluster 2* includes Malaysia, Vietnam, Thailand, and Mongolia, with only Malaysia being close to the leading group.
- *Cluster 3* includes the Philippines, Indonesia, and Cambodia.

Although the choice of three clusters is somewhat arbitrary, figure 2.7 does reasonably

capture the overall location of these countries on the continuum of innovation capabilities. And, as described below, these different levels of capabilities imply that countries in the region need to take differentiated approaches to innovation policy. (Directions for policy are discussed further in chapter 6.)

Effectively fostering innovation—both diffusion and invention—requires a graduated approach of moving firms toward the frontier, recognizing their heterogeneous capacities to innovate

An NIS comprises a multiplicity of actors, institutions, and policies, which poses significant challenges when identifying weaknesses in innovation policy frameworks and, especially, when deciding where to focus public policy efforts to encourage innovation.

FIGURE 2.7 Developing East Asian countries occupy three distinct clusters with respect to innovation capabilities

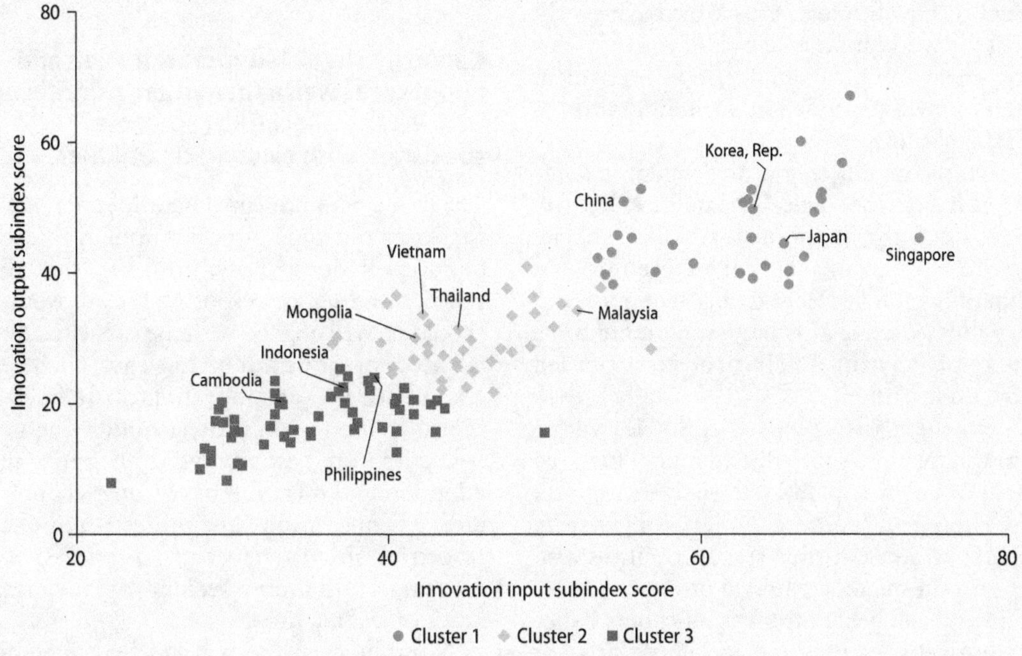

Source: World Bank elaboration from Global Innovation Index (GII) data (https://www.globalinnovationindex.org/).
Note: The "innovation input" subindex scores aspects such as infrastructure, institutions, research and development, and human capital quality. The "innovation output" subindex scores the quality of knowledge, technology, and creative outputs of the economy. Among the 10 developing East Asia countries in this study (Cambodia, China, Indonesia, Lao PDR, Malaysia, Mongolia, Myanmar, the Philippines, Thailand, and Vietnam), Lao PDR and Myanmar are excluded for lack of data.

This is especially the case for most low- and middle-income economies, where multiple elements of the NIS are underdeveloped or have significant weaknesses, including a lack of well-functioning agencies and institutions, mistargeted policies, and a lack of enabling conditions or complementary factors. Innovation policy thus becomes complex, and the critical question is, therefore, how to prioritize policies that will be effective in enabling innovation given the country's capabilities, which in turn depend on the abilities of firms to innovate and of agencies to design and implement appropriate policies.

Based on the experiences of successful East Asian economies such as Japan, Korea, and Singapore, an effective way of addressing this problem and guiding policies is to use a graduated approach. These economies achieved rapid technological convergence based on policies that addressed their innovation capabilities gaps (Cirera and Maloney 2017). (See chapter 6, table 6.3, for the evolution of Korean policies.) For firms to reach the technological frontier, policies and institutions must focus on building the capabilities of the private sector and developing the innovation system elements that are absent, not functional, or poorly aligned with need.

Cirera and Maloney (2017) propose assessing the adequacy of policies and institutions through the lens of a "capabilities escalator"—to reflect the capacity of firms and country systems to absorb and use knowledge (figure 2.8). At the lower level of capabilities, firms have mostly productive, but few technological, capabilities; hence the policy objective should be to build those capabilities. On this lowest step of the escalator, policies should focus on developing management quality, skills, and national quality infrastructure. Where the business climate is weak, policies should focus on creating an environment conducive to investment and knowledge diffusion, including through FDI and trade.

On the middle step of the escalator, some firms have technological capabilities, but few have R&D and invention capabilities. Policies in those countries should therefore focus on expanding and strengthening technological capabilities while also supporting more firms in implementing R&D projects oriented toward invention.

On the highest step, in countries where firms have more sophisticated capabilities, the goal of policy should be to enable invention by supporting more complex, longer-term R&D projects. At this stage, countries also require adequate intellectual property protection and will benefit from significant collaboration between industry and universities or other knowledge providers.

Figure 2.8 presents an illustrative set of policy instruments, corresponding to the different levels of the capabilities escalator.

Countries should support diffusion and adoption as well as invention, prioritizing policies and allocating resources consistent with existing capabilities

The framework presented here does not imply that only one type of policy applies to each country. It does imply, however, that the policies and public resources for innovation should be well aligned with the capacities and the needs of the private sector. Thus, countries with relatively low innovation capabilities—typically the region's lower-middle-income countries—are best advised to prioritize the adoption and diffusion of existing technologies. As innovation capabilities rise, policy priorities should also shift, progressively focusing on the more technically advanced needs of leading firms.

Notably, even the region's high-income, high-capacity countries such as Japan, Korea,

FIGURE 2.8   **Appropriate policy instruments to foster innovation differ depending on the level of innovation capabilities**

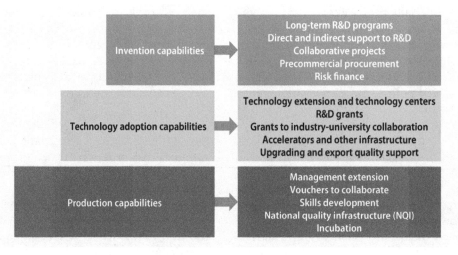

Source: Adapted from Cirera and Maloney 2017. ©World Bank. Further permission required for reuse.
Note: R&D = research and development.

and Singapore—as well as the United States and Canada—offer support for technology adoption as well as invention, with different sets of policies to encourage both dimensions of innovation. At any level of capabilities, the point is not to focus policies only on either adoption or invention but rather to allocate more resources in a way commensurate with innovation capabilities.

Taking a graduated approach ensures that the different parts of the NIS can effectively support the development of the needed capabilities. The capacities of public agencies to design and implement effective policies also evolve with increasing capabilities in the private sector.

Supporting basic forms of innovation also pays off

Finally, it is important to emphasize that, contrary to some popular beliefs, more-basic forms of innovation, including imitation of products and processes, adoption of new technologies, or increases in product quality are important for productivity growth. Thus, policies that successfully encourage innovations that are new to the firm or new to the domestic market can have significant returns. This is clear from some growth models such as presented in Madsen, Islam, and Ang (2010) but also from microeconomic evidence.

Studies looking at the relationship between innovation and productivity rarely distinguish between types of innovation and largely find a positive impact of innovation on productivity. (See Mohnen and Hall [2013] for a survey of the evidence from OECD countries.) In one of the few studies looking at this more directly, using a panel of Turkish firms, Fazlioğlu, Dalgiç, and Yereli (2019) find positive returns to innovations that are new to the firm or new to the local market only. This less sophisticated type of innovation, in addition to allowing firms to remain competitive, also generates positive returns.

Conclusions

Rapid technological change, along with the diverse shocks that developing East Asia is experiencing, means that technology adoption for higher productivity needs to happen faster and more broadly than in the past. Climbing the capabilities escalator requires efforts to develop firms' and countries' innovation capabilities and to progressively address the key barriers on the supply of knowledge and firm absorption.

Developing and implementing policies that are comprehensive yet proportional to local capabilities can pay large dividends in addressing existing constraints and enhancing innovation and technological development. It is important, however, that policy makers be realistic about the current strength of their countries' institutions and policy-making capacity. If there is a mismatch between countries' capabilities and the types of policies and institutional reforms implemented, such reforms can be both costly and ineffective (Cirera and Maloney 2017).

This chapter has highlighted some key elements for understanding how policy makers can accelerate innovation in developing East Asia:

- Innovation needs to be understood in its broad sense, ranging from basic upgrading to invention, and from imitation and adoption of new technologies to discovery.

- Innovation and technology are not static concepts; they change over time and have accelerated during certain historical periods through the invention of general purpose technologies that enable the multiplication and use of new technologies that change production processes. The world is currently undergoing one such period—the fourth industrial revolution, or Industry 4.0.

- Supporting innovation and technology adoption requires understanding the systemic nature of innovation and building the private sector's innovation capabilities, as demonstrated by the rapid technological catch-up in Japan, Korea, and Singapore. This process is often gradual but needs to be accelerated.

- Designing policies and institutions to achieve this transition to a more innovation-based growth model requires keeping in mind the capabilities of the private sector. Most developing East Asian countries are clustered in two main groups on the capabilities escalator—those on the bottom step and those in the middle. These groups likely require a different mix of policy instruments and associated allocations of public resources.

- Policies should support both diffusion and invention, but for most of developing East Asia, the priority should be the diffusion of existing technologies and the building of managerial practices while maintaining some instruments to support invention among those few firms capable of pushing the frontier.

- There is no evidence that convergence to the technological frontier can happen quickly. On the contrary, there are reasons to expect a greater divergence if governments do not (a) act fast, (b) prioritize diffusion, (c) remove policy biases against services, and (d) support innovation in business models and organizational changes, especially given the risk of technological disruptions in some markets.

Notes

1. An important empirical literature in knowledge functions estimates the elasticity of patenting with respect to R&D. Trajtenberg (2001) and Griliches (1990) offer as a stylized fact that, in cross-section, patents are probably roughly proportional to R&D, implying an elasticity of unity. The elasticities decrease when using panel data estimation and for low- and middle-income countries (see Bosch, Lederman, and Maloney 2005), suggesting some decreasing returns to scale to knowledge.

2. Figure 2.2 excludes the 10 developing East Asia countries in this study (Cambodia, China, Indonesia, the Lao People's Democratic Republic, Malaysia, Mongolia, Myanmar, the Philippines, Thailand, and Vietnam) because, although their Enterprise Survey data distinguish between innovations that are new to the firm and new to the market, they do not distinguish between innovations that are new to the local market and those that are new to the international market.

3. Although the preceding discussion focuses on countries as a unit, there is significant heterogeneity within countries regarding innovation activity. Even in countries such as Korea that have reached the technological frontier (based on several metrics, such as R&D, robotization, patents, and income per capita), there is considerable heterogeneity in firms' innovation performance. This heterogeneity and its relevance to promoting innovation-led growth in developing East Asia is examined in more detail in chapter 3.

4. Hallward-Driemeier and Nayyar (2019), for example, find that the intensity of robot use in high-income countries has a positive impact on FDI growth in low- and middle-income countries up to some threshold, after which increased robotization negatively affects FDI in these countries. Most countries in their study are still below the inflection point, however. Artuc, Bastos, and Rijkers (2018) find that greater use of robots in Organisation for Economic Co-operation and Development (OECD) economies increases demand for imports from low- and middle-income countries. Dachs, Kinkel, and Jäger (2019) find a positive relationship between Industry 4.0 technologies and reshoring of production for a sample of European manufacturing firms. De Backer et al. (2016) also find some evidence, albeit weak, of reshoring affecting capital investment. For an overview of the literature on reshoring and its impact on investment, see Wan et al. (2019).

5. Comin and Mestieri (2018) define "Western countries" to include Australia, Austria, Belgium, Canada, Denmark, Finland, France, Germany, Italy, Japan, the Netherlands, New Zealand, Norway, Sweden, Switzerland, the United Kingdom, and the United States.

6. The CHAT dataset (http://www.nber.org/data/chat) is an unbalanced panel dataset with information on the adoption of over 100 technologies in more than 150 countries since 1800.

7. Nelson and Rosenberg (1993) define the NIS narrowly as "a set of institutions whose interactions determine the innovative performance of national firms," especially those supporting R&D. Other authors, such as Lundvall (1992), include a broader set of institutions such as national education systems, labor markets, financial markets, intellectual property rights policies, competitive product markets, and welfare regimes. A challenge with applying some of the variations of these frameworks is that they can be too broad and lead to different interpretations of what matters for innovation, including the key actors and policies. This makes analyzing policy and formulating clear recommendations difficult.

8. Maloney (2017) offers a way of conceptualizing the NIS that has two major advantages: (a) it is more specific about which elements to include and assess (where to set the boundaries), and (b) it includes some important considerations related to the costs of doing business and investment barriers, which can be important deterrents of innovation and have often been omitted from previous analyses.

References

Acemoglu, Daron. 2010. "When Does Labor Scarcity Encourage Innovation?" *Journal of Political Economy* 118 (6): 1037–78.

Acemoglu, Daron, Ufuk Akcigit, Harun Alp, Nicholas Bloom, and William Kerr. 2018. "Innovation, Reallocation, and Growth." *American Economic Review* 108 (11): 3450–91.

Acemoglu, Daron, and Pascual Restrepo. 2018. "The Race between Man and Machine: Implications of Technology for Growth, Factor Shares, and Employment." *American Economic Review* 108 (6): 1488–542.

Acemoglu, Daron, and Fabrizio Zilibotti. 2001. "Productivity Differences." *Quarterly Journal of Economics* 116 (2): 563–606.

Alm, Richard, and W. Michael Cox. 1996. "The Economy at Light Speed: Technology and Growth in the Information Age and Beyond." In *Annual Report 2016, Federal Reserve Bank of Dallas*, 2–17.

Artuc, Erhan, Paulo Bastos, and Bob Rijkers. 2018. "Robots, Tasks and Trade." Policy Research Working Paper 8674, World Bank, Washington, DC.

Autor, David H., and David Dorn. 2013. "The Growth of Low-Skill Service Jobs and the Polarization of the U.S. Labor Market." *American Economic Review* 103 (5): 1553–97.

Bosch, Mariano, Daniel Lederman, and William F. Maloney. 2005. *Patenting and Research and Development: A Global View*. Washington, DC: World Bank.

Bresnahan, Timothy. 2010. "General Purpose Technologies." In *Handbook of the Economics of Innovation*, vol. 2, edited by Bronwyn H. Hall and Nathan Rosenberg, 761–91. Amsterdam: Elsevier.

Caselli, Francesco, and Wilbur John Coleman II. 2006. "The World Technology Frontier." *American Economic Review* 96 (3): 499–522.

Cirera, Xavier, Marcio Cruz, Stefan Beisswenger, and Gregor Schueler. 2017. "Technology Adoption in Developing Countries in the Age of Industry 4.0." Unpublished manuscript, World Bank, Washington, DC.

Cirera, Xavier, and William F. Maloney. 2017. *The Innovation Paradox: Developing-Country Capabilities and the Unrealized Promise of Technological Catch-Up*. Washington, DC: World Bank.

Comin, Diego A., and Bart Hobijn. 2009. "The CHAT Dataset." NBER Working Paper No. 15139, National Bureau of Economic Research, Cambridge, MA.

Comin, Diego, Bart Hobijn, and Emilie Rovito. 2006. "Five Facts You Need to Know About Technology Diffusion." NBER Working Paper No. 11928, National Bureau of Economic Research, Cambridge, MA.

Comin, Diego, and Martí Mestieri. 2018. "If Technology Has Arrived Everywhere, Why Has Income Diverged?" *American Economic Journal: Macroeconomics* 10 (3): 137–78.

Dachs, Bernhard, Steffen Kinkel, and Angela Jäger. 2019. "Bringing It All Back Home? Backshoring of Manufacturing Activities and the Adoption of Industry 4.0 Technologies." *Journal of World Business* 54 (6): 101017.

De Backer, Koen, Carlo Menon, Isabelle Desnoyers-James, and Laurent Moussiegt. 2016. "Reshoring: Myth or Reality?" Science, Technology and Industry Policy Papers No. 27, Organisation for Economic Co-operation and Development, Paris.

DFKI (German Research Centre for Artificial Intelligence). 2011. "Industrie 4.0: Mit dem Internet der Dinge auf dem Weg zur 4. Industriellen Revolution."

Fazlıoğlu, Burcu, Başak Dalgıç, Ahmet Burçin Yereli. 2019. "The Effect of Innovation on Productivity: Evidence from Turkish Manufacturing Firms." *Industry and Innovation* 26 (4): 439–60.

Ford, Martin. 2015. *The Rise of the Robots: Technology and the Threat of a Jobless Future.* New York: Basic Books.

Frey, Carl Benedikt, and Michael A. Osborne. 2017. "The Future of Employment: How Susceptible Are Jobs to Computerisation?" *Technological Forecasting and Social Change* 114: 254–80.

Goñi, Edwin, and William F. Maloney. 2017. "Why Don't Poor Countries Do R&D? Varying Rates of Factor Returns across the Development Process." *European Economic Review* 94: 126–47.

Gort, Michael, and Steven Klepper. 1982. "Time Paths in the Diffusion of Product Innovations." *Economic Journal* 92 (367): 630–53.

Griliches, Zvi. 1957. "Hybrid Corn: An Exploration in the Economics of Technological Change." *Econometrica* 25 (4): 501–22.

Griliches, Zvi, 1990. "Patent Statistics as Economic Indicators: A Survey." *Journal of Economic Literature* 28 (4): 1661–707.

Hall, Bronwyn H. 2006. "Innovation and Diffusion." In *The Oxford Handbook of Innovation*, edited by Jan Fagerberg, David C. Mowery, and Richard R. Nelson, 459–84. Oxford and New York: Oxford University Press.

Hall, Bronwyn H., and Beethika Khan. 2003. "Adoption of New Technology." NBER Working Paper No. 9730, National Bureau of Economic Research, Cambridge, MA.

Hallward-Driemeier, Mary, and Gaurav Nayyar. 2018. *Trouble in the Making? The Future of Manufacturing-Led Development.* Washington, DC: World Bank.

Hallward-Driemeier, Mary C., and Gaurav Nayyar. 2019. "Have Robots Grounded the Flying Geese? Evidence from Greenfield FDI in Manufacturing." Policy Research Working Paper 9097, World Bank, Washington, DC.

Hobday, Michael. 1995. "East Asian Latecomer Firms: Learning the Technology of Electronics." *World Development* 23 (7): 1171–93.

Lundvall, Bengt-Åke, ed. 1992. *National Systems of Innovation: Towards a Theory of Innovation and Interactive Learning.* London: Pinter.

Madsen, Jakob B., Md. Rabiul Islam, and James B. Ang. 2010. "Catching Up to the Technology Frontier: The Dichotomy between Innovation and Imitation." *Canadian Journal of Economics* 43 (4): 1389–411.

Maloney, William. 2017. "Revisiting the National Innovation System in Developing Countries." Policy Research Working Paper 8219, World Bank, Washington, DC.

Mansfield, Edwin. 1961. "Technical Change and the Rate of Imitation." *Econometrica* 29 (4): 741–66.

Mohnen, Pierre, and Bronwyn H. Hall. 2013. "Innovation and Productivity: An Update." *Eurasian Business Review* 3 (1): 47–65.

Nelson, Richard R., and Nathan Rosenberg. 1993. "Technical Innovation and National Systems." In *National Innovation Systems: A Comparative Analysis*, edited by Richard R. Nelson, 3–21. Oxford and New York: Oxford University Press.

OECD and Eurostat. 2018. *Oslo Manual 2018: Guidelines for Collecting, Reporting and Using Data on Innovation.* 4th ed. Paris: OECD; Luxembourg: Eurostat.

Schwab, Klaus. 2016. *The Fourth Industrial Revolution.* Geneva: World Economic Forum.

Skinner, Jonathan, and Douglas Staiger. 2007. "Technology Adoption from Hybrid Corn to Beta-Blockers." In *Hard-to-Measure Goods and Services: Essays in Honor of Zvi Griliches*, edited by Ernst R. Berndt and Charles R. Hulten, 545–70. Chicago: University of Chicago Press.

Stoneman, Paul, and Giuliana Battisti. 2010. "The Diffusion of New Technology." In *Handbook of the Economics of Innovation*, vol. 2, edited by Bronwyn H. Hall and Nathan Rosenberg, 733–60. Amsterdam: Elsevier.

Tether, Bruce S. 2003. "The Sources and Aims of Innovation in Services: Variety between and within Sectors." *Economics of Innovation and New Technology* 12 (6): 481–505.

Trajtenberg, Manuel. 2001. "Government Support of Commercial R&D: Lessons from the Israeli Experience." Working Papers from Tel Aviv No. 2001–8, Tel Aviv University, Israel.

Wan, Li, Guido Orzes, Marco Sartor, and Guido Nassimbeni. 2019. "Reshoring: Does Home Country Matter?" *Journal of Purchasing and Supply Management* 25 (4): 100551.

Weking, Jörg, Maria Stöcker, Marek Kowalkiewicz, Markus Böhm, and Helmut Krcmar. 2019. "Leveraging Industry 4.0—A Business Model Pattern Framework." *International Journal of Production Economics* 225: 107588.

Technology Adoption and Diffusion: A Firm-Level Perspective

Introduction

As emphasized in previous chapters, developing East Asia is facing great challenges associated with changing production structures and global shocks that require the region to accelerate its diffusion of technologies and its rate and sophistication of innovation. Chapter 2 argued that moving to a more innovation-led growth model requires a focus on facilitating the diffusion of technology as well as on building the capabilities within firms to enable more sophisticated forms of innovation and discovery.

Building on the benchmarking exercise presented in chapter 1, this chapter looks more deeply at where the region stands in terms of innovation and technology. It first discusses the extent of technology adoption and diffusion and analyzes how ready the region is to meet the new challenges ahead. The chapter then examines the considerable heterogeneity in innovation performance across the region's firms. Given their capabilities, firms' innovation in the region is primarily about adoption and imitation, but there are also frontier firms and locations engaged in discovery and generating new technologies. Finally, the chapter describes some of the potential drivers of adoption and the reasons why firms in developing East Asia may not be innovating and adopting new technologies. Understanding the extent of technology adoption and diffusion, along with the heterogeneity across firms, is critical to determining the right combination of policies that can help accelerate technology diffusion and adoption as well as invention in the region.

Is East Asia converging with, or diverging from, the technological frontier? Why diffusion matters

Although inventions and new technologies push the technological frontier and offer the possibility for large increases in productivity, it is the diffusion of these innovations and new technologies that ultimately determines the pace of income and productivity growth (Hall and Khan 2003). Historical estimates by Comin and Mestieri (2018) suggest that differences in the evolution of technology diffusion since the industrial revolution have generated an annual difference in growth between countries of 0.75 percentage points—responsible for 80 percent of the Great

Divergence (also known as the "European miracle") starting in the 19th century as European countries moved ahead of other high-income countries. The post–World War II growth experience of Western Europe and Japan can be explained, in large part, by the rapid adoption of existing foreign technologies (Comin and Hobijn 2010).

Similarly, estimates by Santacreu (2015), using imports of intermediate goods, suggest that technology diffusion is an especially important source of growth for less-developed countries. She estimates that between 1996 and 2007, 65 percent of overall labor productivity growth in low- and middle-income countries can be explained by foreign innovations embodied in imports, whereas for Organisation for Economic Co-operation and Development (OECD) countries, this figure is 35.5 percent. This process of technological catch-up is also true for the advanced economies in East Asia: historical evidence suggests that the development miracles of Japan and then the Four Asian Tigers—Hong Kong SAR, China; the Republic of Korea; Singapore; and Taiwan, China—over the past 50 years all involved substantial reduction in technology adoption lags relative to the OECD (Comin and Hobijn 2011).

Developing East Asia is converging in adoption lags but diverging in intensity of use

Recent evidence suggests, however, that while new technology is arriving in developing East Asia at an accelerating pace, the region's gaps with high-income economies in the *intensity* of technology use may be increasing.

As discussed in chapter 2, Comin and Mestieri (2018) suggest that the technology adoption lag—defined as the number of years it takes for a technology to arrive to a country after invention—has narrowed significantly between high-income and lower-income countries. Using their estimates (from chapter 2, figure 2.5), the same pattern appears to hold true for developing East Asia (figure 3.1, panel a). For example, the median adoption lag for

older technologies such as steamships (invented in the later 1700s) was almost 170 years in developing East Asia, compared with 60 years in OECD countries. In contrast, the gap in the median adoption lag for the internet (invented in the 1980s) was merely five years.

At the same time, gaps in intensity of technology use—how widely new technologies have been adopted—have widened over time (figure 3.1, panel b). Comin and Mestieri (2018) suggest this gap is a main driver of the divergence in income between Western countries and the rest of the world in the past 200 years. For developing East Asia, the estimated intensity of technology use has declined at an annual rate of 0.50 percent relative to OECD countries, implying a divergence in the intensity of use of new technologies during the same period.

Different technologies diffuse at different speeds

A more nuanced view of technological convergence highlights heterogeneity across technologies. Figure 3.2 shows the diffusion in East Asia and the United States of two different technologies: the internet and industrial robots.

The internet—a general purpose technology (GPT) that enables many other technologies—has diffused rapidly, becoming ubiquitous in all countries in recent years. However, the diffusion path for robots in the region is different. At the forefront, Japan and Korea started adopting robots at the same time and now use robots in industry at higher intensity—that is, more widely—than in the United States. China's adoption of industrial robots has been the fastest in the region, growing exponentially in the past 20 years. However, many other countries in the region seem unlikely to converge with the frontier anytime soon, probably because few of them are currently specialized in sectors that can use robots intensively. This suggests that when thinking about specific technologies, one also needs to understand their uses within the firm.

FIGURE 3.1   Technology adoption lags in developing East Asia are converging with those of OECD countries, but intensity of technology use is diverging

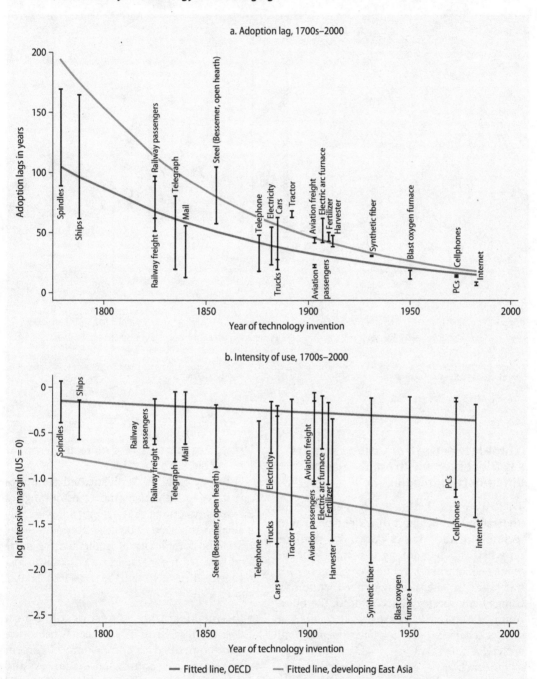

Source: World Bank, using country technology-level estimates from Comin and Mestieri 2018.

Note: Adoption lag (the number of years for a technology to arrive to a country after invention) and the intensive margin, or usage intensity (how widely new technologies are adopted), are both country-specific model parameters estimated structurally using the Cross-Country Historical Adoption of Technology (CHAT) database developed by Comin and Hobijn (2004). The blue and orange lines are fitted, respectively, to Organisation for Economic Co-operation and Development (OECD) and developing East Asian countries (the sample here including Cambodia, China, Indonesia, Malaysia, Mongolia, the Philippines, Thailand, and Vietnam). The bars show the median adoption lags (panel a) or intensive margins (panel b) of the two country groups for each labeled technology. PCs = personal computers.

FIGURE 3.2   **Data on internet and robot use in East Asia tell two different tales of diffusion and convergence with the frontier**

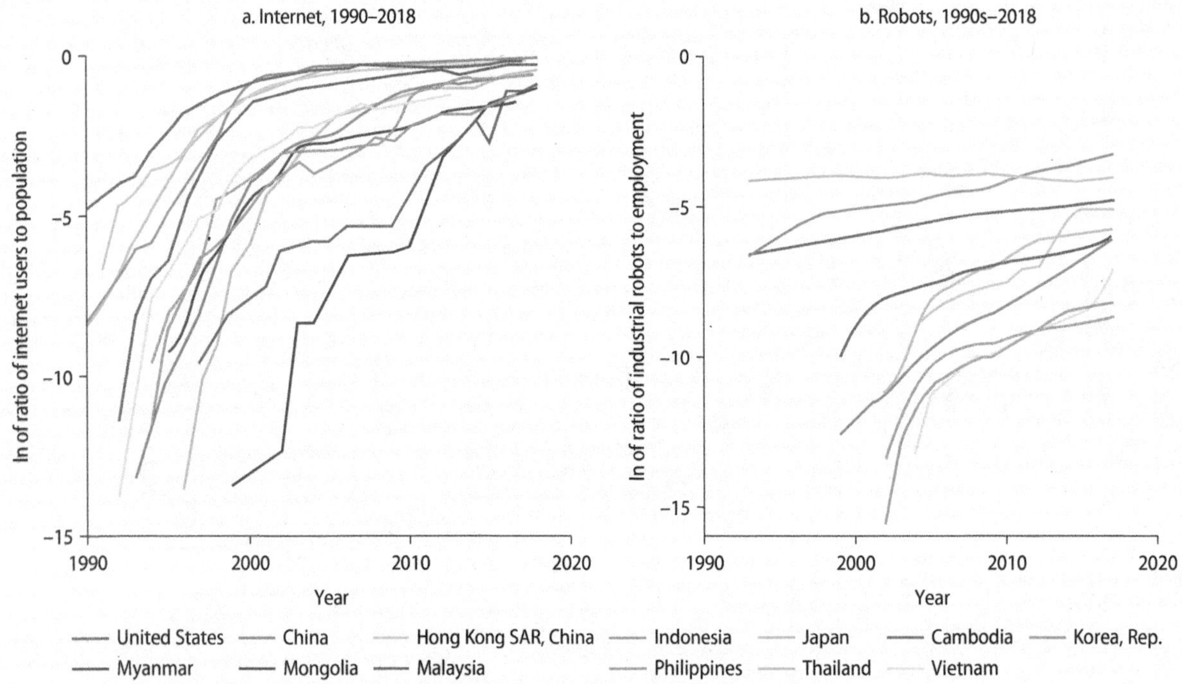

Source: Internet data from the Cross-Country Historical Adoption of Technology (CHAT) database (Comin and Hobjin 2010), updated using the World Development Indicators (WDI) database for more recent years; robot data from the International Federation of Robotics; employment data from the WDI database.
Note: ln = natural logarithm.

A firm-level view of diffusion suggests a ladder of complexity in the use of different technologies

To fully unpack this heterogeneity and understand diffusion, a firm's perspective of technology adoption is necessary. A focus on whether a technology is being used, for what task, and how intensively, is needed if one wants to measure whether technology brings better performance. Indeed, the question is not only whether a firm uses internet or blockchain but also for what purpose and with what intensity.

For each task, a firm can use different types of technologies, which can range from less to more sophisticated. This can be seen using data from the Firm-level Adoption of Technology (FAT) survey of Vietnamese firms (Cirera, Comin, Cruz, and Lee 2020), which shows the most frequently used technology,

by business function. (For more details on the FAT survey, see annex 3A.)

Moving to more sophisticated technologies may require capabilities across a range of business functions that are not immediately available and need to be developed within the firm. The complexity of implementing more sophisticated technologies translates into low intensity of use, as the Vietnam FAT results show:

• *In manufacturing*, for fabrication, most Vietnamese firms (70 percent) use operator-controlled machines, only 9 percent use computer-controlled machines, and less than 1 percent use more-advanced technologies like robots, 3D-printers, or additive manufacturing (figure 3.3).

• *In retail services*, for inventory management, 63 percent of firms use computer databases with manual updates,

FIGURE 3.3   **The intensive use of cutting-edge technology for manufacturing, retail, and agriculture remains limited in Vietnam**

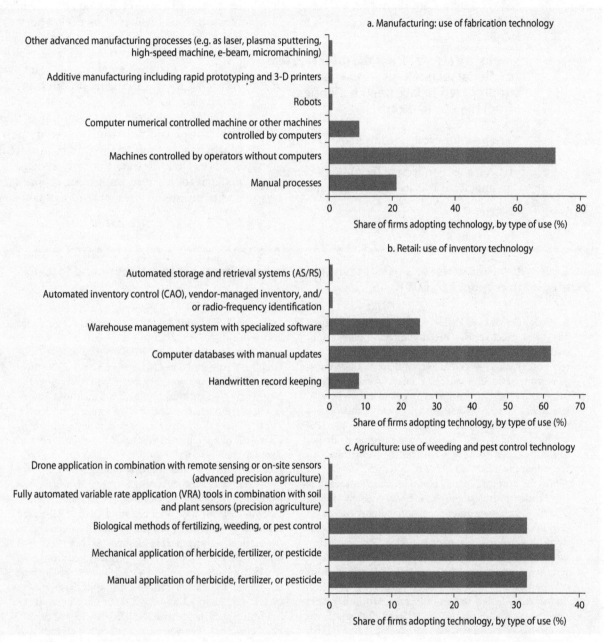

a. Manufacturing: use of fabrication technology

b. Retail: use of inventory technology

c. Agriculture: use of weeding and pest control technology

Source: World Bank estimates, using the 2020 Firm-level Adoption of Technology (FAT) survey of Vietnamese firms (Cirera, Comin, Cruz, Lee, and Martins-Neto 2020).

25 percent use warehouse management systems with specialized software, while only 1 percent use advanced technologies such as automated storage and retrieval systems.

- *In agriculture,* almost one-third of firms still use manual weeding and pest techniques as the predominant technology, whereas the use of automated precision agricultural techniques is almost nonexistent.

These results illustrate the quality ladder in technology use and indicate that most firms are at a significant distance from the technological frontier.

Firms are also far from the intensive use of digital technologies and were largely unprepared to face new challenges from the COVID-19 crisis

The need for accelerated technology diffusion has become more apparent with the recent COVID-19 pandemic. Technology can play an important role in containing transmission of the virus, as Korea has demonstrated (box 3.1). Social-distance measures have also led to a need for more flexibility in the implementation of business functions and tasks: firms are facing challenges associated with moving certain functions to home-based work, increasing "contactless" sales, and enforcing social distancing on the manufacturing shop floor.

Technologies to solve or minimize these challenges include digital e-commerce platforms and more flexible manufacturing processes. Despite the early evidence of a sharp increase in the use of online sales and platforms as a response to the pandemic

---

BOX 3.1   Republic of Korea's use of technology to implement contact tracing and testing strategies in response to COVID-19

In its fight against COVID-19, the Republic of Korea has made effective use of technology and innovation. Using the country's information and communication technology (ICT) infrastructure and accumulated outputs from national research and development (R&D) programs, the Korean government acted swiftly to use advanced technologies and innovative approaches in its response measures (Oh et al. 2020). In particular, its contact tracing and aggressive testing strategies are considered to have significantly contributed to flattening the coronavirus curve in Korea.

At the core of Korea's contact tracing strategy is the Epidemic Investigation Support System (EISS). The Korean government introduced this data system in March 2020 to support rapid, accurate epidemiological investigations in close coordination with the Korean National Police Agency, Credit Finance Association of Korea, telecommunications companies, and credit card companies. Information and data collected from these information partners become available on the COVID-19 data platform to enable epidemiological researchers and health officials to identify transmission routes and conduct "big data" analyses for the prediction of areas where people may be vulnerable to infection (Park et al. 2020). Additionally, the EISS enables (a) automated analysis of the movement of confirmed cases within 10 minutes, (b) close interinstitutional coordination through real-time information exchanges,

and (c) efficient management of access to personal information (MOEF 2020).

Complementary to the EISS are the mobile Self-Diagnosis App and Self-Quarantine Safety Protection App, which the government developed to support the monitoring of inbound travelers and those under self-quarantine, respectively (Republic of Korea 2020). These digital tools support government officials and researchers throughout the four stages of contact tracing: investigation, risk assessment, contact classification, and contacts management.

Korea's COVID-19 testing strategy also benefited from technology and innovation. For instance, domestic biotech firms used artificial intelligence (AI)-based big data systems and high-performance computing to dramatically shorten development of a coronavirus diagnostic kit (from several months to around two weeks), which was aided by the government's swift emergency use authorization. This rapid development of test kits enabled universal testing in the country from the early phases of the COVID-19 pandemic. Furthermore, Korea was one of the first countries that established walk-through and drive-through screening stations. This innovative approach to testing, along with the rapid development of diagnostic kits, helped the country meet its extensive testing needs while minimizing the risks involved.

Source: Frias, Lee, and Shin 2020.

(Apedo-Amah et al. 2020), a key question is how well firms in developing East Asia are equipped to use them and to adapt to both preexisting and newly emerging challenges.

To better assess firms' readiness to adopt technology, a "digital readiness index" was developed, using the FAT survey for Vietnam (Cirera, Comin, Cruz, Lee, and Martins-Neto 2020). The index measures the extent of firms' digitalization by business function.[1] Figure 3.4 shows the results of the indexes (ranging between 0 and 100) for Vietnam. Panel a focuses on use of digital infrastructure and platforms, while panel b focuses on the extent of digitalization of general business functions.

Regarding digital infrastructure use, figure 3.4, panel a, shows that almost all firms have access to the internet, but far fewer firms have their own websites or use social media for marketing or sales. Large firms have a 60 percent probability of having their own website, in contrast to slightly more than

30 percent of small firms. Access to online platforms is also relatively low relative to its potential, especially for small and medium-size firms. Moreover, only 7 percent of firms have adopted cloud computing for their business processes.

As for the use of digital technologies in general business functions (figure 3.4, panel b), the indexes—percentages of firms that use a digital technology as the main one for the specified business function—similarly suggest substantial room for increased digitalization. On average across different business functions, only 20 percent of Vietnamese firms use fully digitalized processes to perform general business functions ranging from marketing, payment methods, and production planning to sales and supply chain management.[2]

The results show considerable room for improvement in digitalization across different firm functions and tasks. For example, most firms in Vietnam do not use digital technologies as their main tool for sales. Although

FIGURE 3.4   **Digital readiness indexes show widespread internet access among Vietnamese firms, but few are fully equipped to use digitalized processes for primary business functions**

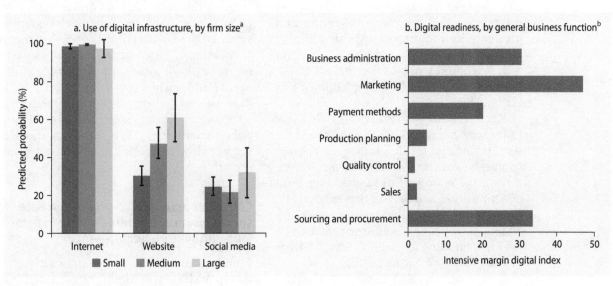

Source: Cirera, Comin, Cruz, Lee, and Martins-Neto 2020.
Note: The indexes were developed using data from the Firm-level Adoption of Technology (FAT) survey of Vietnamese firms in manufacturing, retail, and agriculture. For more details about the FAT data, see annex 3A.
a. Panel a shows the predicted probability of firms with internet, own website, and social media on size—small (5–19 employees); medium (20–99); and large (100+)—from the Probit regressions, while controlling for sector and region. All estimates are weighted by sampling and country weights. Vertical lines show confidence intervals.
b. Panel b shows the percentages of firms that use a digital technology as the main one for the specified business function.

around 30 percent of the firms can do some sales online, only 2.5 percent of those firms that sell directly to consumers use some digital sales method—either social platforms or (most often) their own websites—more intensively than other methods.

Nearly half (47 percent) of Vietnamese firms use digital technologies for marketing and advertising. The current use of digital technologies in business administration remains low (31 percent), however, implying low ability to provide the flexibility to enable workers to cope with potential disruptions created by COVID-19 or other shocks.

Technology adoption generates a positive productivity dividend

To make the most of existing and emerging technologies, it will be important for firms in developing East Asia to continue accumulating innovation capabilities—first by upgrading their processes using digital technologies, and then by adopting more sophisticated Industry 4.0 tools.

The dividends from doing so, in terms of productivity and competitiveness gains, can be large. As discussed in previous chapters, the empirical literature that examines the relationship between innovation and productivity indicates that innovation *of all types* generally has a positive impact on firm-level productivity. (For surveys of the evidence, see Hall [2011] and Mohnen and Hall [2013].)

Recent analysis using World Bank Enterprise Survey (WBES) data produces similar findings for developing East Asian countries. Product and process innovation among the region's firms, including both new-to-market and new-to-firm innovation, is associated with higher labor productivity and higher revenue total factor productivity (TFP), controlling for firm-level and market characteristics (de Nicola 2019).

Data from the FAT survey in Vietnam reinforce the positive relationship between technology adoption—a type of diffusion—and productivity at the firm level. Figure 3.5 shows the conditional prediction from regressing the logarithm of value added per worker on a technology index and sector dummies to control for different production functions, by sector. Firms that use more sophisticated technologies in general business functions such as human resource (HR) management, supply chain management, or sales (the extensive margin, shown in panel a) and use them more intensively (the intensive margin, shown in panel b) tend to have higher value added per worker. As expected, the more intensively the sophisticated technology is used (panel b), the stronger the relationship.

Heterogeneity in the pattern and diffusion of innovation across space, sectors, and firms

As argued earlier, what matters most for a country's growth performance is how rapidly technology and innovation diffuse across enterprises in a country. Indeed, the productivity and technological divide between the leading and lagging firms in developing East Asia is likely the consequence of slow diffusion *within* countries. And as Andrews, Criscuolo, and Gal (2016) suggest, this technological divide is a likely cause of the global productivity slowdown since 2000. This section shows that there is substantial heterogeneity in the pattern of technology adoption and innovation across and within countries, sectors, and in some cases, even within the same firms. This heterogeneity merits the concerns of policy makers because, if persistent, it could further slow the region's productivity and growth.

Countries across developing East Asia show significant heterogeneity in firm-level innovation performance

Firm-level measures of innovation activities, using WBES data, highlight considerable heterogeneity in firm-level innovation activity across the region. Close to 60 percent of Chinese firms introduce a product or service innovation, and 20 percent have a

FIGURE 3.5   **Technology adoption brings labor productivity gains to Vietnamese firms**

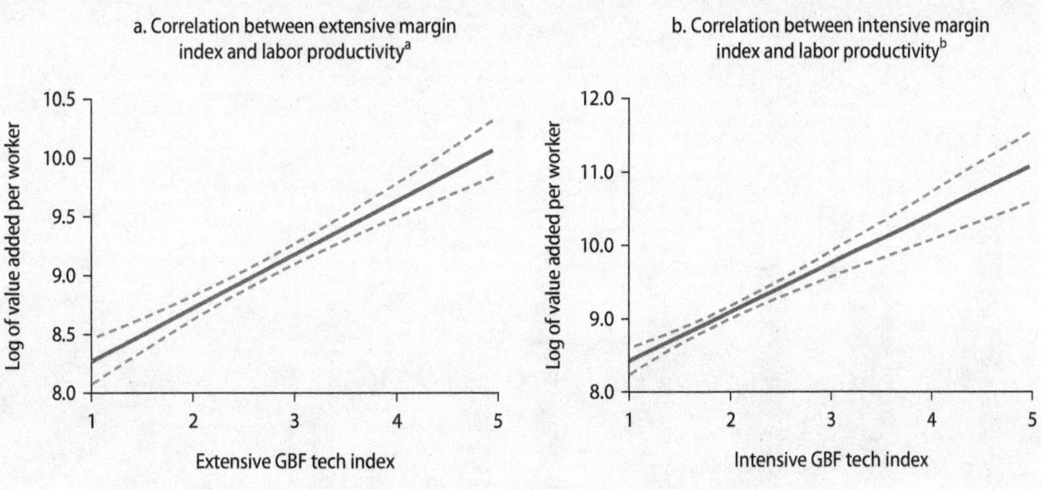

a. Correlation between extensive margin index and labor productivity[a]

b. Correlation between intensive margin index and labor productivity[b]

Source: Cirera, Comin, Cruz, Lee, and Martins-Neto 2020.

Note: The figures show the conditional predictions (solid lines) and 95 percent confidence levels (dashed lines) from regressing the log of labor value added per worker on a technology index and sector dummy variables. The index (from 1 to 5) measures the sophistication of technology—1 being the least sophisticated and 5 the most sophisticated technology for a set of general business functions (GBF) including business administration (human resources, accounting, and so on); production or service operations planning; sourcing, procurement, and supply chain management; marketing and product development; sales; payments; and quality control. The indexes were developed using data from the Firm-level Adoption of Technology (FAT) survey of Vietnamese firms in manufacturing, retail, and agriculture. For more details about the FAT data, see annex 3A.

a. The "extensive" index refers to the average among all GBFs of the most sophisticated technology used in each business function, even if marginally used.

b. The "intensive" index refers to average among all GBFs of the most sophisticated technology used more intensively for each business function—that is, the main technology used by the firm.

foreign-licensed technology (figure 3.6). At the other end of the spectrum, less than 15 percent of firms in countries such as Myanmar and Thailand report having a product or service innovation, and a mere 5 percent have any technology licensed from foreign companies. As discussed in chapter 2 (figure 2.7), with the exception of China, countries in the region are located in the lower two (out of three) clusters of innovation capabilities.

Innovation activity also varies widely across sectors

Firms in developing East Asia also differ substantially in innovation outcomes across sectors—as measured by the incidence of firms implementing or adopting a new product, process, or organizational or marketing approach. Evidence from the WBES data suggests that manufacturing firms are significantly more likely than firms in the

services sector to undertake a product or process innovation.

However, these findings may paint a biased picture of the true extent of innovation in manufacturing and services, being partly driven by the different nature of innovation in these sectors (box 3.2). Among more narrowly defined sectors, the share of firms that undertook a product or process innovation is highest in computer and related activities (ICT) and other high-tech industries such as machinery and equipment, electronics, and chemicals (figure 3.7).

Firms are not technology savvy in everything

Finally, even within firms, there can be significant heterogeneity in the process of technology adoption. Evidence from the FAT survey in Vietnam offers new insights about the complexities of firms' technology

FIGURE 3.6   **Developing East Asian countries vary widely in firm-level innovation activity**

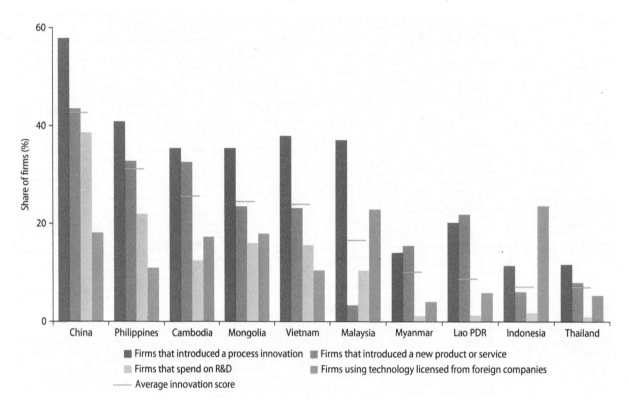

Source: World Bank calculations using latest World Bank Enterprise Survey data.
Note: The innovation score captures both innovation outputs and inputs. It is calculated as the average of the likelihood that firms have a product innovation, a process innovation, positive research and development (R&D) spending, or license technology from foreign companies.

adoption decisions. The data suggest that the use of sophisticated technologies can differ significantly across business functions even within a given firm.

The radar diagrams in figure 3.8 illustrate both between- and within-firm heterogeneity in technology adoption, using data from a large and a medium-size firm in the food processing sector. They show that, for the same business administration functions, these two firms can be very different in the extensive margin of technology use (figure 3.8, panel a), but the gap is minimal when use intensity is considered (figure 3.8, panel b). Moreover, the same firm (for example, Firm 1) can be near the frontier in its use of food storage technology but far from the frontier in the use of input testing technology (figure 3.8, panel d). Cirera, Comin, Cruz, Lee, and Martins-Neto (2020)

show, in fact, that within-firm variation in the use of technology (figure 3.8, panels b and d) is larger than the cross-firm variation (figure 3.8, panels a and c).

The pattern of heterogeneity in innovation activity is also spatial, demanding different policies across geographical areas

The unevenness of technological discovery and diffusion across the region's countries is mirrored by innovation performance within these countries. Using data from Crunchbase, an investment and funding platform, map 3.1 shows the spatial distribution of companies that have received early-stage equity between 2007 and 2019—a proxy for the incidence of innovative start-ups—across cities in

BOX 3.2   **Innovation in manufacturing versus services**

There are major differences in the *observed* innovation rates between manufacturing and services firms. Measured by having implemented a product or process innovation, services firms in developing East Asia (and elsewhere) appear to be significantly less innovative than manufacturing firms (figure B3.1.1). At the same time, the most salient innovations portrayed in the region's popular press are examples from service companies such as those providing ride-sharing services (Grab, Go-Jek); e-commerce (Alibaba); or gaming and payment platforms (Tencent).

Reasons for this innovation gap between manufacturing and services firms

What can explain this apparent discrepancy? One reason is the huge underlying heterogeneity in services. Services subsectors are very different from each other in their input-to-output process and the levels of technology of the inputs used (Pires, Sarkar, and Carvalho 2008). Detailed examination of service activities suggests, for example, that knowledge-intensive business services are just as likely as the high-technology manufacturing subsectors to have a product or process innovation. (See Pires, Sarkar, and Carvalho [2008] and Iacovone, Mattoo, and Zahler [2013] for evidence from Portugal and Chile.) This likelihood of innovation also holds true for the computer and related activities (ICT) services sector in developing East Asia (figure 3.7). However, because this sector accounts for only a small share (around 3 percent) of firms in the services sector, the overall rate of innovation in services is driven by more traditional subsectors such as wholesale and retail.

Second, innovations in the services and manufacturing sectors are inherently different from each other. Ettlie and Rosenthal (2011) argue that key differences concern the alternative ways in which services sector enterprises implement the innovative process (often with less-formal research and development (R&D) processes or piloting and testing); the unique way in which service providers test customer concepts (given that services are often unique to the specific customer); and the more pronounced role of informal sourcing of innovation ideas by enterprise managers.

Difficulty of measuring services innovation

Service activities have a range of characteristics that render measurement extremely difficult (Pires, Sarkar, and Carvalho 2008): the intangible nature of most services, the overlap of the moment of production and consumption, nonstorability, and the strong user-producer links. Intangibility, in particular, means that service products often cannot be displayed in advance, and their qualities are not easily explained to the customer. These same characteristics hinder efforts toward standardization. Therefore, intangible services lack the ability to create a temporary monopoly with the help of some sort of patent protection to redeem the innovation annuities. This lack of potential for protection may reduce the incentive for innovation activities in the services sector (Hipp and Grupp 2005).

Because of the differences between manufacturing and services innovation, traditional measures to capture technological innovations have a manufacturing bias and do not adequately capture the full extent of innovations in services. Innovation in services has been

FIGURE B3.1.1   **Manufacturing and services firms differ in rates of innovation, especially of new products or processes**

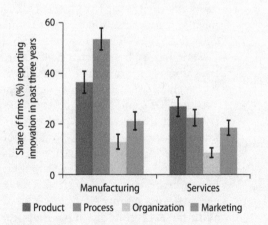

Source: World Bank Enterprise Survey data, latest round.
Note: The figure shows the average share and 95 percent confidence interval in the pooled sample, accounting for country fixed effects. Data include manufacturing and services sector firms surveyed by the Enterprise Surveys in all 10 middle-income countries covered in this study: Cambodia, China, Indonesia, Lao PDR, Malaysia, Mongolia, Myanmar, the Philippines, Thailand, and Vietnam.

box continues next page

BOX 3.2 **Innovation in manufacturing versus services** (continued)

characterized as "soft" or nontechnological, more likely to be incremental, and more on the organizational side. (For a review, see Doloreux, Shearmur, and Rodriguez [2016].) As a result, measures such as R&D and patents tend to systematically overlook innovation activities in services sectors (Hall 2011; Hipp and Grupp 2005).[a] When looking at other measures of organizational and marketing innovations, however, services firms in East Asia are not significantly different from those in the manufacturing sector (figure B3.1.1).

There appear to be some differences in the returns from different types of innovation in services relative to manufacturing, but the evidence has been very mixed. In general, empirical evidence so far has suggested that the returns to innovation are similar between these two sectors (Audretsch et al. 2018; Musolesi and Huiban 2010).

In both the nature and returns to innovation, the line between manufacturing and services innovations

has become increasingly blurred to the extent that innovation in manufacturing assumes the form of "servicification." At least 20 percent of Spanish manufacturing firms have introduced services in the recent past (Santamaría, Nieto, and Miles 2012). And the vast majority of French manufacturers sell services in addition to producing goods (Crozet and Milet 2017). In a contrasting phenomenon in the United States, sourcing and design activities are now performed by "factoryless goods producers" whose activities were once done within manufacturing (Bernard and Fort 2017). In addition, innovation of services has been found to increase productivity for manufacturing activities, both within the firms and for downstream sectors using services inputs (Crozet and Milet 2017).

a. A firm's accounting practices can also play a role. Perhaps the most extreme example of how reported R&D can underestimate innovation is in the case of Amazon. Amazon reports only "technology and content" investment, with no separate reporting of R&D efforts (Hernández et al. 2020).

developing East Asia. Across all countries and sectors, innovative companies are concentrated in a few urban hubs but remain absent in large areas of all countries. The incidence of innovative start-ups in China, in particular, appears consistent with the pattern of patent filings, which suggest that technological and design capabilities are concentrated in a few locations in Eastern China (Prud'homme and Zhang 2019).

These patterns affirm that despite a level of technological achievement in major cities that might rival that of high-income countries, low levels of technological advancement in lagging areas mean that, in aggregate, the countries in the region are not as technologically advanced as high-income economies.

Although innovation, especially in tech companies, tends to concentrate in specific tech hubs, spatial inequality suggests the need for countries to have a differentiated development strategy for firms outside these hubs and to build on preexisting endowments in other subregions within developing East Asia.

There is a high concentration of the most-inventive activities

Another form of within-country heterogeneity is the duality of firm-level R&D investment and concentration of the most-inventive activities. Figure 3.9 shows the distribution of R&D intensity for selected East Asian countries and uses Israel as a benchmark country. Each country has a separate sample year between 2012 and 2016. Across all countries, the vast majority of firms perform no R&D at all (figure 3.9, panel a). Notably, of those firms that do invest in R&D, the distribution of R&D intensity (as measured by R&D expenditure per employee) differs significantly across countries (figure 3.9 panel b). With the exception of China, it appears that the share of firms investing in R&D as well as R&D intensity among these firms tends to increase with a country's income level, both on average and across the whole distribution.

This result is not surprising: an empirical regularity in any economy is that the most-inventive activities—those resulting from

FIGURE 3.7   Firm-level innovation in East Asia also differs across sectors

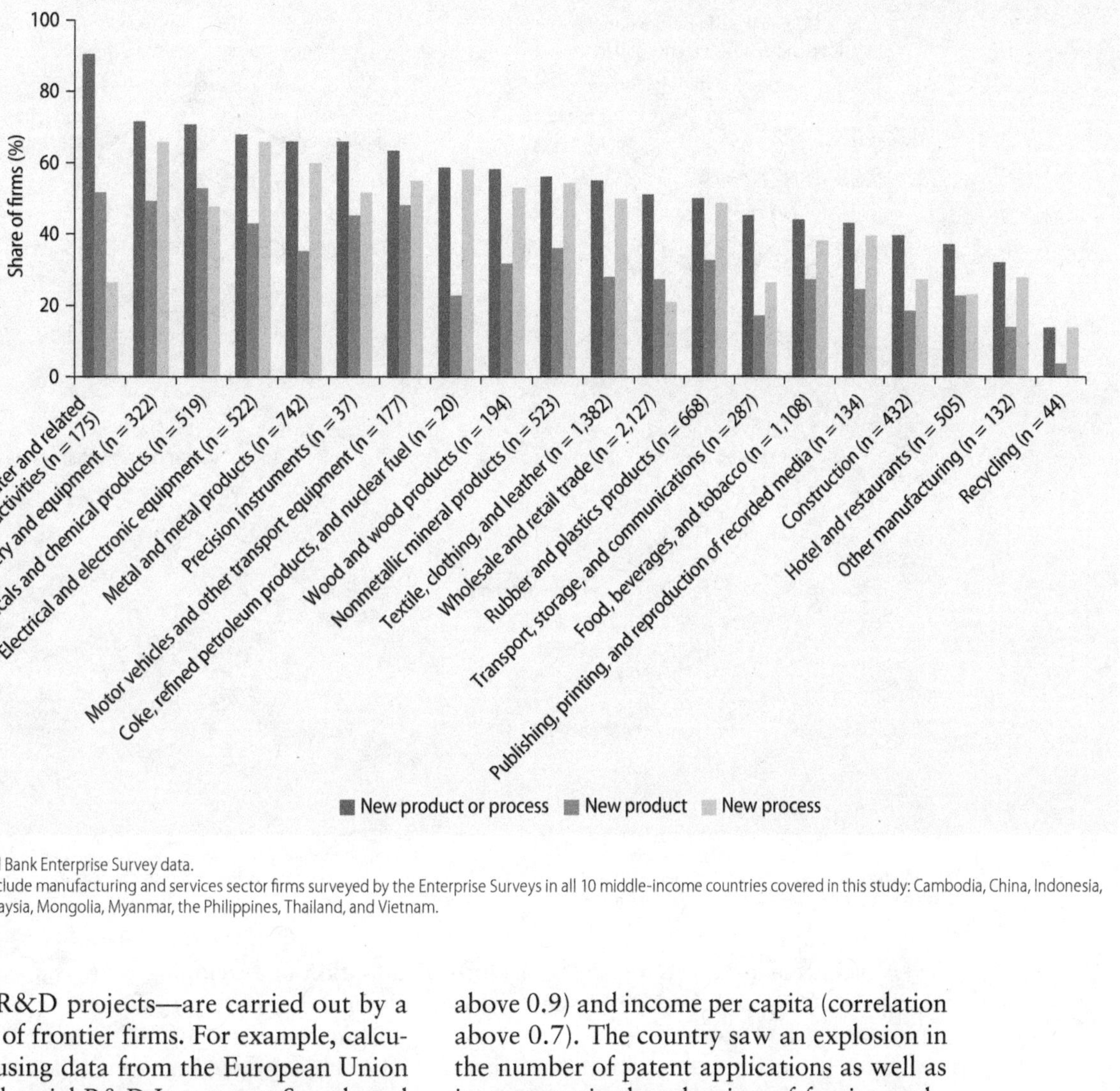

Legend: ■ New product or process   ■ New product   ■ New process

Source: World Bank Enterprise Survey data.
Note: Data include manufacturing and services sector firms surveyed by the Enterprise Surveys in all 10 middle-income countries covered in this study: Cambodia, China, Indonesia, Lao PDR, Malaysia, Mongolia, Myanmar, the Philippines, Thailand, and Vietnam.

formal R&D projects—are carried out by a handful of frontier firms. For example, calculations using data from the European Union (EU) Industrial R&D Investment Scoreboard suggest that the top 10 public companies account for just under 20 percent of aggregate private sector R&D spending in the United States and close to 10 percent in China (Hernández et al. 2020).

The explosion of patents mentioned earlier for China's manufacturing sector, similarly, can be accounted for by a tiny, highly select group of Chinese companies in the ICT equipment industry (Eberhardt, Helmers, and Yu 2011). The companies' growth in patent applications closely mirrors the countries' growth in R&D expenditures (correlation is above 0.9) and income per capita (correlation above 0.7). The country saw an explosion in the number of patent applications as well as investment in the adoption of foreign technologies, as measured by aggregate payments for technology licensing fees (figure 3.10). In fact, in 2011, China overtook the United States as the country with the most patent filings.

Moreover, tracking the growth in different types of patents and foreign citations suggests that Chinese patent quality also exhibits a real and robust improvement over time (Wei, Xie, and Zhang 2017). The extent of innovation and improvements over time have been considerably lower and slower in other developing East Asian countries, however.

FIGURE 3.8   Radar diagrams show substantial heterogeneity in technological sophistication within firms

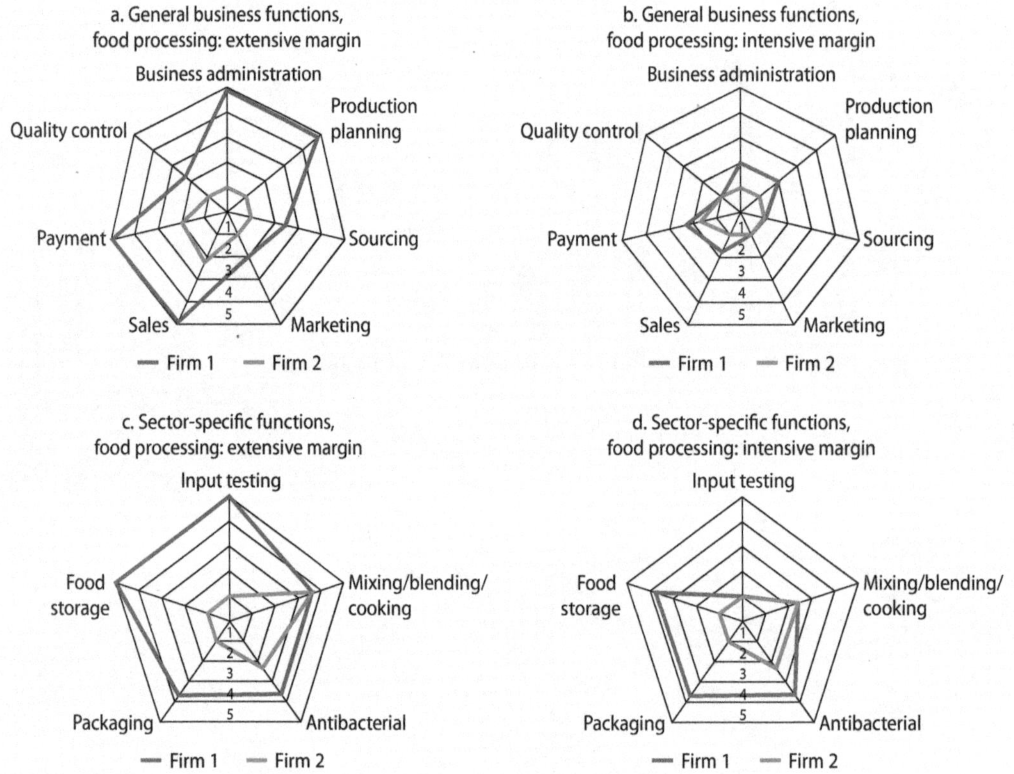

a. General business functions,
food processing: extensive margin

b. General business functions,
food processing: intensive margin

c. Sector-specific functions,
food processing: extensive margin

d. Sector-specific functions,
food processing: intensive margin

Source: Cirera, Comin, Cruz, Lee, and Martins-Neto 2020.
Note: In each radar diagram, the values 1–5 indicate relative distance from the frontier in a firm's use of technology for a given business function (1 being the most distant and 5 representing the frontier). Firm 1 and Firm 2 are Vietnamese food-processing firms that provided data for the Firm-level Adoption of Technology (FAT) survey. For more details about the FAT data, see annex 3A.

Overall, this large heterogeneity in innovation activities and the high concentration of invention and more-complex innovation activities in only a few locations and firms suggests that diffusion is not occurring (or at least not occurring fast or broadly enough to support higher productivity growth), which is slowing the creation of higher-quality jobs that could significantly boost incomes in the region. A policy priority should be to promote the diffusion of knowledge and technology from frontier firms, domestic or foreign, to the rest of the economy.

What inhibits innovation?

Evidence from the previous section has highlighted that the process of invention and adoption in developing East Asia is not only diverse across countries but also uneven within countries. To facilitate the diffusion of technology and innovation, countries need more nuanced policies that can target key areas of underperformance. The challenge for policy makers is to understand the drivers of this heterogeneity. In other words, what inhibits firms from adopting technology and innovating more?

Who innovates?

The first element in understanding what inhibits innovation is the profile of innovators. Firms that innovate look consistently different from non-innovators in several dimensions. WBES data suggest that, on average, East

MAP 3.1   **The spatial distribution of innovative start-ups in developing East Asia shows a concentration in urban hubs, excluding large areas of all countries**

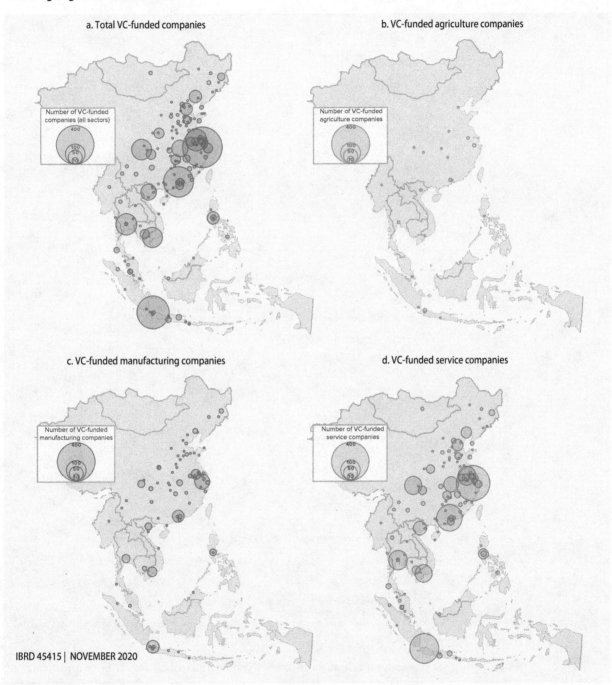

a. Total VC-funded companies

b. VC-funded agriculture companies

c. VC-funded manufacturing companies

d. VC-funded service companies

IBRD 45415 | NOVEMBER 2020

Source: World Bank elaboration using Crunchbase data (https://www.crunchbase.com/).
Note: The maps show distribution of innovative start-ups—defined as currently operating companies that received early-stage equity deals between 2007 and 2019—across cities in developing East Asia (Cambodia, China, Indonesia, Lao PDR, Malaysia, Mongolia, Myanmar, the Philippines, Thailand, and Vietnam). The size of the circles is proportional to the number of companies. City names were extracted from companies' addresses and merged into a geographic information system (GIS) dataset using a fuzzy match algorithm; hence a subsample of companies is not included because of nonmatches. VC = venture capital.

FIGURE 3.9   **There is significant duality in firm-level R&D investment**

a. Distribution of firm-level R&D investment, selected countries[a]

b. Concentration of high R&D activities, selected countries[b]

─── Israel ─── China ─── Cambodia ─── Malaysia ─── Philippines

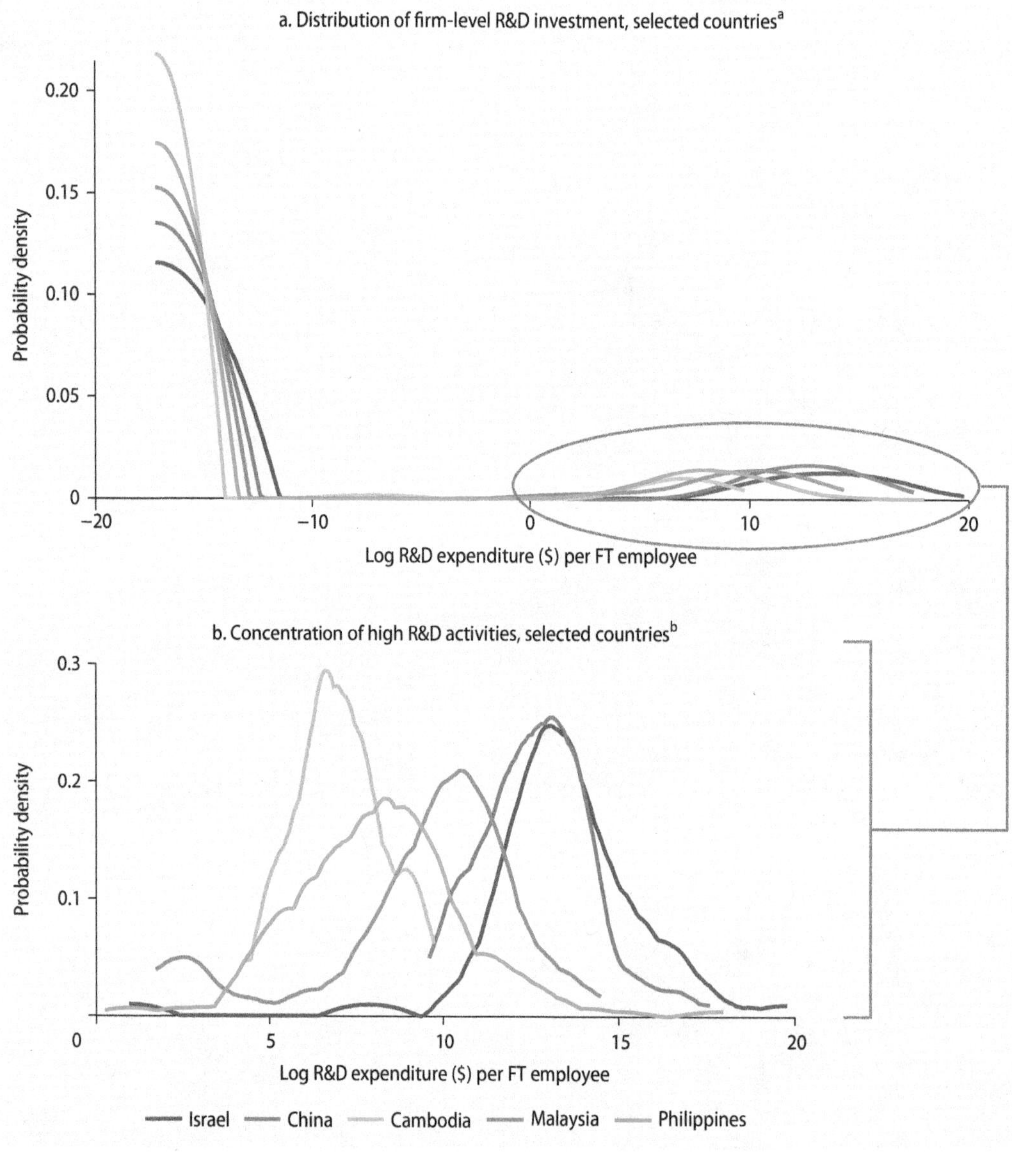

Source: World Bank Enterprise Survey data.
Note: In both panels, Israel (dark solid line) represents the benchmark. FT = full-time; R&D = research and development.
a. Panel a illustrates the distribution of R&D investment across all firms, by country.
b. Panel b (an enlarged portion of panel a) illustrates the distribution of R&D intensity (R&D expenditure per employee) among firms that do invest in R&D, by country.

Asian firms that engage in all or at least one dimension of innovation—product, process, organization, or marketing—tend to be larger, more likely to export, and more likely to be located in larger cities (table 3.1).

Market size appears to be particularly important for firms engaged in multiple dimensions of innovation. Conditional on country, sector, and other firm characteristics, exporters are 3.6 times more likely than nonexporters to have some innovation in all four dimensions. In addition, firms in cities with populations exceeding 1 million are four times more likely than those in cities with

FIGURE 3.10   **Inventions and foreign technology adoption have increased over time, by country, 2000–19**

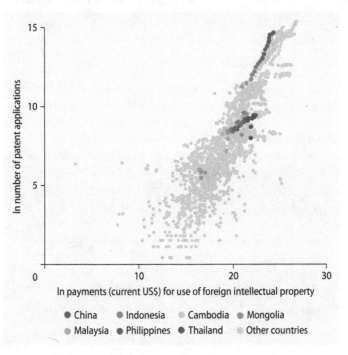

Source: World Development Indicators database.
Note: "Inventions" reflects the number of patent applications. "Foreign technology adoption" reflects aggregate fees (in current US$) paid to other countries for technology licenses. The darker the shade, the more recent the year of data. ln = natural logarithm.

populations below 50,000 to engage in all four dimensions of innovation.

Considering other characteristics, young and foreign-owned firms do not tend to innovate more than other firms. However, firm size is highly correlated with innovation propensity, particularly innovations in multiple dimensions. Compared with small and medium-size firms, large firms are eight times and three times more likely, respectively, to participate in all four types of innovation.

Factors internal to the firm: firm capabilities and uncertainty

One potentially important inhibitor of innovation is a lack of absorptive capabilities. Innovation requires a range of capabilities that enable firms to respond to market conditions, identify new technological opportunities, develop a plan to exploit them, and then cultivate the necessary resources to do so.

Case study research about the adoption of ICT in the United States, for example, has pointed out that the adoption of many GPTs often involves major reorganization and co-investment in new products or business models (Bresnahan and Trajtenberg 1995; Brynjolfsson, Hitt, and Yang 2002).

These requirements are likely even more intense for Industry 4.0 technologies, as described in chapter 2. The acquisition or the lack of these capabilities—and specifically, managerial and organizational practices—is fundamental to the process of upgrading (Sutton 2012) and other basic forms of innovation.

Poor management quality is a deterrent to innovation
Evidence from a detailed matched employer-employee survey for China supports this view: the degree of a firm's innovativeness—as measured by a firm's incidence of having

TABLE 3.1 **Firms that innovate in developing East Asia tend to be larger, exporters, and located in larger cities**

Firm characteristic	Innovate in all four dimensions[a]	Innovate in at least one dimension[a]
Firm age	0.992	0.988
	(0.0132)	(0.00820)
Share (%) of foreign ownership	0.989*	1.004
	(0.00638)	(0.00318)
Exporter	3.595***	1.535**
	(1.509)	(0.294)
Firm size: Medium (20–99 employees)	2.699**	1.852***
	(1.136)	(0.285)
Firm size: Large (≥ 100 employees)	8.046***	2.533***
	(3.628)	(0.444)
Location size: > 1 million population	4.434**	3.617***
	(2.567)	(1.450)
	2.559	2.838**
Location size: 250,000–1 million population	(1.881)	(1.164)
Location size: 50,000–250,000 population	1.422	6.354***
	(1.196)	(2.743)
N	6,344	9,555

Source: World Bank Enterprise Survey data.
Note: Odds ratio from logistic regression of firm innovation on firm characteristics, conditional on country (Cambodia, China, Indonesia, Lao PDR, Malaysia, Mongolia, Myanmar, Philippines, Thailand, Vietnam) and sector (manufacturing, trade, construction, transport, other services) fixed effects. The base for firm size is "Small (< 20 employees)" and for location size, "less than 50,000" population. Robust standard error in parentheses.
a. Firms can introduce an innovation in all or any of the following four dimensions: product/service, process, organization, and marketing.
*** $p < 0.01$ ** $p < 0.05$ * $p < 0.1$

a product or process innovation, R&D project, or patent—is positively associated with the firm's management quality and share of highly (college) educated workers (Park and Xuan 2020). Data from the World Management Survey (WMS) show, however, that compared with US firms—a proxy for the global frontier—firms in selected developing East Asian countries are significantly less-well-managed on average and along the whole distribution (figure 3.11).[3]

Moreover, poor overall innovation performance appears to be driven by management quality gaps that are generally larger for the top firms.[4] That is, the frontier firms in developing East Asia perform disproportionally worse than the frontier firms in the United States. This gap in management capabilities likely contributes to the innovation gaps both (a) between the region and the global frontier, and (b) between firms within the same countries.

Informational constraints and uncertainty are barriers to innovation and technology adoption

Innovation is an inherently risky endeavor. The process of technology adoption, for example, is often characterized by significant uncertainty (as to the future path of the technology and its benefits) and by limited information about the benefits, costs, and even the technology's viability (Hall 2004).

Informational constraints. In this environment, informational failures may constitute a significant barrier to technology adoption and innovation. A study of large Indian textile plants, for example, argues that "informational constraints" are an important factor leading firms not to adopt simple, apparently beneficial practices that are widespread elsewhere (Bloom et al. 2013). The work of Atkin et al. (2017) on barriers to technology adoption provides a possible microfoundation for such informational constraints.

Their evidence suggests that misalignment of incentives between different types of workers within firms can impede the flow of information on the benefits of a new technology between the shop-floor workers and managers.

Informational failures can also manifest in misperceptions about firms' own technological sophistication. Evidence from outside the region suggests that firms significantly overestimate their own management capabilities, and those with worse

FIGURE 3.11   Firms in developing East Asian countries score lower on management capabilities than firms at the global frontier

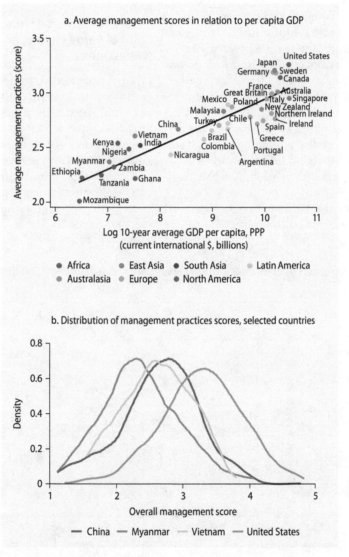

Source: World Management Survey (WMS), Centre for Economic Performance.
Note: The WMS scores (collected over several years) range from 1 (worst practice) to 5 (best practice) across key management practices used by organizations in different sectors. These practices are grouped into five areas: Operations Management, Performance Monitoring, Target Setting, Leadership Management, and Talent Management. GDP = gross domestic product; PPP = purchasing power parity.

management capabilities are more likely to be overconfident (Del Carpio and Taskin 2016). Firms in developing East Asia are no exception. The FAT survey in Vietnam suggests that most firm managers are overconfident about their firms' technological capabilities: they routinely assess their own companies' relative technology levels to be higher than what's revealed in the benchmarking data (figure 3.12).

Uncertainty about returns from technology. The often-high fixed cost of innovation and technology adoption also means that uncertainty about returns—for example, because of uncertainty about demand for new products or the efficiency of new technologies—will lead to low initial adoption of new technologies (as explained in Atkin et al. 2017). Evidence of increased investment in quality upgrading in response to new export demand offers empirical support for this argument (Atkin, Khandelwal, and Osman 2017).

Data from the FAT survey in Vietnam confirms that firms consider uncertainty to be an important factor in their technology adoption decisions. Well over 50 percent of surveyed firms, regardless of size, indicated that they are deterred by uncertainty of demand and high cost along with doubts about value of the new technologies (figure 3.13). More than half also cited lack of capabilities in terms of skills and available information as a critical constraint to adoption.

External drivers of innovation: trade, global value chains, and foreign direct investment

Firms' decisions to adopt technologies and innovate are not made in a vacuum. Their external environment shapes the returns and their incentives to innovate, depending on market size, prices of and access to complementary inputs, competitive pressure with both domestic and foreign firms, the flows of information and opportunities for learning-by-doing, and the quality of regulations, including intellectual property protection. For extensive

FIGURE 3.12 **Managers of Vietnamese firms express overconfidence about their firms' technological capabilities**

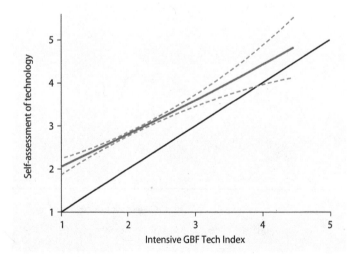

Source: Cirera, Comin, Cruz, Lee, and Martins-Neto 2020.
Note: The blue line shows the quadratic fit with a 95 percent confidence interval (dotted red lines). The black 45-degree line shows where expectations and index are equal. The technology index is regressed on the firms' self-assessment of sophistication relative to other firms in the country. The technology index applied here covers the most-used technologies in general business functions (GBF), which include business processes, production planning, supply chain management, marketing, sales, payment methods, and quality control. The index was developed using data from the Firm-level Adoption of Technology (FAT) survey of Vietnamese firms in manufacturing, retail, and agriculture. For more details about the FAT data, see annex 3A.

FIGURE 3.13   Lack of demand and uncertainty is the top self-reported barrier to technology adoption among Vietnamese firms of all sizes

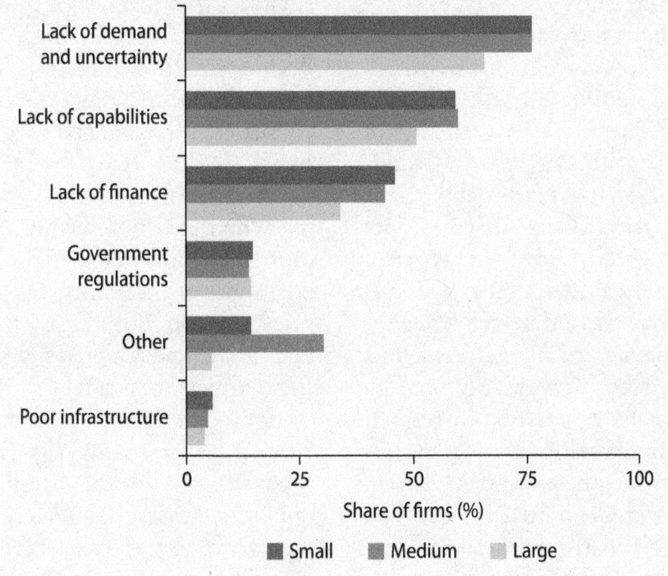

Source: Cirera, Comin, Cruz, and Lee 2020.
Note: Firm sizes small (5–19 employees), medium (20–99), and large (100+). Data were gathered from the Firm-level Adoption of Technology (FAT) survey of Vietnamese firms in manufacturing, retail, and agriculture. For more details about the FAT data, see annex 3A.

discussions, see Syverson (2011), Verhoogen (2020), and Zanello et al. (2016).

The cost of capital relative to labor (especially low-skilled labor) also plays a role in determining the direction of innovation toward more or less labor savings. Evidence from China suggests that minimum-wage increases lead firms to upgrade to more labor-saving, capital-intensive technologies (Hau, Huang, and Wang 2020). At the same time, in urban areas that receive a higher influx of low-skilled workers, firms tend to use less human-capital-intensive technologies and produce fewer patents (Imbert et al. 2018).

It is not possible to empirically assess the extent to which lack of innovation in developing East Asia is driven by relative factor prices. (Chapter 4 looks at the supply of human capital and finance in more detail.) Nevertheless, for many countries in the region, low labor cost has supported an outward-oriented development strategy,

which in turn has facilitated a diffusion of innovation to the region that often complements low labor cost. At the same time, diffusion within countries remains slow, consistent with the heterogeneity described earlier. This strategy will likely have decreasing returns without serious efforts to address firms' capability constraints—efforts that are essential to reaping the spillover benefits from trade and investment flows.

Trade and global value chains can enable innovation, but benefits are concentrated in the most-productive firms

Theory and evidence suggest trade can be a major channel for knowledge diffusion and a driver of domestic innovation. Exports can create incentives to innovate through increased market size—by spreading the fixed cost of innovation across markets—and enable innovation through learning-by-doing (Aghion et al. 2018; Aghion et al. 2019; Atkin et al. 2017).

Meanwhile, lowering import barriers can create competitive pressure, which induces firms to innovate to "escape competition" (Aghion et al. 2005) and gain market share (Raith 2003). Imports are also a source of access to foreign knowledge, some of which is embedded in the goods traded (Acharya and Keller 2009). Empirically, evidence of increasing domestic innovation and quality upgrading following trade liberalization episodes supports the positive impact of import competition on innovation (Amiti and Khandelwal 2013; Bustos 2011; Gorodnichenko, Svejnar, and Terrell 2010).

Empirical evidence from East Asia has been somewhat mixed, however. Exporting has been found to be positively correlated with R&D and innovation among manufacturing firms in Indonesia and Malaysia (Lee 2004; Yang and Chen 2012). Increased import penetration also positively affects innovation in China, making firms more likely to engage in incremental innovation (Lu and Ng 2012). Similarly, Chen, Zhang, and Zheng (2017) report a surge in R&D intensity when Chinese firms import from high-income sources or when private high-tech firms use these imports. In contrast, reductions in input tariffs after China's accession to the World Trade Organization (WTO) have reduced firms' patent applications because high-quality imports have substituted for internal innovation (Liu and Qiu 2016).

Import penetration correlates with innovation, but host firms need some minimum innovation capabilities
New analysis for developing East Asia carried out for this study indicates that import penetration is positively associated with innovation. (For results, see annex 3B, tables 3B.2, 3B.3, and 3B.4.) For example, among Vietnamese firms engaged in international trade, the reduction in tariffs brought about by accession to the WTO is associated with a significant increase in the number of R&D projects and research topics implemented (annex 3B, table 3B.4).

For the region, on average, increased import penetration is positively associated with both innovation outputs and R&D investment. The positive association between import penetration and innovation is apparent for firms in mature industries but more muted for firms in high-tech industries. Because mature industries arguably enjoy a narrower technology gap with high-income countries, the evidence suggests that laggard firms further away from the technological frontier are discouraged from innovating when pre-innovation rents are low and increased competition primarily reduces post-innovation rents. This is consistent with evidence from both high-income and low- to middle-income countries, which suggests that firms must have adequate capabilities for these positive impacts from imports to materialize (Zanello et al. 2016). Evidence in China is consistent with the international evidence: only the most-productive firms increased their patenting rates and R&D expenditures after the country's accession to the WTO (Bombardini, Li, and Wang 2017).

Global value chains can help in increasing innovation capabilities, but spillovers do not happen automatically
Global value chains (GVCs) represent another important channel for the diffusion of innovation. The relational aspect of GVCs, where firms form longer-term relationships and share an interest in specializing in specific tasks, means that trading firms have even stronger incentives to exchange knowledge (World Bank 2020). Indeed, survey evidence from Vietnam suggests that domestic firms with stronger links to foreign buyers (that is, those with exclusive selling relationships) are more likely to receive assistance from lead firms, especially through sharing knowledge and know-how. Case study research of IKEA's suppliers in China and Southeast Asia shows similarly that many suppliers take advantage of this relationship to improve their "adaptive" capabilities by learning about new products and their process requirements (Ivarsson and Alvstam 2011).

The relational nature of GVCs does not automatically result in technology transfer, however, but depends critically on the governance of value chains and local absorptive capacity. New capabilities may be especially difficult to gain when lead firms in GVCs tightly control their technology (World Bank 2020) or when technology gaps are too large (De Marchi, Giuliani, and Rabellotti 2018; Nocke and Yeaple 2008).

Experience from the electronics industry in Vietnam illustrates these barriers. Although Vietnam has been remarkably successful in gaining global market shares for electronic equipment, it has struggled to increase its domestic value-added share, because local suppliers have been slow to climb the quality ladder. Driving this outcome is a mix of inadequate domestic capabilities and difficulties in breaking into global supply chains with hyperspecialized parts suppliers (World Bank 2017).

Trade flows and GVC activities increase the probability of co-invention

Beyond technological spillovers, GVCs may also promote innovation through co-invention (De Backer and Flaig 2017). By trading in goods and services, firms can build a rapport that may later induce collaboration on R&D and ultimately co-invention. New analysis from the OECD's Trade in Value Added (TiVA) database reveals interesting, stylized facts that support the interplay between GVCs and global innovation networks (GINs)—globally organized networks of firms and nonfirm organizations that develop and diffuse innovations.

First, GINs have grown denser in developing East Asia over the past 30 years, suggesting an improvement in the region's ability to collaborate and innovate (map 3.2). Second, although GINs are still not as developed as GVC networks, GVC hubs also tend to be key nodes in GINs. Econometric evidence from bilateral trade and patent data further suggests that co-invention increases in the presence of a trading relationship (see annex 3B, table 3B.5), in line with the evidence from OECD countries documented in De Backer and Flaig (2017). The results illustrate that the benefits of GVCs for co-invention also depend on the capacity of local firms relative to their trading partners: the incidence of co-invention is proportional to the innovative activities of the country and its partners and is inversely related to the technological distance between the partner countries.

FDI can also facilitate innovation, but spillover benefits are uneven

A large body of theoretical and empirical evidence has documented how foreign direct investment (FDI) can facilitate technology spillovers. (For a review, see Aghion and Tirole 1994; Görg and Greenaway 2004; and Keller 2010.) The literature identifies two types of spillovers: horizontal (or intraindustry) and vertical (or interindustry). The latter can be further differentiated into backward (depending on upstream suppliers) or forward (depending on downstream customers) spillovers.

Horizontal spillovers may arise when the multinational affiliate generates technological learning spillovers to other firms in the industry through its business operation. Similarly, (backward) vertical spillovers may arise when the multinational affiliate provides technology to its suppliers at below-market prices. The evidence on these spillovers is mixed, however. There is firm-level evidence of positive spillovers for some high-income countries, as shown by Keller and Yeaple (2009) for the United States; Javorcik (2004) for Lithuania; or Haskel, Pereira, and Slaughter (2007) for the United Kingdom. The evidence appears less likely to be positive in less-advanced economies, however. The impact of FDI on technological change in Chinese domestic firms could also be negative (Fu and Gong 2011). This result could depend on crowding-out effects in product and human-capital markets as well as on the technology gap between foreign and domestic firms.

Brahmbhatt and Hu (2010) provide an overview of the diverse diffusion patterns of FDI in East Asia. On one end of the spectrum are economies like Singapore's, whose development has largely been driven by FDI. On the other end of the spectrum, Korea (and to a lesser extent, Taiwan, China) tended to restrict FDI and favored the use of other

MAP 3.2 **Global innovation networks with developing East Asia have grown denser in recent decades**

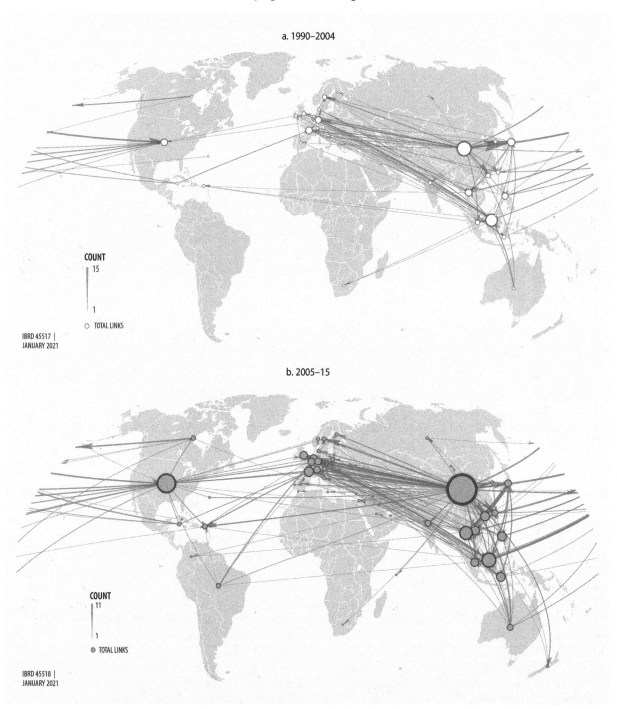

a. 1990–2004

COUNT

15

1

○ TOTAL LINKS

IBRD 45517 |
JANUARY 2021

b. 2005–15

COUNT

11

1

⊚ TOTAL LINKS

IBRD 45518 |
JANUARY 2021

Source: World Bank elaboration using the REGPAT database 2018 of the Organisation for Economic Co-operation and Development (OECD).
Note: The flows of global innovation networks correspond to the number of international co-inventions by country pairs during the selected period. The OECD REGPAT database presents patent data that have been linked to regions according to the addresses of applicants and inventors. REGPAT data were available for the following countries in developing East Asia: Cambodia, China, Indonesia, Malaysia, the Philippines, Thailand, and Vietnam. Plots created using flowmap.blue.

instruments to spread innovation—such as through the licensing of foreign technology and upgrading of domestic technological capabilities (including through domestic R&D and strengthening of technical education and labor force skills). Between these extremes are Indonesia, Malaysia, the Philippines, and Thailand, which have also drawn substantial FDI inflows since the 1980s.

The diverse country experience in East Asia suggests that the business environment as well as firm-specific characteristics are likely to affect the formation and diffusion of FDI spillovers. An enabling business environment is more likely to attract foreign investors. But to ensure that FDI supports diffusion and technology adoption, adequate absorptive capacity on the part of local firms is also needed.

To target spillovers, some countries have considered conditions for FDI entry—so-called forced technology transfer policies. China provides a noteworthy, if unique, example of how governments use policies such as mandated formation of international joint ventures (IJVs) (box 3.3) or quid pro quo requirements for foreign firms to transfer technology domestically in return for access to China's domestic market. Recent evidence suggests that such policies have led to significant gains in innovation for China but might impose significant costs on its FDI partners (Girma et al. 2015; Holmes, McGrattan, and Prescott 2015; Jiang et al. 2018). Given China's market size, there is also a question about the replicability of this approach for most countries in the region, given fierce global competition for FDI, especially in the current context of potential reshoring of production.

New evidence from the most recent World Bank Enterprise Surveys for developing East Asia points to negative effects of horizontal linkages on innovation, possibly because of competition effects, across all the dimensions of innovation considered. (See further details in annex 3B, table 3B.7.) Evidence of positive backward linkages, especially in

the case of R&D investments, suggests that the increased presence of foreign firms in the downstream sectors provides an incentive for domestic firms to innovate. Increased competition for foreign customers or the ability to exploit economies of scale may raise incentives for domestic suppliers to improve the quality of their products.

As in the case of import penetration, the evidence supports the idea that local firms' ability to take advantage of FDI spillovers depends on their absorptive capacity and more precisely on their level of technology efficiency. Firms that are closer to the technological frontier are more likely to benefit from the presence of foreign firms (see results in annex 3B, table 3B.7).

Conclusions

This chapter has argued that although developing East Asia has been home to some leading innovative companies that might rival those in high-income countries, there remains a large technological divide between and within the region's countries. By and large, firms are far from the global frontier and are underprepared for rapid technological changes such as the shift to digital and flexible manufacturing technologies.

The slow process of innovation diffusion and the presence of lagging firms is a stylized fact that is not unique to the region. Nevertheless, it highlights the role of innovation policy to not only support firms pushing the frontier but also those firms investing in catching up. Given that the aggregate contribution made by innovation and new technologies to productivity, growth, and welfare is largely determined by how well and how rapidly innovations diffuse within countries, policy needs to actively promote diffusion by nurturing and developing domestic innovation capacity.

Understanding the drivers of firms' innovation decisions is key to inform policy. A potential explanation for low diffusion is a lack of firm capabilities—a set of

BOX 3.3   International joint ventures and technology transfer in China

Inward foreign direct investment (FDI) may take the form of joint ventures—legal partnerships between a foreign investor and a domestic firm to create a new operation in the domestic market. China's government mandates the formation of international joint ventures (IJVs) for foreign investors in certain industries that seek to invest domestically. Despite its policy relevance, robust empirical evidence about its effectiveness has emerged only recently.

Girma et al. (2015) find that increased foreign acquisitions following FDI liberalization episodes in China significantly raise the research and development (R&D) activities of domestic firms, driven primarily by joint ventures. Jiang et al. (2018) provide the most comprehensive assessment of the role of IJVs in China to date. They rely on administrative data on all IJVs from 1998 to 2007, with direct information on firm-to-firm linkages, and document several interesting findings:

- First, IJVs have a positive significant effect on firm innovation (as measured by patents) and productivity.

- Further, this positive effect is present through both intrafirm (the joint venture) and interfirm (the domestic partner firm and other firms in the industry) channels. The IJV partner seems to matter, however. Among different FDI source countries, IJVs with US firms appear to have the strongest spillover effects.
- Moreover, the companies chosen to be IJV partners are systematically different: they are larger, more connected to government officials, and tend to be more innovative and productive.

These results might suggest that the same policy will not automatically yield the same impact elsewhere, depending on local markets and the existing stock of domestic firms. Even in China, new research by Chen and Lawell (2020) warns that more nuanced results can be found in the automobile industry: whether positive technology transfer for firms in IJVs materializes depends on the country of origin of the international partner.

"know-hows" that enable firms to respond to market conditions, identify relevant new technologies, develop plans to exploit them, and then acquire the necessary resources to do so. These capabilities are often linked to management quality; however, the data show substantial gaps between the region's firms and the global frontier as well as tremendous heterogeneity within countries. New survey data on firm-level technologies also offer a glimpse into the complexities of the technology adoption decisions: multiple technologies exist for different business functions, and the same firms can be technologically advanced or laggards in different functions. Navigating these decisions requires substantial knowledge and entails a great deal of uncertainty. Evidence suggests that these informational constraints and

uncertainties may constitute major barriers to firms' investments in technological upgrading.

Traditionally, East Asia's openness to trade and foreign investments has helped reduce these barriers by facilitating the flow of knowledge and expanding firms' access to both input and output markets. However, the extent of spillover benefits has been somewhat limited and will continue to depend on the absorptive capacity of domestic firms. With the restructuring of global GVCs, there is enormous uncertainty about the potential future gains from the region's growth strategy. Uncertainty has only intensified because of the COVID-19 pandemic. In this context, continued investment in building firm capabilities for innovation represents a critical no-regrets policy option.

Annex 3A The Firm-level Adoption of Technologies survey

The goal of the World Bank's Firm-level Adoption of Technologies (FAT) survey is to collect comprehensive information about the technologies used in each of the key business functions for a representative sample of companies. The survey is comprehensive in three different dimensions:

- It covers a large number of business functions.
- For each business function, the survey includes a wide range of technologies, requiring different levels of sophistication to accomplish the tasks needed to fulfill the function.
- It collects sufficient information to measure the various dimensions of the technology adoption process (for example, range of technologies, most-used technology, and adoption lag).

The survey is stratified to ensure the representativeness of the sample by sector, firm size, and region. This feature enables construction of representative statistics about technology adoption and use along those three dimensions as well as at the country- and firm-levels.

The FAT survey comprises five modules:

- *Module A:* Collects general information about the characteristics of the establishment
- *Module B:* Covers the technologies used in eight generic business functions
- *Module C:* Covers the use of technologies for functions that are specific to each of 10 industry and services functions
- *Module D:* Includes questions about the drivers of and barriers to technology adoption
- *Module E:* Collects information on employment, balance sheet, and performance, which enables computation of labor productivity and other measures at the company level.

Modules B and C collect the information to measure technology adoption, while the other modules collect information on firm characteristics, performance, and other variables that can provide information on the barriers to and drivers of technology adoption.

In addition to Vietnam, the survey has been carried out in Bangladesh, the state of Ceará in Brazil, Malawi, and Senegal, and it is currently being implemented in India, Kenya, Korea, and Poland.

Annex 3B Supplementary tables

TABLE 3B.1   **Management scores of selected East Asian countries relative to the United States, by quantile**

Country	Kolmogorov-Smirnov Test	Differences relative to the United States at					
		Mean	q5	q10	q50	q90	q95
China	0.426	−0.577***	−0.472***	−0.444***	−0.583***	−0.694***	−0.651***
	(0)	(0.0272)	(0.0755)	(0.0594)	(0.0375)	(0.0544)	(0.0589)
Vietnam	0.418	−0.616***	−0.500***	−0.611***	−0.611***	−0.750***	−0.833***
	(0)	(0.0519)	(0.105)	(0.117)	(0.0578)	(0.0563)	(0.0732)
Myanmar	0.601	−1.175***	−1.111***	−1.167***	−1.333***	−1.083***	−0.722**
	(0)	(0.0918)	(0.103)	(0.0973)	(0.128)	(0.234)	(0.289)

Source: Worldwide Management Survey (WMS), Centre for Economic Performance of the London School of Economics and Political Science.
Note: WMS sample of firms with at least 100 workers. Results from the Kolmogorov-Smirnov distribution test, ordinary least squares (OLS), and quantile (q) regressions (at q5, q10, q50, q90, q95) of the management score on country dummies, with United States as the baseline. *** 1%; ** 5%, and * 10% confidence level.

TABLE 3B.2   **Import penetration is positively associated with innovation in developing East Asia**

Independent variables	Innovation score (1)[a]	Innovation score (2)[b]	Innovation score (3)[c]	New or improved process	New or improved product/service	R&D expenses	Use of foreign technology
	OLS			LPM			
	0.475***	0.496***	0.461***	0.284	0.793***	0.903***	0.0972
Import penetration	(3.53)	(3.69)	(3.29)	(1.28)	(3.65)	(3.65)	(0.41)
Capital stock	Yes	Yes	Yes	Yes	Yes	Yes	Yes
Firm characteristics	Yes	Yes	Yes	Yes	Yes	Yes	Yes
City FE	Yes	Yes	Yes	Yes	Yes	Yes	Yes
Country FE	Yes	Yes	Yes	Yes	Yes	Yes	Yes
Survey FE	Yes	Yes	Yes	Yes	Yes	Yes	Yes
Observations	5,620	5,628	5,348	4,031	4,098	4,078	5,516
R^2	0.249	0.251	0.255	0.152	0.137	0.145	0.121

Source: World Bank Enterprise Survey data for East Asian countries, latest round.
Note: "Developing East Asia" refers to the 10 middle-income countries covered in this study: Cambodia, China, Indonesia, Lao PDR, Malaysia, Mongolia, Myanmar, the Philippines, Thailand, and Vietnam. Firms are asked four questions. One question asks whether a firm has introduced a product innovation; a second question asks if the firm has introduced a process innovation; a third question asks if the firm has introduced an organizational innovation; and a fourth question asks if the firm has introduced a marketing innovation. The firm may answer "yes" or "no" to each of these questions individually, and the score(s) depend on how many of the firm responses are a "yes." Results from instrumental variable (IV) regression where import penetration is instrumented for with the average of import penetration among firms belonging to the same industry but located in other cities within the same country. Standard errors are robust and clustered at the sample stratification level. The sample is stratified by industry, size of firm, and region. *t* statistics are reported in parentheses. FE = fixed effects; LPM = linear probability model; OLS = ordinary least squares; R&D = research and development.
a. For innovation score (1), the numerator is given by the number of "yes" responses to the four questions listed above and the denominator is four.
b. For innovation score (2), where the numerator is given by the number of "yes" responses to the four questions listed above and the denominator is the number of questions answered by the firm.
c. For innovation score (3), the numerator is given by the number of "yes" responses to the four questions listed above, and the denominator is the number of nonmissing answers from each firm.
* $p < 0.10$ ** $p < 0.05$ *** $p < 0.01$

TABLE 3B.3   The discouraging effect for laggard industries in developing East Asia

	a. Mature industries						
Independent variables	Innovation score (1)[a]	Innovation score (2)[b]	Innovation score (3)[c]	New or improved process	New or improved product/ service	R&D expenses	Use of foreign technology
	OLS				LPM		
	0.247***	0.247***	0.250***	0.358***	0.361***	0.332***	0.00154
Import penetration	(3.55)	(3.53)	(3.54)	(4.03)	(3.98)	(3.71)	(0.01)
Firm characteristics	Yes	Yes	Yes	Yes	Yes	Yes	Yes
Country FE	Yes	Yes	Yes	Yes	Yes	Yes	Yes
Survey FE	Yes	Yes	Yes	Yes	Yes	Yes	Yes
Observations	4,124	4,140	3,961	2,902	2,945	2,933	4,062
R^2	0.259	0.260	0.259	0.136	0.110	0.167	0.137
	b. High-tech industries						
Independent variables	Innovation score (1)[a]	Innovation score (2)[b]	Innovation score (3)[c]	New or improved process	New or improved product/ service	R&D expenses	Use of foreign technology
	OLS				LPM		
	0.484	0.484	0.482	1.558**	1.426	1.897**	0.119
Import penetration	(1.50)	(1.50)	(1.50)	(2.02)	(1.57)	(2.38)	(0.59)
Firm characteristics	Yes	Yes	Yes	Yes	Yes	Yes	Yes
Country FE	Yes	Yes	Yes	Yes	Yes	Yes	Yes
Survey FE	Yes	Yes	Yes	Yes	Yes	Yes	Yes
Observations	1,364	1,366	1,305	1,033	1,053	1,043	1,341
R^2	0.232	0.232	0.232	0.202	0.209	0.140	0.125

Source: World Bank Enterprise Survey data for East Asian countries, latest round.
Note: "Developing East Asia" refers to the 10 middle-income countries covered in this study: Cambodia, China, Indonesia, Lao PDR, Malaysia, Mongolia, Myanmar, the Philippines, Thailand, and Vietnam. Firms are asked four questions. One question asks whether a firm has introduced a product innovation; a second question asks if the firm has introduced a process innovation; a third question asks if the firm has introduced an organizational innovation; and a fourth question asks if the firm has introduced a marketing innovation. The firm may answer "yes" or "no" to each of these questions individually, and the score(s) depend on how many of the firm responses are a "yes." Standard errors are robust and clustered at the sample stratification level. The sample is stratified by industry, size of firm, and region. *t* statistics are reported in parentheses. FE = fixed effects; LPM = linear probability model; OLS = ordinary least squares; R&D = research and development.
a. For innovation score (1), the numerator is given by the number of "yes" responses to the four questions listed above and the denominator is four.
b. For innovation score (2), where the numerator is given by the number of "yes" responses to the four questions listed above and the denominator is the number of questions answered by the firm.
c. For innovation score (3), the numerator is given by the number of "yes" responses to the four questions listed above and the denominator is the number of nonmissing answers from each firm.
* $p < 0.10$ ** $p < 0.05$ *** $p < 0.01$

TABLE 3B.4   Effects of WTO accession: Innovation and import-export activity in Vietnam

Independent variables	R&D expense	R&D projects implemented	R&D expense	R&D projects implemented
	Revenue per workers		TFPR (Levinsohn Petrin)	
	3391261.6	86.29	3396545.1	87.38*
Imports-exports × after 2007	(1.06)	(1.66)	(1.06)	(1.68)
	−397631.3	−265.6*	−395125.5	−266.6*
Imports-exports	(−1.08)	(−1.87)	(−1.07)	(−1.89)
	−388899934.4	−44351.4	−440548810.5	−40509.8
After 2007	(−0.30)	(−1.13)	(−0.35)	(−1.03)

table continues next page

TABLE 3B.4   **Effects of WTO accession: innovation and import-export activity in Vietnam** *(continued)*

Independent variables	R&D expense	R&D projects implemented	R&D expense	R&D projects implemented
	Revenue per workers		TFPR (Levinsohn Petrin)	
	540.9	−1.104	177039888.2	−46610.0
Productivity	(0.08)	(−0.81)	(0.63)	(−0.96)
	1375.0	0.0669	1346.8	0.0709
Total investment	(0.97)	(0.92)	(0.97)	(0.99)
	462395.0	275.2*	448843.9	276.7*
Number of workers	(1.14)	(1.85)	(1.11)	(1.86)
ISIC FE	Yes	Yes	Yes	Yes
Year FE	Yes	Yes	Yes	Yes
Observations	20,738	11,454	26,183	15,171
R^2	0.203	0.536	0.202	0.530

Source: World Bank Enterprise Survey, Vietnam, 2004–16.
Note: Ordinary least squares (OLS) model. Standard errors are robust and clustered at the sample stratification level. The sample is stratified by industry, size of firm, and region.
t statistics are reported in parentheses. The sample excludes firms reporting negative values for (a) total assets, at either the beginning or the end of the year; (b) fixed assets, at either the beginning or the end of the year; (c) revenues; (d) total payroll payable; (e) total investment; (f) cost of goods and services; or (g) number of employees. Firms reporting zero or missing values for the total assets are also dropped. ISIC = International Standard Industrial Classification; R&D = research and development; TFPR = revenue total factor productivity; WTO = World Trade Organization.
* $p < 0.10$ ** $p < 0.05$ *** $p < 0.01$

TABLE 3B.5   **Co-inventions gravity model for developing East Asia countries**

Independent variables	OLS				PPML			
Log(Patent stock country)	0.13***	0.12***	0.13***	0.12***	0.597***	0.779***	0.600***	0.778***
	(0.01)	(0.00)	(0.01)	(0.00)	(0.039)	(0.040)	(0.039)	(0.040)
Log(Patent stock partner)	0.12***	0.11***	0.12***	0.11***	0.562***	0.674***	0.569***	0.676***
	(0.00)	(0.00)	(0.00)	(0.00)	(0.045)	(0.057)	(0.043)	(0.056)
Log(Technological distance)	−0.13***	−0.13***	−0.13***	−0.13***	−0.090***	−0.078***	−0.098***	−0.088***
	(0.01)	(0.01)	(0.01)	(0.01)	(0.020)	(0.020)	(0.019)	(0.019)
Bilateral trade	0.22***	0.22***	0.22***	0.22***	−0.004***	−0.004***	−0.004***	−0.005***
	(0.01)	(0.01)	(0.01)	(0.01)	(0.001)	(0.001)	(0.001)	(0.001)
No bilateral trade	−0.09***	−0.12***	−0.09***	−0.11***	−6.074***	−5.984***	−6.353***	−6.273***
	(0.01)	(0.01)	(0.01)	(0.01)	(0.311)	(0.308)	(0.309)	(0.308)
Contiguity?	0.42***	0.41***	0.42***	0.41***	0.301***	0.305***	0.353***	0.357***
	(0.07)	(0.07)	(0.07)	(0.07)	(0.111)	(0.112)	(0.103)	(0.104)
Common language?	0.15***	0.15***	0.15***	0.15***	1.084***	1.076***	1.088***	1.080***
	(0.03)	(0.03)	(0.03)	(0.03)	(0.085)	(0.081)	(0.082)	(0.078)
Pair ever in colonial relationship?	−0.12***	−0.12***	−0.12***	−0.12***	−0.914***	−0.918***	−0.953***	−0.957***
	(0.04)	(0.04)	(0.04)	(0.04)	(0.098)	(0.096)	(0.096)	(0.095)
Physical distance	−0.00***	−0.00***	−0.00***	−0.00***	−0.000***	−0.000***	−0.000***	−0.000***
	(0.00)	(0.00)	(0.00)	(0.00)	(0.000)	(0.000)	(0.000)	(0.000)
Time difference	0.04***	0.04***	0.04***	0.04***	0.008	0.007	−0.041**	−0.042***
	(0.00)	(0.00)	(0.00)	(0.00)	(0.015)	(0.014)	(0.016)	(0.016)
No time difference	0.06***	0.07***	0.07***	0.07***	0.405***	0.398***	0.427***	0.418***
	(0.01)	(0.01)	(0.01)	(0.01)	(0.110)	(0.107)	(0.105)	(0.103)
WTO deep agreement			0.01*	0.01*			−0.266***	−0.264***
			(0.01)	(0.01)			(0.036)	(0.035)
Year FE	Yes	Yes	Yes	Yes	Yes	Yes	Yes	Yes
Origin FE	Yes	Yes	Yes	Yes	Yes	Yes	Yes	Yes

table continues next page

TABLE 3B.5   **Co-inventions gravity model for developing East Asia countries** *(continued)*

Independent variables	OLS				PPML			
Destination FE	Yes	Yes	Yes	Yes	Yes	Yes	Yes	Yes
Sector FE	No	Yes	No	Yes	No	Yes	No	Yes
Mean dep. var.	0.13	0.13	0.13	0.13	0.16	0.16	0.16	0.16
R^2	0.05	0.05	0.05	0.05	0.47	0.49	0.49	0.51
Adjusted-within-R^2	0.03	0.03	0.03	0.03				
Observations	765,952	765,952	765,952	765,952	650,947	650,947	650,947	650,947

Sources: Trade in Value Added (TiVA) and REGPAT databases, 2018, Organisation for Economic Co-operation and Development.
Note: Sample includes 63 economies. All pairs include one of 10 middle-income "developing East Asia" countries: Cambodia, China, Indonesia, Lao PDR, Malaysia, Mongolia, Myanmar, the Philippines, Thailand, and Vietnam. Robust standard errors in parentheses. The dependent variable is the number of international co-inventions for the origin-destination pair in a given sector and year. Distance is the absolute value of the difference between the stock of patents in countries. FE = fixed effects; OLS = ordinary least squares; PPML = Poisson pseudo maximum likelihood; R&D = research and development; WTO = World Trade Organization.
* $p < 0.10$ ** $p < 0.05$ *** $p < 0.01$

TABLE 3B.6   **FDI spillover effects on innovation in developing East Asia**

Independent variables	New or improved process	New or improved product or service	R&D expenses	Use of foreign technology
Forward linkage	0.500	−0.600	−0.328	−0.00904
	(0.88)	(−1.39)	(−0.74)	(−0.03)
Backward linkage	0.233	1.056*	2.188***	0.501
	(0.36)	(1.96)	(3.08)	(1.32)
Horizontal linkage	−0.325***	−0.441***	−0.310***	−0.213**
	(−2.75)	(−5.90)	(−2.67)	(−2.32)
% Material inputs imported	0.000971*	0.00318***	0.00112*	0.0000914
	(1.71)	(5.42)	(1.88)	(0.22)
% Sales exported indirectly	0.00222***	0.00351***	0.00293***	0.000877
	(2.79)	(3.62)	(3.56)	(1.10)
% Sales exported directly	0.00111*	0.000831	0.000748	0.00170***
	(1.79)	(1.32)	(1.19)	(3.51)
Medium (20–99)	0.182***	0.0737**	0.0590**	0.0721***
	(5.61)	(2.42)	(2.26)	(3.29)
Large (≥ 100)	0.253***	0.166***	0.187***	0.203***
	(7.29)	(5.02)	(5.66)	(7.05)
Age	−0.00656***	−0.00204	−0.000544	0.000702
	(−4.04)	(−1.31)	(−0.33)	(0.55)
100% domestic ownership	0.0537	−0.0526	−0.0209	−0.177***
	(1.23)	(−1.14)	(−0.45)	(−4.23)
No female owners	−0.00183	−0.0663**	0.0339	0.00396
	(−0.07)	(−2.32)	(1.01)	(0.19)
Access to finance: minor obstacle	0.138***	0.180***	0.00530	0.0459**
	(4.53)	(5.83)	(0.20)	(2.14)
Access to finance: moderate obstacle	0.117***	0.155***	0.137***	0.0282
	(2.76)	(3.97)	(3.65)	(0.93)
Access to finance: major obstacle	0.0826	0.0353	0.173***	0.0219
	(1.36)	(0.67)	(3.21)	(0.46)
Country FE	Yes	Yes	Yes	Yes
Survey FE	Yes	Yes	Yes	Yes
Observations	5,620	5,704	5,675	7,808
R^2	0.149	0.149	0.132	0.106

Source: World Bank Enterprise Survey data for East Asian countries, latest round.
Note: Linear probability model. Standard errors are robust and clustered at the sample stratification level. The sample is stratified by industry, size of firm, and region. *t* statistics are reported in parentheses. "Developing East Asia" refers to the 10 middle-income countries covered in this study: Cambodia, China, Indonesia, Lao PDR, Malaysia, Mongolia, Myanmar, the Philippines, Thailand, and Vietnam. FDI = foreign direct investment; FE = fixed effects; R&D = research and development.
* $p < 0.10$ ** $p < 0.05$ *** $p < 0.01$

TABLE 3B.7   **Effect of firms' distance from the frontier on the strength of spillovers in developing East Asia**

Independent variables	Innovation score (1)[a]	Innovation score (2)[b]	Innovation score (3)[c]	Improved process	New product/service	R&D	Foreign technology
Forward linkage	0.791	0.849	0.562	0.957	1.149	−0.0284	1.028
	(1.24)	(1.31)	(0.92)	(0.88)	(1.47)	(−0.04)	(1.35)
Backward linkage	−0.750	−0.710	−0.493	−1.211	−2.249**	−1.195	1.703
	(−1.06)	(−1.00)	(−0.71)	(−0.85)	(−2.30)	(−1.05)	(1.51)
Horizontal linkage	−0.451***	−0.454***	−0.504***	−0.690***	−0.328*	−0.569***	−0.238
	(−4.40)	(−4.38)	(−5.04)	(−3.18)	(−1.88)	(−3.85)	(−1.21)
Forward linkage × distance	−0.856*	−0.909**	−0.729	−0.569	−1.292**	−0.990*	−0.586
	(−1.89)	(−1.99)	(−1.63)	(−0.80)	(−2.24)	(−1.84)	(−1.07)
Backward linkage × distance	0.568	0.588	0.421	0.324	1.421**	0.574	−0.0247
	(1.18)	(1.22)	(0.88)	(0.39)	(2.10)	(0.79)	(−0.04)
Horizontal linkage × distance	−0.158**	−0.158**	−0.132*	−0.123	−0.237**	−0.207**	−0.0520
	(−2.24)	(−2.23)	(−1.87)	(−0.98)	(−2.11)	(−2.06)	(−0.44)
Distance	0.0438*	0.0461*	0.0399	0.0204	0.0558	0.0482	0.0488
	(1.69)	(1.77)	(1.49)	(0.51)	(1.40)	(1.18)	(1.20)
Firm characteristics	Yes	Yes	Yes	Yes	Yes	Yes	Yes
N	2,904	2,910	2,775	2,850	2,880	2,873	2,859
R²	0.208	0.204	0.207	0.171	0.145	0.139	0.099

Source: World Bank Enterprise Survey data for East Asian countries, latest round.

Note: "Developing East Asia" refers to the 10 middle-income countries covered in this study: Cambodia, China, Indonesia, Lao PDR, Malaysia, Mongolia, Myanmar, the Philippines, Thailand, and Vietnam. Standard errors are robust and clustered at the sample stratification level. The sample is stratified by industry, size of firm, and region. t statistics are reported in parentheses. Firm controls include percentage of material inputs imported, percentage of sales exported indirectly, percentage of sales exported directly, size of the firm, age of the firm, dummy for 100 percent domestic ownership, dummy for no female owners, and a categorical variable for access to finance. Distance with the frontier for local firms is a Mahalanobis distance between local and foreign firms' productivity. R&D = research and development.

a. For innovation score (1), the numerator is given by the number of "yes" responses to the four questions listed above and the denominator is four.

b. For innovation score (2), where the numerator is given by the number of "yes" responses to the four questions listed above and the denominator is the number of questions answered by the firm.

c. For innovation score (3), the numerator is given by the number of "yes" responses to the four questions, one each for (whether they have introduced (1) a product innovation, (2) a process innovation, (3) an organizational innovation, and/or (4) a marketing innovation. The denominator is the number of nonmissing answers from each firm.

* $p < 0.10$ ** $p < 0.05$ *** $p < 0.01$

Notes

1. A firm can be digital in several tasks. For example, it can process sales online but also manage the supply chain digitally. The business functions included in the FAT survey capture the extent of digitalization not only in a firm's ability to process sales online but also to perform other management tasks in an integrated system, including remotely. The "digital readiness index" focuses on the intensive margin. Thus, for example, a value of 100 in sales corresponds to a firm processing all sales on online platforms or on the firm's website.

2. A comparable index in the state of Ceará in Brazil is 42 percent (Cirera, Comin, Cruz, and Lee 2020).

3. The WMS (https://worldmanagementsurvey.org/), operated by the Centre for Economic Performance of the London School of Economics and Political Science, is conducted through in-depth interviews of over 20,000 firms in 35 countries. The WMS captures several aspects of management, including firms' practices in target setting, monitoring, and human resource management. It is not specific to innovation, but is a proxy for firms' overall capabilities.

4. These differences are statistically significant and hold true for different quantiles of the overall management score distribution. See additional results in annex 3B, table 3B.1.

References

Acharya, Ram C., and Wolfgang Keller. 2009. "Technology Transfer through Imports." *Canadian Journal of Economics* 42 (4): 1411–48.

Aghion, Philippe, Antonin Bergeaud, Timothee Gigout, Matthieu Lequien, and Marc Melitz. 2019. "Spreading Knowledge across the World: Innovation Spillover through Trade Expansion." Manuscript, Harvard University, Cambridge, MA.

Aghion, Philippe, Antonin Bergeaud, Matthieu Lequien, and Marc J. Melitz. 2018. "The Heterogeneous Impact of Market Size on Innovation: Evidence from French Firm-Level Exports." NBER Working Paper No. 24600, National Bureau of Economic Research, Cambridge, MA.

Aghion, Philippe, Nick Bloom, Richard Blundell, Rachel Griffith, and Peter Howitt. 2005. "Competition and Innovation: An Inverted-U Relationship." *Quarterly Journal of Economics* 120 (2): 701–28.

Aghion, Philippe, and Jean Tirole. 1994. "The Management of Innovation." *Quarterly Journal of Economics* 109 (4): 1185–209.

Amiti, Mary, and Amit K. Khandelwal. 2013. "Import Competition and Quality Upgrading." *Review of Economics and Statistics* 95 (2): 476–90.

Andrews, Dan, Chiara Criscuolo, and Peter N. Gal. 2016. "The Best versus the Rest: The Global Productivity Slowdown, Divergence across Firms and the Role of Public Policy." Productivity Working Papers No. 5, Organisation for Economic Co-operation and Development, Paris.

Apedo-Amah, Marie Christine, Besart Avdiu, Xavier Cirera, Marcio Cruz, Elwin Davies, Arti Grover, Leonardo Iacavone, et al. 2020. "Unmasking the Impact of COVID-19 on Businesses: Firm Level Evidence from Across the World." Policy Research Working Paper 9434, World Bank, Washington, DC.

Atkin, David, Azam Chaudhry, Shamyla Chaudry, Amit K. Khandelwal, and Eric Verhoogen. 2017. "Organizational Barriers to Technology Adoption: Evidence from Soccer-Ball Producers in Pakistan." *Quarterly Journal of Economics* 132 (3): 1101–64.

Atkin, David, Amit K. Khandelwal, and Adam Osman. 2017. "Exporting and Firm Performance: Evidence from a Randomized Experiment." *Quarterly Journal of Economics* 132 (2): 551–615.

Audretsch, David B., Marian Hafenstein, Alexander S. Kritikos, and Alexander Schiersch 2018. "Firm Size and Innovation in the Service Sector." Discussion Paper No. 12035, Institute of Labor Economics (IZA), Bonn.

Bernard, Andrew B., and Teresa C. Fort. 2017. "Factoryless Goods Producers in the USA." In *The Factory-Free Economy: Outsourcing, Servitization, and the Future of Industry*, edited by Lionel Fontagné and Ann Harrison, 136–68. Oxford: Oxford University Press.

Bloom, Nicholas, Benn Eifert, Aprajit Mahajan, David McKenzie, and John Roberts. 2013. "Does Management Matter? Evidence from India." *Quarterly Journal of Economics* 128 (1): 1–51.

Bombardini, Matilde, Bingjing Li, and Ruoying Wang. 2017. "Import Competition and Innovation: Evidence from China." Unpublished.

Brahmbhatt, Milan, and Albert Hu. 2010. "Ideas and Innovation in East Asia." *The World Bank Research Observer* 25 (2): 177–207.

Bresnahan, Timothy F., and Manuel Trajtenberg. 1995. "General Purpose Technologies 'Engines of Growth'?" *Journal of Econometrics* 65 (1): 83–108.

Brynjolfsson, Erik, Lorin M. Hitt, and Shinkyu Yang. 2002. "Intangible Assets: Computers and Organizational Capital." *Brookings Papers on Economic Activity* 2002 (1): 137–81.

Bustos, Paula. 2011. "Trade Liberalization, Exports, and Technology Upgrading: Evidence on the Impact of MERCOSUR on Argentinian Firms." *American Economic Review* 101 (1): 304–40.

Chen, Yuan, and C.-Y. Cynthia Lin Lawell. 2020. "Supply and Demand in the Chinese Automobile Market: A Random Coefficients Mixed Oligopolistic Differentiated Products Model." Working paper, Cornell University, Ithaca, NY.

Chen, Zhiyuan, Jie Zhang, and Wenping Zheng. 2017. "Import and Innovation: Evidence from Chinese Firms." *European Economic Review* 94: 205–20.

Cirera, Xavier, Diego A. Comin, Marcio Cruz, and Kyung Min Lee. 2020. "Technology Within and Across Firms." NBER Working Paper No. 28080, National Bureau of Economic Research, Cambridge, MA.

Cirera, Xavier, Diego A. Comin, Marcio Cruz, Kyung Min Lee, and Antonio Soares Martins-Neto. 2020. "Firm-Level Technology Adoption in Vietnam." Unpublished manuscript, World Bank, Washington, DC.

Comin, Diego, and Bart Hobijn, 2004. "Cross-Country Technology Adoption: Making the Theories Face the Facts." *Journal of Monetary Economics*, 51 (1): 39–83.

Comin, Diego, and Bart Hobijn. 2010. "An Exploration of Technology Diffusion." *American Economic Review* 100 (5): 2031–59.

Comin, Diego, and Bart Hobijn. 2011. "Technology Diffusion and Postwar Growth." *NBER Macroeconomics Annual* 25 (1): 209–46.

Comin, Diego, and Martí Mestieri. 2018. "If Technology Has Arrived Everywhere, Why Has Income Diverged?" *American Economic Journal: Macroeconomics* 10 (3): 137–78.

Crozet, Matthieu, and Emmanuel Milet. 2017. "Should Everybody Be in Services? The Effect of Servitization on Manufacturing Firm Performance." *Journal of Economics & Management Strategy* 26 (4): 820–41.

De Backer, Koen, and Dorothee Flaig. 2017. "The Future of Global Value Chains: Business as Usual or 'A New Normal'?" Science, Technology and Innovation Policy Papers No. 41, OECD Publishing, Paris.

De Marchi, Valentina, Elisa Giuliani, and Roberta Rabellotti. 2018. "Do Global Value Chains Offer Developing Countries Learning and Innovation Opportunities?" *European Journal of Development Research* 30 (3): 389–407.

de Nicola, Francesca. 2019. "Assessing How Returns to Innovation Vary Depending on the Business Environment and Firms' Characteristics." Background paper for this study, World Bank, Washington, DC.

Del Carpio, Ximena, and Temel Taskin. 2016. "Management Quality Matters: Measuring and Benchmarking the Quality of Firms' Management in Turkey." *Private Sector Development Blog*, November 14. https://blogs.worldbank.org/psd/management-quality-matters-measuring-and-benchmarking-quality-firms-management-turkey.

Doloreux, David, Richard Shearmur, and Mercedes Rodriguez. 2016. "Determinants of R&D in Knowledge-Intensive Business Services Firms." *Economics of Innovation and New Technology* 25 (4): 391–405.

Eberhardt, Markus, Christian Helmers, and Zhihong Yu. 2011. "Is the Dragon Learning to Fly? An Analysis of the Chinese Patent Explosion." Research Paper 11/16, Centre for Research on Globalisation and Economic Policy, University of Nottingham, UK.

Ettlie, John E., and Stephen R. Rosenthal. 2011. "Service versus Manufacturing Innovation." *Journal of Product Innovation Management* 28 (2): 285–99.

Frias, Jaime, Jin Lee, and Kyeyoung Shin. 2020. "Innovation Policy Learning from Korea: Lessons for Design and Execution of Innovation Policies in Emerging Economies." World Bank, Washington, DC.

Fu, Xiaolan, and Yundan Gong. 2011. "Indigenous and Foreign Innovation Efforts and Drivers of Technological Upgrading: Evidence from China." *World Development* 39 (7): 1213–25.

Girma, Sourafel, Yundan Gong, Holger Görg, and Sandra Lancheros. 2015. "Estimating Direct and Indirect Effects of Foreign Direct Investment on Firm Productivity in the Presence of Interactions between Firms." *Journal of International Economics* 95 (1): 157–69.

Görg, Holger, and David Greenaway. 2004. "Much Ado about Nothing? Do Domestic Firms Really Benefit from Foreign Direct Investment?" *The World Bank Research Observer* 19 (2): 171–97.

Gorodnichenko, Yuriy, Jan Svejnar, and Katherine Terrell. 2010. "Globalization and Innovation in Emerging Markets." *American Economic Journal: Macroeconomics* 2 (2): 194–226.

Hall, Bronwyn H. 2004. "Innovation and Diffusion." NBER Working Paper No. 10212, National Bureau of Economic Research, Cambridge, MA.

Hall, Bronwyn H. 2011. "Innovation and Productivity." NBER Working Paper No. 17178, National Bureau of Economic Research, Cambridge, MA.

Hall, Bronwyn H., and Beethika Khan. 2003. "Adoption of New Technology." NBER Working Paper No. 9730, National Bureau of Economic Research, Cambridge, MA.

Haskel, Jonathan E., Sonia C. Pereira, and Matthew J. Slaughter. 2007. "Does Inward Foreign Direct Investment Boost the Productivity of Domestic Firms?" *Review of Economics and Statistics* 89 (3): 482–96.

Hau, Harald, Yi Huang, and Gewei Wang. 2020. "Firm Response to Competitive Shocks: Evidence from China's Minimum Wage Policy." *Review of Economic Studies* 87 (6): 2639–71.

Hernández, Hector, Nicola Grassano, Alexander Tübke, Sara Amoroso, Zoltan Csefalvay, and Petros Gkotsis. 2020. *The 2019 EU Industrial R&D Investment Scoreboard*. Luxembourg: European Union.

Hipp, Christiane, and Hariolf Grupp. 2005. "Innovation in the Service Sector: The Demand for Service-Specific Innovation Measurement Concepts and Typologies." *Research Policy* 34 (4): 517–35.

Holmes, Thomas J., Ellen R. McGrattan, and Edward C. Prescott. 2015. "Quid Pro Quo: Technology Capital Transfers for Market Access in China." *Review of Economic Studies* 82 (3): 1154–93.

Iacovone, Leonardo, Aaditya Mattoo, and Andrés Zahler. 2013. "Trade and Innovation in Services: Evidence from a Developing Economy." Policy Research Working Paper 6520, World Bank, Washington, DC.

Imbert, Clément, Marlon Seror, Yifan Zhang, and Yanos Zylberberg. 2018. "Migrants and Firms: Evidence from China." Working Paper No. 7440, CESifo, Munich.

Ivarsson, Inge, and Claes Göran Alvstam. 2011. "Upgrading in Global Value-Chains: A Case Study of Technology-Learning among IKEA-Suppliers in China and Southeast Asia." *Journal of Economic Geography* 11 (4): 731–52.

Javorcik, Beata Smarzynska. 2004. "Does Foreign Direct Investment Increase the Productivity of Domestic Firms? In Search of Spillovers through Backward Linkages." *American Economic Review* 94 (3): 605–27.

Jiang, Kun, Wolfgang Keller, Larry D. Qiu, and William Ridley. 2018. "International Joint Ventures and Internal vs. External Technology Transfer: Evidence from China." NBER Working Paper No. 24455, National Bureau of Economic Research, Cambridge, MA.

Keller, Wolfgang. 2010. "International Trade, Foreign Direct Investment, and Technology Spillovers." In *Handbook of the Economics of Innovation*, vol. 2, edited by Bronwyn H. Hall and Nathan Rosenberg, 793–829. Amsterdam: Elsevier.

Keller, Wolfgang, and Stephen R. Yeaple. 2009. "Multinational Enterprises, International Trade, and Productivity Growth: Firm Level Evidence from the United States." *Review of Economics and Statistics* 91 (4): 821–31.

Lee, Cassey. 2004. "The Determinants of Innovation in the Malaysian Manufacturing Sector: An Econometric Analysis at the Firm Level." *ASEAN Economic Bulletin* 21 (3): 319–29.

Liu, Qing, and Larry D. Qiu. 2016. "Intermediate Input Imports and Innovations: Evidence from Chinese Firms' Patent Filings." *Journal of International Economics* 103: 166–83.

Lu, Yi, and Travis Ng. 2012. "Do Imports Spur Incremental Innovation in the South?" *China Economic Review* 23 (4): 819–32.

MOEF (Ministry of Economy and Finance, Republic of Korea). 2020. "Safeguarding Economic Resilience: In Responding to the Economic Impact of COVID-19." Report, MOEF, Seoul.

Mohnen, Pierre, and Bronwyn H. Hall. 2013. "Innovation and Productivity: An Update." *Eurasian Business Review* 3 (1): 47–65.

Musolesi, Antonio, and Jean-Pierre Huiban. 2010. "Innovation and Productivity in Knowledge Intensive Business Services." *Journal of Productivity Analysis* 34 (1): 63–81.

Nocke, Volker, and Stephen Yeaple. 2008. "An Assignment Theory of Foreign Direct Investment." *Review of Economic Studies* 75 (2) 529–57.

Oh, Juhwan, Jong-Koo Lee, Dan Schwarz, Hannah L. Ratcliffe, Jeffrey F. Markuns, and Lisa R. Hirschhorn. 2020. "National Response to COVID-19 in the Republic of Korea and Lessons Learned for Other Countries." *Health Systems & Reform* 6 (1): e1753464.

Park, Albert, and Wenshi Xuan. 2020. "Skills for Innovation in China." Background paper for this report, Hong Kong University of Science and Technology, Hong Kong SAR, China.

Park, Young Joon, Sang Yun Cho, Jin Lee, Ikjin Lee, Won-Ho Park, Seungmyeong Jeong, Seongyun Kim, Seokjun Lee, Jaeho Kim, and Ok Park. 2020. "Development and Utilization of a Rapid and Accurate Epidemic Investigation Support System for COVID-19." *Osong Public Health and Research Perspectives* 11 (3): 118–27.

Pires, Cesaltina Pacheco, Soumodip Sarkar, and Luísa Carvalho. 2008. "Innovation in Services– How Different from Manufacturing?" *The Service Industries Journal* 28 (10) : 1339–56.

Prud'homme, Dan, and Taolue Zhang. 2019. *China's Intellectual Property Regime for Innovation: Risks to Business and National Development*. Cham, Switzerland: Springer.

Raith, Michael. 2003. "Competition, Risk, and Managerial Incentives." *American Economic Review* 93 (4): 1425–36.

Republic of Korea. 2020. "Preventing the Inflow and Spread of the Virus." COVID-19 response information, Coronavirus-19 website of the Republic of Korea. http://ncov.mohw.go.kr/en/baroView.do?brdId=11&brdGubun=111.

Santacreu, Ana Maria. 2015. "Innovation, Diffusion, and Trade: Theory and Measurement." *Journal of Monetary Economics* 75: 1–20.

Santamaría, Lluís, María Jesus Nieto, and Ian Miles. 2012. "Service Innovation in

Manufacturing Firms: Evidence from Spain." *Technovation* 32 (2): 144–55.

Sutton, John. 2012. *Competing in Capabilities: The Globalization Process*. Oxford: Oxford University Press.

Syverson, Chad. 2011. "What Determines Productivity?" *Journal of Economic Literature* 49 (2): 326–65.

Verhoogen, Eric. 2020. "Firm-Level Upgrading in Developing Countries." Working paper No. 83, Center for Development Economics and Policy and Center on Global Economic Governance, School of International and Public Affairs, Columbia University, New York.

Wei, Shang-Jin, Zhuan Xie, and Xiaobo Zhang. 2017. "From 'Made in China' to 'Innovated in China': Necessity, Prospect, and Challenges." *Journal of Economic Perspectives* 31 (1): 49–70.

World Bank. 2017. "Vietnam: Enhancing Enterprise Competitiveness and SME Linkages: Lessons from International and National Experience." Working paper, World Bank, Washington, DC.

World Bank. 2020. *World Development Report 2020: Trading for Development in the Age of Global Value Chains*. Washington, DC: World Bank.

Yang, Chih-Hai, and Ying-Hui Chen. 2012. "R&D, Productivity, and Exports: Plant-Level Evidence from Indonesia." *Economic Modelling* 29 (2): 208–16.

Zanello, Giacomo, Xiaolan Fu, Pierr Mohnen, and Marc Ventresca. 2016. "The Creation and Diffusion of Innovation in Developing Countries: A Systematic Literature Review." *Journal of Economic Surveys* 30 (5): 884–912.

Skills and Finance for Innovation | 4

Introduction

The ability of firms to innovate depends on numerous factors that fall outside the realm of innovation policy, strictly defined. As discussed in previous chapters, these include policy and institutional factors that establish business and regulatory environments conducive to firms investing in innovation. Other key complementary factors include the availability of a sufficiently skilled workforce and adequate financing to support firms'—often risky—innovation activities. This chapter focuses on the roles of, and challenges associated with, the adequate supply of skills and finance in enabling innovation.

Skills for innovation

Strong workforce skills are critical to enabling innovation among firms

A significant literature highlights the importance of workers' human capital and skills in enabling innovation. This is not surprising, as greater education and skill levels provide workers with the cognitive abilities needed to absorb knowledge, develop and interact with new technologies, and create new products and processes at the frontier (Acemoglu, Aghion, and Zilibotti 2006; Toner 2011).

Several studies find a significant positive relationship between workers' human capital and firms' innovation in high-income economies.[1] Analysis of World Bank Enterprise Survey data from across developing East Asia also finds that employees' human capital—both education and firm-level training—is positively correlated with the intensity of their research and development (R&D) investment (ADB 2020; de Nicola 2019).

Moreover, the effects of workers' human capital on innovation appear to be sizable. A recent report by the Asian Development Bank finds, for example, that a 1 percent increase in worker education, as proxied by secondary school enrollment, is associated with a 2 percent increase in innovation as measured by patent flows (ADB 2020).

While the positive effect of education and skills on innovation appears to cut across categories of workers, one strand of the literature focuses on the impact of managers' human capital. Maloney and Sarrias (2017) find that managers' education is a key driver of differences in managerial quality—an important determinant of innovation—across countries (Cirera, Maloney, and Sarrias 2020).[2] Having highly educated managers is also directly associated with greater firm-level innovation (Ayyagari,

Demirgüç-Kunt, and Maksimovic 2011). Interestingly, a recent study of Japanese start-ups finds that a firm founder's level of human capital is, likewise, positively associated with the firm's innovation outcomes (Kato, Okamuro, and Honjo 2015).

A range of workforce skill types are important to fostering innovation

Which types of human capital—and skills, in particular—are important for innovation? Until recently, analysis of skills for innovation has focused predominantly on the role and importance of science, technology, engineering, and mathematics (STEM) skills (see, for example, World Bank 2012). STEM skills are still considered important. Over time, however, there has been a growing understanding that a broader set of skills are needed to foster innovation, including not only technical knowledge but also advanced problem solving; creative decision making; and the abilities to manage complexity, to communicate effectively, and to work well in teams.

Recent studies of the skills needed to support innovation and to enable successful adoption of new technologies thus recognize the importance of a wider set of skills and disciplines beyond those related to STEM (Deming and Khan 2018; Green, Jones, and Miles 2007; OECD 2011, 2016).

These include technical skills, higher-order cognitive skills, noncognitive skills, and managerial and entrepreneurial skills, as summarized in table 4.1 and further described below. With rapid technological change, there is a growing demand for the higher-order cognitive skills required to carry out nonroutine tasks (Mason and Shetty 2019; World Bank 2016). In addition, across the literature, there is a consensus that noncognitive skills, also called socioemotional skills, are of increasing importance to enabling innovation.[3]

Technical skills. Several types of technical skills can be important in fostering innovation. At a basic level, digital literacy is increasingly critical to innovation-related tasks. Along with the knowledge and ability to use basic digital business tools and applications, there is a growing need for specialized skills to develop, operate, and maintain information and communication technology (ICT) systems. Demand for these digital and technical capabilities is high in developing East Asia, yet workers with such skills remain in short supply; indeed, employers across the region report difficulty in finding employees with the required technical skills (Mason, Kehayova, and Yang 2018).

Higher-order cognitive skills. Skills such as problem solving, critical thinking, creative thinking, and logical thinking are becoming

TABLE 4.1   **A range of workforce skills are important for enabling innovation**

Skill type	Description
Technical	These are specific skills needed in an occupation, are often discipline-specific, and may include knowledge of certain tools or processes such as common software (for example, Microsoft Excel) and specific software (for example, Java).
Higher-order cognitive	These include skills such as problem solving, critical thinking, learning to learn, and the ability to manage complexity. These more-advanced cognitive skills must be built on a strong foundation of basic cognitive skills (that is, literacy and numeracy).
Noncognitive (socioemotional)	These noncognitive skills include the ability to work and interact effectively in teams, communicate, motivate oneself, take initiative, and be able to read and manage one's own emotions and reactions to others' behaviors.
Managerial and entrepreneurial	These competencies are needed to implement innovative ideas and enable organizations to adapt and respond in competitive environments. They also include leadership skills like team building, negotiation, motivation, and coordination.

Source: Adapted from Kataoka and Alejo 2019.
Note: STEM = science, technology, engineering, and mathematics.

increasingly valuable relative to basic cognitive skills like literacy and numeracy. The higher-order cognitive skills needed for innovation also include the ability to learn and adapt. Technology, for instance, is only useful to the extent that people can use it. Individuals also need the ability to accumulate knowledge and skills to operate new processes, create new knowledge, and improve adopted innovations. Such "trainable" individuals who can learn are valuable to innovative firms. Higher-order cognitive skills are often not included in traditional school curricula, however.

Socioemotional skills. Numerous personal attributes are essential to one's performance and effectiveness in the workplace and in social situations. These attributes encompass a wide range of nonroutine social and behavioral skills (table 4.2). Socioemotional skills, particularly "conscientiousness," are positively correlated with job performance dimensions such as task orientation and

TABLE 4.2 Socioemotional skills reflect personal attributes that are essential to workplace performance

Domain	Skills or characteristics
Conscientiousness (task performance)	• Achievement focus • Self-discipline • Responsibility • Perseverance
Extraversion (interpersonal engagement)	• Sociability • Assertiveness • Energy • Enthusiasm
Agreeableness (collaboration)	• Empathy • Trust • Cooperation • Straightforwardness
Openness (open-mindedness)	• Curiosity • Imagination • Creativity • Tolerance
Emotional stability (emotion regulation)	• Stress resistance • Optimism • Control of one's emotions

Source: Adapted from Kataoka and Alejo 2020.

organizational citizenship behavior, and negatively correlated with counterproductive work behavior (OECD 2017). With jobs becoming increasingly intensive in nonroutine interpersonal tasks, the demand by firms for strong socioemotional skills, including communication and leadership, is also expected to increase (Bughin et al. 2018).[4]

Managerial and entrepreneurial skills. The importance of managerial skills to innovation is well emphasized in the literature. Even after controlling for inputs such as R&D, for instance, managerial and organizational practices are important predictors of innovation across countries, firm sizes, and income levels (Cirera and Maloney 2017). Managerial skills are an essential input of management quality. Moreover, managerial talent—the ability to build teams, communicate, motivate people, identify talent, and strategize—influences innovation because it enables firms to identify productive opportunities, evaluate their feasibility, and allocate human resources effectively. Entrepreneurship skills are similarly valuable to innovation, particularly in the ability to manage risks.

Evidence on skills for innovation

Evidence from high-income economies suggests that advanced cognitive, socioemotional, and technical skills are all important to fostering innovation

To date, most evidence on the skills that enable innovation comes from high-income countries and reinforces the idea that a range of advanced skills are important to fostering innovation. A survey of employees in 20 Organisation for Economic Co-operation and Development (OECD) economies finds, for example, that those working in firms that innovate use more nonroutine cognitive skills than employees in firms that do not innovate (Avvisati, Jacotin, and Vincent-Lancrin 2013). The skills found to most distinguish those working in innovating firms include "coming up with new ideas and solutions" (creativity); "willingness to question ideas" (critical thinking); and "ability to present new ideas or products to an audience" (communication).

Firm-level studies from Ireland and Norway underscore the importance of higher-order technical skills—those associated with greater R&D capabilities—for fostering innovation at the technological frontier (Doran and Ryan 2014; Engen and Holen 2014).

Recent research also highlights the key role of socioemotional skills in fostering innovation. One study of innovation in the biotech industry in Taiwan, China, finds that greater conscientiousness (task performance), openness (open-mindedness), extraversion (interpersonal engagement), and emotional stability (emotion regulation) are all associated with firms' overall innovation performance, while conscientiousness, agreeableness (collaboration), and extraversion are associated specifically with technological innovation (Hsieh, Hsieh, and Wang 2011). Moreover, a study on innovation in the marine tourism industry in Taiwan, China, finds that greater agreeableness, extraversion, and openness are all significantly correlated with three key innovative skills: "idea generation," "idea promotion," and "idea implementation" (Chen, Wu, and Chen 2010).

New evidence from developing East Asia also indicates that innovative firms demand workers with a range of advanced skills

New evidence, based on data from recent employer-employee linked surveys in China and Vietnam, sheds further light on how skills differ across more- and less-innovative firms in developing East Asia. The analysis of these surveys, carried out for this study, benefits from unusually rich data on (a) firms' characteristics and innovation activities; (b) employees' education, training, cognitive achievement (in Vietnam), and socioemotional skills; and (c) employees' job-related tasks (box 4.1).

Both employer-employee surveys include data on multiple dimensions of firm innovation, such as whether a firm carries out product and process innovation, whether it has an R&D department, and whether it has generated new patents. Based on these multiple indicators of firm-level innovation activity, an innovation score—or "innovation intensity index"—is generated to help clarify the types and levels of skills demanded by highly innovative versus less or non-innovative firms.

BOX 4.1 Employer-employee linked survey data from China and Vietnam on skills for innovation

The analysis of skills for innovation presented in this chapter draws on two recent employer-employee linked surveys from China and Vietnam. These surveys contain detailed firm-level data, including on innovation, drawing on lessons from the World Bank Enterprise Surveys. They also provide unusually rich data on employee skills and task allocation, building on the lessons from other recent surveys on workers' skills, such as the Organisation for Economic Co-operation and Development's (OECD) Programme for the International Assessment of Adult Competencies (PIAAC) and the World Bank's Employer Skills Toward Employability and Productivity (STEP) surveys.

China Employer-Employee Survey
In 2018, the China Employer-Employee Survey (CEES) collected responses of 2,001 manufacturing firms and 16,379 workers from five Chinese prov-

inces: Guangdong, Jiangsu, Jilin, Hubei, and Sichuan. The survey samples are designed to be representative at the province level.

The CEES 2018 data include multiple measures of firm innovation, including measures of product and process innovation, whether a firm has an R&D department, whether it has generated invention patents in the past three years, and whether it is a high-tech firm. These multiple measures facilitate the creation of an innovation score—or "innovation intensity index"—for each firm, against which it is possible to analyze the skills and characteristics demanded of workers in more-innovative firms compared with those in less-innovative firms.

The survey also includes multiple measures of workers' human capital, including education levels, fields of study (among those with vocational and higher education), training, and socioemotional

box continues next page

skills, as well as detailed measures related to workers' tasks on the job (Park and Xuan 2020).

Enterprise Survey on Innovation and Skills, Vietnam
The 2019 Enterprise Survey on Innovation and Skills (ESIS) data for Vietnam was implemented in five Vietnamese provinces: Hanoi, Bac Ninh, Da Nang, Ho Chi Minh City, and Binh Duong. This survey was designed to be representative of firms in the manufacturing and information and communication technology (ICT) services sectors and included state-owned enterprises. From four strategic sectors—high-skilled innovator, medium-skilled innovator, labor intensive, and ICT services—201 firms were randomly selected from the Vietnam Enterprise Registry 2017 data.

Given the sampling design, it is likely that the firms surveyed are more engaged in innovation activities than the average Vietnamese firm. ESIS collected information on firm characteristics from 201 managers and on employee background and skills from 849 staff in four occupational categories: managers, professionals, technicians, and clerks. The survey was designed to capture firms' engagement in the four main types of innovation defined in the third edition of the *Oslo Manual*: product, process, organizational, and marketing innovations (OECD and Eurostat 2005).

The survey collected data on a range of firm-level variables, including innovation activities and managers' perceptions about factors that hamper innovation. It also collected detailed data on workers' human capital and skills, including through an assessment of employees' literacy and cognitive skills. The literacy assessment measured cognitive achievement using internationally recognized proficiency levels, as in the International Adult Literacy and Life Skills (IALS) and Adult Literacy and Life (ALL) skills surveys. ESIS also implemented an assessment of workers' socioemotional skills (Miyamoto and Sarzosa 2020).

Using the innovation intensity index, firms in both the China Employer-Employee Survey (CEES) and Vietnam's Enterprise Survey on Innovation and Skills (ESIS) were divided into three categories:

- *Low-innovation firms:* those that have carried out only one or no innovation activities identified in the survey
- *Medium-innovation firms:* those that have carried out two or three innovation activities
- *High-innovation firms:* those that have carried out four or five innovation activities.

Education in innovative firms. Using this categorization, consistent patterns were found regarding the education and skills profiles of high-innovation firms relative to medium- or low-innovative firms in China and Vietnam. In both countries, high-innovation firms tend to employ younger workers, more-educated workers (specifically, those with a college education), and more workers with STEM-related degrees (figure 4.1).[5] Indeed, average employee education levels rise with firms' levels of innovation intensity.

Cognitive abilities. In Vietnam, the survey measured employees' cognitive skills using direct assessment of literacy linked to two internationally recognized proficiency scales: the International Assessment of Adult Competencies (PIAAC) and the Adult Literacy and Life Skills Survey (ALL). Scaled from 0 to 5, a score of 2 captures basic proficiency, whereas a proficiency level 3 denotes the minimum level required for individuals to autonomously perform nonroutine tasks—often taken as the level of literacy required to function effectively in 21st-century workplaces (Miyamoto and Sarzosa 2020).[6]

Consistent with the educational composition of the workforce found in more-innovative firms, an analysis of employees' cognitive skills indicates that advanced cognitive skills—problem solving ability, capacity for critical

FIGURE 4.1 **More-innovative firms in China and Vietnam have more highly educated employees and a higher share with STEM degrees**

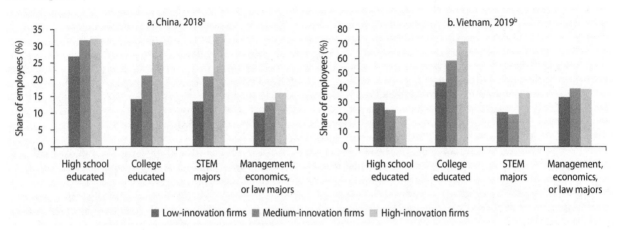

Sources: World Bank elaboration, based on Park and Xuan 2020 and Miyamoto and Sarzosa 2020, using, respectively, the 2018 China Employer-Employee Survey (CEES) and the 2019 Enterprise Survey on Innovation and Skills (ESIS) for Vietnam.
Note: Firms are categorized on the basis of "innovation intensity," measured by the number of innovation activities undertaken, as captured in the respective surveys. Scaled from 0–5, low-, medium-, and high-innovation are defined, respectively, as those undertaking 0–1, 2–3, and 4–5 innovation activities as defined in the CEES and ESIS. STEM = science, technology, engineering, and mathematics.
a. The CEES collected responses of 2,001 manufacturing firms and 16,379 workers from five Chinese provinces: Guangdong, Jiangsu, Jilin, Hubei, and Sichuan.
b. ESIS collected responses from 201 manufacturing and information and communication technology (ICT) services firms and 849 staff in five Vietnamese provinces: Hanoi, Bac Ninh, Da Nang, Ho Chi Minh City, and Binh Duong.

FIGURE 4.2 **Stronger cognitive and socioemotional skills are associated with greater innovation intensity among firms in Vietnam, 2019**

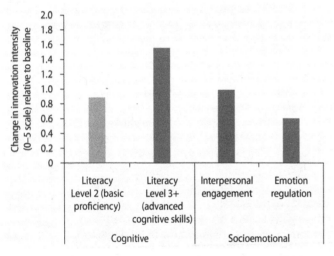

Source: Miyamoto and Sarzosa 2020, using 2019 Enterprise Survey on Innovation and Skills (ESIS) data for Vietnam.
Note: ESIS collected responses from 201 manufacturing and information and communication technology (ICT) services firms and 849 staff in five Vietnamese provinces: Hanoi, Bac Ninh, Da Nang, Ho Chi Minh City, and Binh Duong. The figure compares the difference in "innovation intensity" between firms based on average employee literacy proficiency and scores from socioemotional skills assessments. For cognitive skills, changes in innovation intensity are measured against a baseline of a literacy proficiency level of 1 and below (omitted category). For socioemotional skills, changes are measured as the estimated effect of a 1 standard deviation increase in the average assessment score. The "innovation intensity index" measures firms by the number of innovation activities undertaken—on a 0–5 scale, where 0 equals no firm-level innovation activities (least innovation intensive) and 5 equals all the measured innovation activities (most innovation intensive) as defined in the ESIS. The darker bars indicate estimates are statistically significant at the 5 percent level or above. Literacy Levels 2 and 3+ capture increasing cognitive skill levels, where Literacy Level 3 represents the minimum proficiency level required for individuals to autonomously perform nonroutine tasks.

thinking, ability to learn, and ability to manage complexity—are associated with higher innovation intensity among Vietnamese firms (figure 4.2). Although one must be careful about asserting a causal relationship from this analysis, the strength of the association between employees' cognitive skills and firm-level innovation is noteworthy. Firms whose employees have advanced cognitive skills—averaging proficiency level 3 or above—score 1.5 points higher on an "innovation intensity index" (on a 0–5 scale) than firms whose employees have an average proficiency level 1 or below. Further analysis of the Vietnam data suggests, moreover, that having employees with advanced cognitive skills is particularly important to firms engaged in invention (Miyamoto and Sarzosa 2020).

Socioemotional skills. As figure 4.2 also shows, greater socioemotional skills in the form of greater interpersonal engagement ("extraversion") and emotion regulation ("emotional stability") are also associated with greater innovation intensity among firms. The association between interpersonal engagement skills and innovation appears to be especially strong with respect to firms engaged in technology adoption and diffusion (Miyamoto and Sarzosa 2020).

These findings on cognitive and socioemotional skills and innovation in Vietnam are consistent with earlier analysis for Vietnam using the 2013 Skills Toward Employability and Productivity (STEP) Employer Survey (Macdonald 2019). Specifically, managers and professionals working in innovating firms (defined as firms having R&D units) report engaging in more activities requiring both routine and nonroutine cognitive skills (reading, math, and complex problem solving) than do managers and professionals working in non-innovating firms. Managers and professionals in innovating firms also report using a greater range of socioemotional skills—engaging regularly in persuading clients or coworkers and interacting with teams—than do their counterparts in non-innovating firms.

Stronger socioemotional skills are significantly associated with greater innovation intensity in China as well (figure 4.3). Specifically, high-innovation firms demonstrate high demand for employees who exhibit strong task performance ("conscientiousness"), interpersonal skills ("extraversion"), and an ability to collaborate and work in teams ("agreeableness"). This higher demand for strong socioemotional skills holds even after controlling for firm and individual worker characteristics (Park and Xuan 2020).[7]

Employees in highly innovative firms perform more nonroutine cognitive tasks
Consistent with higher education and greater cognitive skills, workers in highly innovative firms in China and Vietnam perform more nonroutine analytical and interpersonal cognitive tasks than their counterparts in medium- or low-innovation firms (figure 4.4). In China, the difference between workers in highly innovative and less innovative firms is particularly striking regarding nonroutine analytical tasks (figure 4.4, panel a). In both China and Vietnam, employees in highly innovative firms carry out significantly less routine work than those in less-innovative firms. In Vietnam, the difference in the extent of routine manual tasks between employees in high-innovation firms and those in low- and medium-innovation firms is especially large (figure 4.4, panel b).

FIGURE 4.3 **High-innovation firms in China exhibit high demand for workers with strong socioemotional skills**

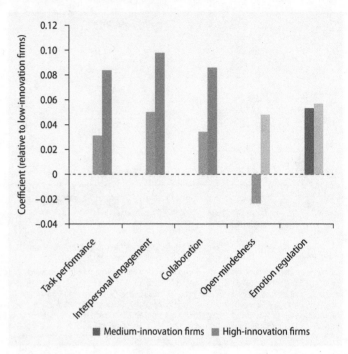

■ Medium-innovation firms ■ High-innovation firms

Source: World Bank elaboration, based on Park and Xuan 2020, using the 2018 China Employer-Employee Survey (CEES).
Note: The CEES collected responses of 2,001 manufacturing firms and 16,379 workers from five Chinese provinces: Guangdong, Jiangsu, Jilin, Hubei, and Sichuan. Firms are categorized based on "innovation intensity," measured by the number of innovation activities undertaken, scaled from 0–5. Low-, medium-, and high-innovation are defined, respectively, as those undertaking 0–1, 2–3, and 4–5 innovation activities as defined in the CEES. Regression coefficients relative to low-innovation firms (the omitted category). Regressions control for firm and individual worker characteristics. Darker bars are statistically significant at the 5 percent level (or above).

Managers' skill sets are particularly important
The data also reinforce the importance of managers' skills to innovation. Analysis of skills across categories of workers in Vietnam—managers, professionals, technicians, and clerks—indicates that managers' capabilities are important contributors to firms' innovation performance.

Specifically, advanced cognitive skills among managers and technicians (as measured by literacy proficiency levels of 3, 4, or higher), along with managers' interpersonal skills, are all positively associated with higher innovation intensity among Vietnamese firms (figure 4.5). The association between managers'—and especially technicians'—cognitive abilities and firm innovation performance is particularly strong.

FIGURE 4.4   **Employees in more-innovative firms in China and Vietnam have jobs that are more intensive in nonroutine cognitive analytical and interpersonal tasks**

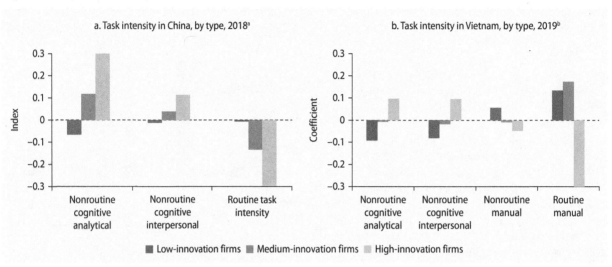

Sources: World Bank elaboration based on Park and Xuan 2020 and Miyamoto and Sarzosa 2020, using, respectively, the 2018 China Employer-Employee Survey (CEES) and the 2019 Enterprise Survey on Innovation and Skills (ESIS) for Vietnam.
Note: Firms are categorized by "innovation intensity," measured by the number of innovation activities undertaken, as captured in the respective surveys. Scaled from 0–5, low-, medium-, and high-innovation are defined, respectively, as those undertaking 0–1, 2–3, and 4–5 innovation activities. The Vietnam analysis does not include an aggregated measure of "routine task intensity;" therefore, panel b shows instead an individual measure of "routine manual" tasks. No information was included in either panel on routine cognitive tasks because none of the related regression coefficients was statistically significant.
a. The CEES collected responses of 2,001 manufacturing firms and 16,379 workers from five Chinese provinces: Guangdong, Jiangsu, Jilin, Hubei, and Sichuan.
b. ESIS collected responses from 201 manufacturing and information and communication technology (ICT) services firms and 849 staff in five Vietnamese provinces: Hanoi, Bac Ninh, Da Nang, Ho Chi Minh City, and Binh Duong.

FIGURE 4.5   **Managers' and technicians' skills are particularly important to firm innovation in Vietnam, 2019**

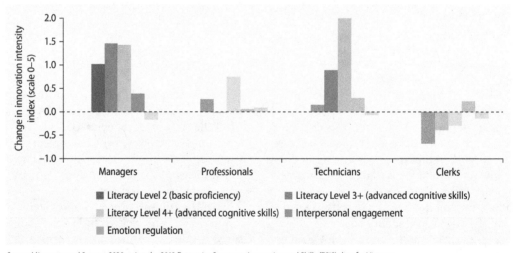

Source: Miyamoto and Sarzosa 2020, using the 2019 Enterprise Survey on Innovation and Skills (ESIS) data for Vietnam.
Note: ESIS collected responses from 201 manufacturing and information and communication technology (ICT) services firms and 849 staff in five Vietnamese provinces: Hanoi, Bac Ninh, Da Nang, Ho Chi Minh City, and Binh Duong. The figure compares the difference in "innovation intensity" between firms based on average literacy proficiency and on socioemotional skills assessment scores of staff in each occupation. For cognitive skills, changes in innovation intensity are measured against a baseline defined as literacy proficiency levels of 1 and below (omitted category). For socioemotional skills, changes are measured as the estimated effect of a 1 standard deviation increase in the average assessment score. The firm innovation intensity index measures the number of innovation activities a firm undertakes on a 0–5 scale, where 0 equals no firm-level innovation activities (least innovation intensive) and 5 equals all measured innovation activities (most innovation intensive). Darker bars indicate estimates that are statistically significant at the 5 percent level or above, except for "interpersonal engagement," which is significant at the 10 percent level. Literacy levels 2, 3, and 4 capture increasing cognitive skill levels, where level 3 represents the minimum proficiency level required for individuals to autonomously perform nonroutine tasks.

Returns to education and advanced skills are especially high in high-innovation firms
Emerging evidence suggests that innovation skills are rewarded in developing East Asia's labor markets. In China, for example, workers in more-innovative firms receive higher wages. The wage gap between low-innovation firms and high-innovation firms is 14–67 percent, depending on the occupation (Park and Xuan 2020). Analysis of the CEES data indicates that returns to college education are higher in high-innovation firms than in low- or medium-innovation firms, as are returns to such socioemotional skills as interpersonal engagement (extraversion) and task performance (conscientiousness), even after controlling for workers' education and experience.

These higher returns appear to be driven by higher wages among the most-skilled workers (such as managers, technical workers, and salesmen) rather than by wages of lower-skilled workers (such as office and production workers). Separate analyses from China and Vietnam also find positive returns to performance of the nonroutine analytical tasks that are critical to innovation, again controlling for workers' education and experience (Bodewig et al. 2014; Du and Park 2017).[8] Whether wage premia in innovative firms always favor high-skilled workers remains an open question. Recent studies in the United Kingdom (Aghion et al. 2019) and Brazil (Cirera and Soares Martins Neto 2020) find positive and significant wage premia associated with innovation, after controlling for education and other worker characteristics. Although the study of the United Kingdom finds that the wage premium is larger for low-skill occupations, the evidence on the distribution of the wage premium in Brazil is inconclusive.

The positive returns associated with more-advanced innovation skills have also raised questions about whether technology adoption and innovation represent an opportunity or a threat to workers and employment more broadly. These questions are of particular interest given evidence from high-income economies of job polarization resulting from technology adoption and automation. Although analysis of the overall employment effects of innovation in low- and middle-income economies is still relatively scarce, the available evidence suggests that innovation raises employment—among high-skilled workers and low- to medium-skilled workers alike—when the productivity gains associated with diffusion or invention enable firms to expand their output and to grow (box 4.2).

BOX 4.2 **The effects of technology adoption and innovation on employment**

One question in the minds of policy makers is how adoption of new technologies and innovation more broadly affect employment, especially among low- and middle-skilled workers. Concerns about the potential employment effects of innovation have been amplified in recent years as a result of research on high-income economies (for example, in Europe and the United States) showing that technology adoption—whether in the form of computers, information and communication technologies (ICTs) or industrial robots—has resulted in labor market polarization (the relative growth of employment in high-skill and low-skill jobs accompanied by a decline in middle-skill jobs) or, alternatively, a shift in demand toward high-skilled labor at the expense of middle- or low-skilled workers (Autor, Dorn, and Hanson 2015; Graetz and Michaels 2018).

At least one recent study on automation also found significant negative effects of robot use on aggregate employment. Examining the effects of robot use on local labor markets in the United States from 1990 to 2007, the study found that each additional robot per 1,000 workers reduced employment on the order of 3.0–5.6 jobs per robot (Acemoglu and Restrepo 2017). Recent research on developing and emerging economies has thus far found little evidence of job polarization, however (Das and Hilgenstock 2018; Maloney and Molina 2016).

Although most research on technology, skills, and jobs has focused on high-income economies,

box continues next page

a growing number of studies are examining these issues in low- and middle-income countries. This evidence generally finds that technology adoption raises relative demand for more-skilled workers (Mason and Shetty 2019). The evidence on employment often paints a more positive picture, however. A recent study of technology adoption among firms in Argentina, Brazil, Chile, Colombia, and Mexico finds, for example, that investments in ICT raised firm productivity, enabling firms to expand their output, which in turn led to net employment growth for both low-skilled and high-skilled workers (Dutz, Almeida, and Packard 2018).

A study of technology adoption (and trade) in Vietnam comes to similar conclusions. Whereas computer use tends to be "labor saving" and raises relative demand for higher-skilled workers, overall employment has increased with rising demand for Vietnamese production and exports (Poole et al. 2017). Cross-country evidence (based on World Bank Enterprise Survey data from 82 low- and middle-income countries) is consistent with the country-level findings: increased adoption of digital technologies is associated with greater firm-level demand for labor, controlling for other factors (Cusolito, Lederman, and Peña 2020).

As with the literature on technology adoption, most research on the effect of innovation on employment to date has focused on high-income economies and finds evidence of "skill-biased technological change"—the relative increase in demand for more-skilled labor resulting from the introduction of a new technology or technology-driven change in production methods or business processes. Nonetheless, the empirical literature that focuses specifically on innovation more consistently finds a positive relationship between product innovation and firm-level employment, often related to expanded demand for firm output.

For example, a study of innovation and employment in France, Germany, Spain, and the United Kingdom finds a positive effect of product innovation on employment, with an estimated elasticity of jobs created close to unity (Harrison et al. 2014). Analysis of a 20-year panel of firms in Germany similarly finds a significant positive relationship between innovation and employment, in the cases of both product and process innovation (Lachenmaier and Rottmann 2011). And an analysis of longitudinal data on Italian manufacturing firms finds a significant positive relationship, albeit relatively small, between innovation and employment (Piva and Vivarelli 2005).

A smaller but growing literature on low- and middle-income countries likewise finds that product innovation is associated with increased employment at the firm level. A recent study of firm-level innovation in Argentina, Chile, Costa Rica, and Uruguay finds, for example, that both process and product innovation have positive effects on employment (Crespi, Tacsir, and Pereira 2019).

These country-level findings are reinforced by a recent study that examines the employment effects of innovation using Enterprise Survey data from 53 low- and middle-income countries (Cirera and Sabetti 2019). This cross-country analysis indicates that product innovation, when successful in raising firm-level sales, also has a positive direct impact on employment. The evidence suggests, moreover, that positive employment effects tend to be larger in low- and middle-income countries, where innovations are commonly more incremental in nature, than in high-income countries. In contrast to product innovation, however, Cirera and Sabetti (2019) find no evidence that either process or organizational innovation have any effect on employment.

The relationship between technology adoption, innovation, and employment is complex. Nonetheless, despite evidence of labor polarization in high-income economies, emerging evidence for low- and middle-income countries suggests that technology adoption and innovation have the potential to increase employment, particularly when increased productivity and profitability results in firm expansion.

Ongoing skills challenges in developing East Asia

Innovative firms cite inadequate skills as a major constraint to their operations

Despite the importance of human capital in fostering innovation, most countries in developing East Asia still face critical skills challenges. These challenges are reflected in numerous human capital and skills-related indicators for the region. Firms throughout the region report a lack of adequate skills as a crucial constraint to their operations. In most of the region's countries, firms that innovate report a lack of adequate skills as a greater constraint to their operations than do non-innovating firms.

More than one-quarter of innovating firms in Cambodia and Indonesia, and nearly one-third of innovating firms in Mongolia, report that inadequate skills are either a major or severe obstacle to their operations.[9] Inadequate skills appear to be an even greater problem when firms try to hire new workers. Indeed, a significant majority of innovating firms in Indonesia, the Philippines, and Vietnam (76 percent, 79 percent, and 64 percent, respectively) report inadequate skills as an obstacle when trying to hire new employees.

Moreover, innovating firms across the region report a range of skills deficits when trying to recruit new employees. The specific skills deficits, as well as the level of severity, differ from country to country, but the magnitude of the problem is often reported to be large. In Indonesia, Malaysia, Myanmar, the Philippines, Thailand, and Vietnam, for example, over 50 percent of all innovative firms cite lack of managerial and leadership skills as a challenge when hiring new workers (figure 4.6). And more than half of all innovative firms in at least three of those six countries also cite a scarcity of interpersonal and communication skills, foreign language skills, computer and information technology (IT) skills, and technical (non-IT) skills as critical challenges when it comes to hiring.[10] Interestingly, the range of skills challenges that innovating firms report facing in hiring workers mirrors the range of cognitive, technical, and socioemotional skills found to be important among high-innovation firms.

Many countries still struggle to build sufficient basic skills among students—the foundation for more-advanced skills among workers

The concerns that firms express about human capital and skills gaps are also reflected in the results of the most recent Programme for International Student Assessment (PISA) tests, administered to 15-year-olds in several developing East Asian countries in 2018.[11] Although PISA scores in four major cities in China are well above those that would be predicted from China's gross domestic product (GDP) per capita, assessment scores on reading, math, and science in Indonesia, Malaysia, the Philippines, and Thailand are considerably below what would be expected given their income levels (figure 4.7).[12] Although the figure presents only reading scores, similar patterns are seen in the 2018 PISA scores for math and science.[13]

Together, these test results suggest that many of the region's countries face continuing challenges in building the "foundational skills" upon which the more-advanced skills for innovation must be built. That most countries' PISA scores have not improved over time is also a matter of concern; indeed, in the case of reading, some countries' performance has even deteriorated (World Bank 2020).

The region's countries must also keep building their technical skills bases

On top of the challenges developing East Asian countries face in building their populations' foundational skills, they need to continue building their technical skills bases, especially if they are to spur innovation at the technological frontier. Although the region's share of tertiary students graduating with degrees in STEM fields is relatively high, tertiary enrollment rates in many countries are lower than would be predicted given their per capita income levels (figure 4.8).

FIGURE 4.6 **Most innovative firms in developing East Asia report difficulties in hiring workers with adequate skills**

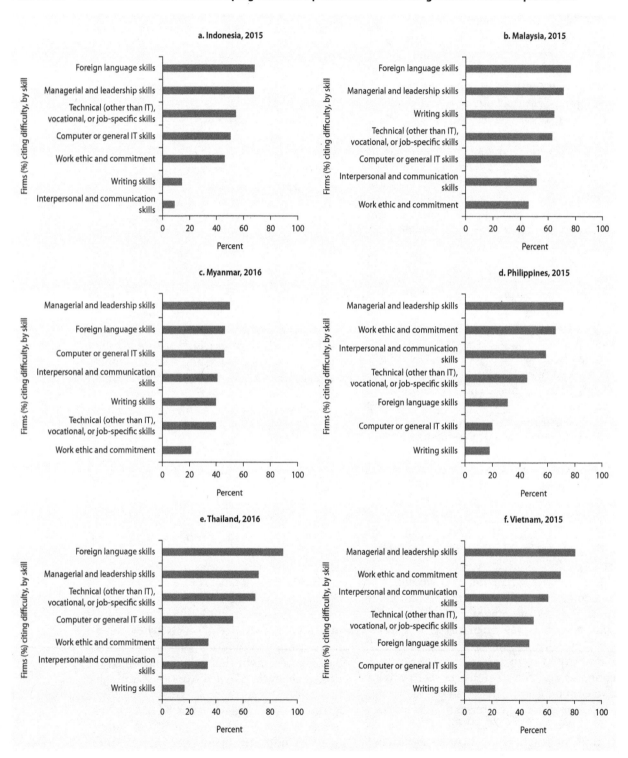

Source: World Bank calculations, based on World Bank Enterprise Surveys.
Note: "Innovative" firms are defined as those that introduced new or significantly improved products or services (product), or adopted new production methods (process), during the past three fiscal years. IT = information technology.

The quality of STEM training remains an issue, however, given the relatively weak development of foundational skills in most of the region's countries. Even in China, where PISA scores are high, rapid expansion in the number of tertiary-level students over the past two decades has posed significant challenges in ensuring quality across the system. Between 1999 and 2016, college enrollments nearly quintupled (from 1.6 million to 7.5 million) in China, while the number of tertiary institutions increased by roughly 2.5 times (from 1,071 to 2,596). Although China has several world-class universities, there remains significant variation in educational quality across institutions, with a sizable share of graduates getting low returns (World Bank and DRC 2019).

Ensuring that countries' education systems support the development of both adequate foundational skills and more-advanced cognitive, socioemotional, and technical skills will be critical to fostering innovation, whether defined as adoption of existing technologies or as invention at the technological frontier.

FIGURE 4.7   Several developing East Asian countries underperform in basic skills formation, creating challenges for the development of more-advanced skills

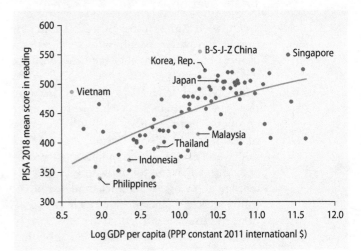

Sources: World Bank elaboration, based on Programme for International Student Assessment (PISA) data and the World Development Indicators database.
Note: The light blue points designate 6 of the 10 "developing East Asia" countries studied in this report. The others (Cambodia, Lao PDR, Mongolia, and Myanmar) did not participate in PISA in either 2018 or 2015. "B-S-J-Z China" scores are not nationally representative but capture test results from urban Beijing, Shanghai, Jiangsu, and Zhejiang only. Vietnam data are from 2015; no PISA results were reported for 2018. GDP = gross domestic product; PPP = purchasing power parity.

FIGURE 4.8   Although developing East Asian countries often produce a higher share of STEM graduates than do countries with similar income levels, most have lower tertiary enrollment rates

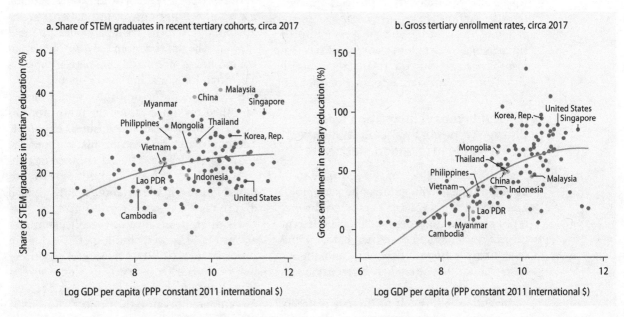

Sources: World Bank elaboration, based on United Nations Educational, Scientific and Cultural Organization (UNESCO), World Development Indicators, and World Economic Forum data.
Note: GDP = gross domestic product; PPP = purchasing power parity; STEM = science, technology, engineering, and mathematics.

Finance for innovation

Financial markets are an enabling factor for innovation

Deep, well-functioning financial markets promote growth through innovation by efficiently allocating capital to the firms with the most promising projects (Levine 2005). Firms with new and better ideas are provided with the means to finance their projects, gaining competitive advantages through increases in productivity (Beck, Levine, and Loayza 2000) and eventually becoming more profitable. Firms that fail to innovate may exit the market, allowing for an efficient allocation of (often scarce) financial resources in the economy. In turn, this efficient allocation leads to higher productivity and, ultimately, growth.

Financial markets also perform important screening and monitoring functions—collecting and processing information that can reduce asymmetric information problems.[14] New innovative projects are evaluated and financed, facilitating development and commercialization. Finance is key at all stages of the innovation process, as the expected monetary returns from innovation are realized with a lag. Specifically, monetary outflows (expenses) for innovation projects precede monetary inflows (revenues), creating a financial gap. The time lag and the amount of the financial gap depend on the type of innovation. Firms can plug the financial gap using either internal or external sources of finance.

Different types of innovation face different types of financing challenges, which may lead to underinvestment

Innovation, as defined in this report, entails both diffusion and adoption of new technologies as well as invention. These two distinct types of innovation commonly have different project timelines and cash-flow patterns and face different financial frictions and agency costs. Thus, they often face different financing challenges.

Invention is difficult to finance in freely competitive markets because cash flows are uncertain and the time line from development to commercialization is often long. Key frictions characteristic to the financing of firm invention include the nonrival nature of knowledge (that is, development by one firm does not prevent the use by another) and asymmetric information between firms and prospective financiers (Hall and Lerner 2010).

Nonrival knowledge. Knowledge spillovers to other firms may make the private rate of return to innovation lower than the socially optimal return to innovation. Lack of full appropriability can reduce investments in innovation. Innovative firms may also be reluctant to share the outcomes of invention in early stages of development with investors for fear of losing the intellectual property right of their innovation to competitors. This reluctance increases information asymmetries in the market, which, together with the high-risk nature of invention, may make investors reluctant to invest, again resulting in underinvestment. Stronger intellectual property rights, accounting standards, and disclosure requirements should help to alleviate this problem.[15] Nevertheless, these frictions may lead to underinvestment in invention.

Asymmetric information. Innovative projects exacerbate asymmetric information between the entrepreneur and the financier. Ex ante, evaluating invention is problematic because returns are highly uncertain and skewed. The time between the development of the business concept and commercialization is also often long, making for an illiquid investment. Although the innovator and financier face the same uncertainty, the innovator has better technological and business expertise, and could also be overoptimistic about the chances of success. Thus, a contingent contract is hard to achieve, and this may lead to moral hazard on the inventor's part,[16] which in turn may lead to underinvestment.

Relative to invention, the diffusion and adoption of new technologies is safer (in terms of probability of success), its timeline is shorter, and firms' loss exposure is more contained. Agency problems are also more limited because the project's novelty is more limited, which makes it easier to collect information to appraise the investment.

TABLE 4.3   **Market frictions have distinct effects on different types of firm innovation**

Innovation type	Returns	Likelihood of success	Loss exposure	Innovation project time line	Asymmetric information	Moral hazard
Diffusion or adoption	Moderate	Moderate	Moderate	Short	Moderate	Moderate
Invention	Large but highly uncertain	Low	Very high	Long	High	High

Source: Original table for this publication.
Note: This table provides a synthetic representation for illustrative purposes.

Technology adoption may nonetheless be costly, depending on the tacit know-how involved as well as country- and firm-level characteristics. If firms cannot absorb this cost with their available resources and cannot find external resources, they may decide to delay or abandon the adoption of the new technology altogether. Table 4.3 summarizes the key market frictions faced by innovating firms, both those inventing and those undertaking diffusion and adoption.

Financial constraints impede firm-level innovation and may hamper project quality
In light of the challenges associated with the financing of firm innovation, both theory and empirical evidence support the view that financial constraints and the type of funding affect firms' decisions to innovate as well as the extent to which they innovate.[17] Financial constraints affect firms' decisions to innovate and adopt new technologies because the propensity of firms to undertake innovative projects depends on their ability to satisfy current capital expenditures and to borrow in the future to meet potentially large adjustment costs during difficult times (Hall and Lerner 2010).[18] There is also the need to accumulate capital over time to finance a new business or firm innovation unless external sources of finance help smooth investment over time (Berger, Molyneux, and Wilson 2020).

In the absence of external finance, financially constrained firms could slow or delay investment in innovative projects or could prematurely stop or abandon such projects altogether. Financial constraints can thus impede the generation of new (novel) innovation and, ultimately, the aggregate level of invention in an industry or economy.[19]

Financial constraints may also hamper the quality of firms' innovation by limiting their abilities to adopt new technologies in production processes and to incorporate them in final products and services. Indeed, financial constraints make firms less likely to invest in risky, exploratory R&D that could lead to productivity-enhancing discovery innovations and more likely to invest in R&D that leads to low-quality patented innovations. This appears to be the case in China, where recent research finds that financially constrained firms orient their R&D toward smaller changes that can raise firms' profits in the short term rather than toward more-significant innovations that could increase firms' longer-term productivity (Cao 2020).

Financial structure is also relevant for firms' innovation processes
The financial structure of firms also influences both the decision to innovate and the quality of innovation. Internal financing—specifically, retained earnings and new equity from existing shareholders—is the main source of funding for most innovation projects (Czarnitzki and Hottenrott 2011). These sources of funding are especially relevant for small and medium-size enterprises and start-ups, which cannot rely on banks or the financial market because of the lack of reputation or lack of the collateral needed to benefit from external sources of finance.

Relying on operating profits for innovation projects is far from ideal, however. Cash flows are volatile sources of finance (Brown, Fazzari, and Petersen 2009), and raising new equity can be costly and sometimes unwarranted (Hottenrott and Peters 2012). As a result, innovative projects with high initial costs may be delayed, postponed, or abandoned for lack of external finance. This issue is likely to be most prominent among smaller, younger firms with greater constraints to accessing external finance.

External sources of finance not only plug the financial gap of innovative firms but also can affect a firm's managerial incentives, governance, and risk-taking behavior, because of the presence of external monitoring by financial intermediaries.[20] In addition, diverse sources of finance have distinct characteristics that can help to reduce market frictions in different manners. Regarding information, for example, capital markets provide price signals and encourage the borrowing firms to publicly release hard data about their enterprises. Banks also fill information gaps by collecting soft information that is mostly held privately. As a result, banks are better equipped to operate in more opaque and risky environments. Moreover, different forms of funding often bring additional benefits to firms beyond the simple provision of finance,

including management skills and expansion of firms' business networks.[21]

Firms in developing East Asia face finance-related obstacles to innovation

Financial systems in much of the region remain bank based, limiting firms' options for financing innovation projects

Differences in firms' access to finance depend, in part, on the level of financial development of each country. Most developing East Asian economies are characterized by bank-based financial systems that lack the necessary diversity to foster firm innovation. Selected indicators of financial market development in developing East Asia show that banks are the dominant source of finance in most of the region's countries except for China (figure 4.9).[22]

In parts of developing East Asia where capital markets are less developed, undertaking invention-oriented innovation may be precluded. Once again, these constraints may

FIGURE 4.9 **Banks remain the dominant source of finance to firms in most of developing East Asia (except China)**

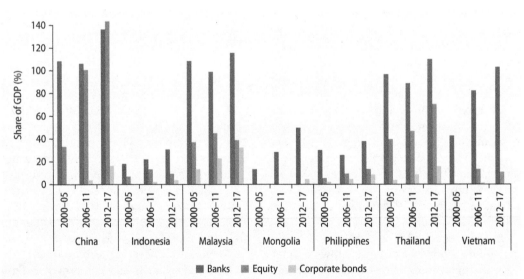

Sources: The World Bank's Global Financial Development and FinDebt databases.
Note: The graph reports averages over the three periods. "Equity" refers to stock market capitalization, "corporate bonds" to the amount outstanding of domestic bonds issued by private entities in industries other than finance, and "banks" to the outstanding amount of private credit granted by domestic banks. "Developing East Asia" refers to the 10 middle-income countries covered in this study: Cambodia, China, Indonesia, Lao PDR, Malaysia, Mongolia, Myanmar, the Philippines, Thailand, and Vietnam. The figure excludes Cambodia, Lao PDR, and Myanmar because of unavailability of data. For Mongolia, data on the corporate bond issuance are not available before 2011.

be particularly severe for younger and smaller firms. Not only do such firms have more limited access to equity financing (because of the small market size), but they also face greater challenges in raising debt financing because asymmetric information problems are commonly worse for smaller and younger firms than for larger and more established firms. Younger and smaller firms are thus more likely than larger firms to allocate investments away from intangible assets and to delay or abstain from innovation projects.

Most firms in the region still rely on internal financing, which can constrain their abilities to finance innovation projects
By far, most of the innovative firms in developing East Asia still use internal funds to finance the purchase of fixed assets (figure 4.10).[23] And this lack of external finance may affect

both the quantity and quality of innovation projects pursued. Interestingly, few countries in the region exhibit significant differences between innovative and non-innovative firms in the financing of fixed assets through external funding sources. Although the lack of external financing may constrain both innovative and non-innovative firms, it may represent a greater constraint on innovative firms—especially those focused on invention—given the potential costs, complexity, and uncertainty of investments associated with such projects.

Improving the availability of external financing would increase the likelihood of firm-level innovation
Low use of external finance may reduce innovation. Indeed, an analysis of a global sample of firms finds that firms with more

FIGURE 4.10 **In developing East Asia, most firms—both innovative and non-innovative—finance fixed assets using internal funds**

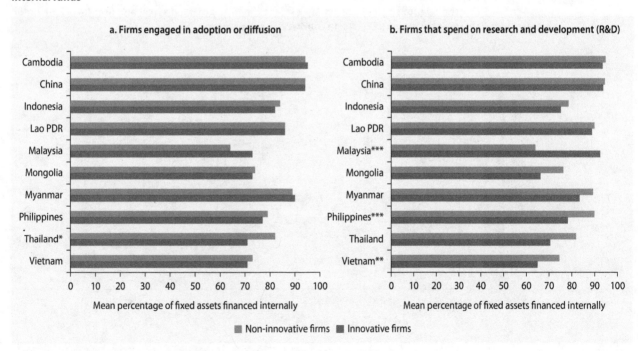

a. Firms engaged in adoption or diffusion

b. Firms that spend on research and development (R&D)

Mean percentage of fixed assets financed internally

Mean percentage of fixed assets financed internally

■ Non-innovative firms ■ Innovative firms

Sources: World Bank elaboration using World Bank Enterprise Survey data.
Note: The graph reports the mean percentage of fixed assets financed through internal funds for firms that either adopt a new product, service, or process (panel a) or spend on research and development (R&D) (panel b). "Developing East Asia" refers to the 10 middle-income countries covered in this study: Cambodia, China, Indonesia, Lao PDR, Malaysia, Mongolia, Myanmar, the Philippines, Thailand, and Vietnam.
Statistically significant difference in the mean value for each regional group in the two reference years, using a two-tailed test: *** $p < 0.01$ ** $p < 0.05$ * $p < 0.1$

diversified financial structures (that is, using external funding instead of retained earnings or other internal resources) are more likely to engage in innovation (Mare, de Nicola, and Liriano 2020). Moreover, firms that use external sources of funding undertake more innovation activities. This appears to be the case for at least a subset of developing East Asian countries, where funding alternatives to internal funds and bank financing are significantly associated with firms' decisions to innovate as well as the extent of firm innovation activity.

The association between financial structure and firm-level innovation is stronger in some countries than in others (figure 4.11). This reinforces the idea that innovation activities and outcomes depend on several country-specific factors—including, from the perspective of innovation finance, the presence of well-developed equity markets (Hsu, Tian, and Xu 2014).

Risk finance is growing in the region, and this could spur firm innovation
Several alternative sources of finance to internal funds and bank lending, commonly known as risk finance (for example, private equity, venture capital, or angel investing), are often associated with firm invention activities because this form of financing specifically targets high-risk, high-return investments.[24] The amount of risk capital financing remains limited around the world, however, especially in low- and middle-income countries. As noted above, most external financing of firms in developing East Asia still comes from banks.

Nonetheless, countries in developing East Asia perform relatively better than those in other regions in attracting risk capital investment, which in 2018 was equivalent to 0.34 percent of GDP on average (totaling approximately US$139 billion) (map 4.1). Moreover, in some

FIGURE 4.11   **The relationship between firms' external financing of fixed assets and firm-level innovation is stronger in some developing East Asian countries than in others**

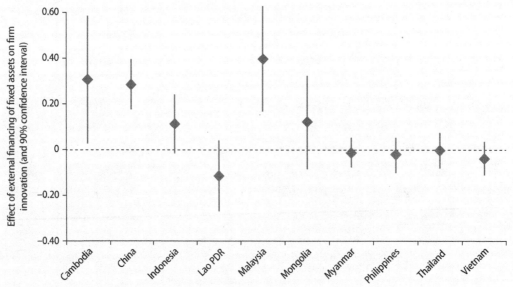

Source: Adapted from Mare, de Nicola, and Liriano forthcoming.
Note: This figure shows the marginal effect (at means, marked with a diamond) of the different sources of working capital funding and fixed assets funding on a country's firm-level innovation score, ranging from 0 (no innovation) to 4 (both adoption and research and development [R&D] expenditures undertaken). The confidence intervals for those coefficients are computed at the 10 percent significance level. The country regressions relate the innovation score for firms in the manufacturing sector to their funding sources, controlling for size, labor productivity, age, and domestic ownership.

MAP 4.1   Countries in developing East Asia attracted relatively large amounts of risk capital financing, as a percentage of GDP, in 2018

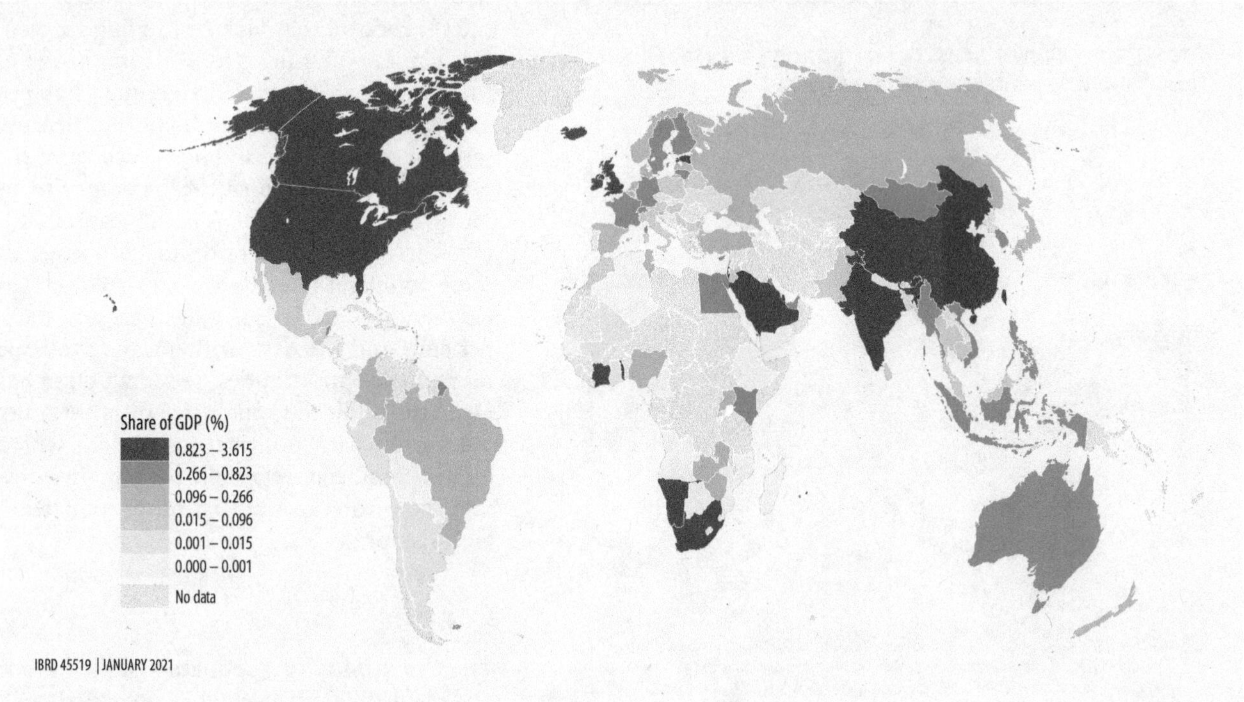

Share of GDP (%)
- 0.823 − 3.615
- 0.266 − 0.823
- 0.096 − 0.266
- 0.015 − 0.096
- 0.001 − 0.015
- 0.000 − 0.001
- No data

IBRD 45519 | JANUARY 2021

Source: World Bank elaboration, using Crunchbase data (https://www.crunchbase.com/),
Note: The map reports the amount of risk capital financing (for example, angel, venture, private, or equity crowdfunding) as a percentage of a country's GDP in 2018. "Developing East Asia" refers to the 10 middle-income countries covered in this study: Cambodia, China, Indonesia, Lao PDR, Malaysia, Mongolia, Myanmar, the Philippines, Thailand, and Vietnam. GDP = gross domestic product.

countries, there are fast-growing private enterprises already valued at more than US$1 billion (also known as "unicorns"), such as in China (for example, Alibaba Group's global parcel tracking platform, Cainiao) and Indonesia (for example, ride-hailing service Go-Jek).

The growth in risk finance is uneven across the region, suggesting a role for financial policy

The growth of risk capital finance is uneven across developing East Asian countries (figure 4.12). Chinese companies have raised a relatively high amount of risk capital since 2007, enabling China to lead the world in its number of unicorns as of June 2019.[25] Before the COVID-19 pandemic began, Indonesia and Vietnam also demonstrated upward trends in the amount of capital raised by

enterprises, whereas the growth of risk capital financing in Thailand has been more limited. The amount of risk financing in Malaysia and the Philippines actually declined recently relative to previous years.

Several factors appear to have contributed to these differential growth patterns, including country-specific differences in the ease of starting a business, investor protection, and the insolvency framework (figure 4.13). Indeed, developing East Asian countries appear to lag behind other regions on several of the World Bank's Doing Business indexes,[26] especially in terms of enforcing contracts and resolving insolvency, which may hamper the development of risk finance and, thus, impede firm innovation.

Country-specific conditions, such as investor preferences and government policies, may also help to explain the observed patterns of risk capital financing. Interviews with venture capitalists in the Philippines, Thailand, and Vietnam identified inexperience of investors and scale (fund sizes) as two of the major challenges to investing in these countries (Scheela et al. 2015). Similarly, Nor (2015) reports that lack of funding for venture capital (VC) firms in Malaysia is one of the main reasons why the country has not seen faster growth of risk financing. Because most of Malaysia's funding comes from the government in the form of loans that firms must repay rather than as equity capital, VC investors do not find it profitable to invest in these companies due to low expected returns (Vivekarajah 2018). Besides investor inexperience and the risk profile of the available investment opportunities, the Philippines has faced the additional challenge of uncertainty associated with political instability, which erodes confidence especially for foreign investors and further reduces incentives to invest in high-risk projects (Lopez 2019).

FIGURE 4.12   Growth in risk capital financing has varied considerably across developing East Asia

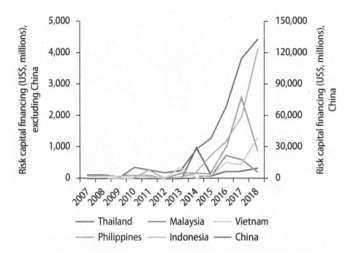

Source: World Bank elaboration, using Crunchbase data (https://www.crunchbase.com/).
Note: The graph reports the amount of risk capital financing (for example, angel, venture, private, or equity crowdfunding) in US$, millions. "Developing East Asia" refers to the 10 middle-income countries covered in this study: Cambodia, China, Indonesia, Lao PDR, Malaysia, Mongolia, Myanmar, the Philippines, Thailand, and Vietnam." The figure excludes Cambodia, Lao PDR, Mongolia, and Myanmar due to lack of data. For all countries except China, the scale is the left y-axis.

Conclusions

The availability of adequately skilled labor and risk-capital finance, while not strictly falling under the purview of innovation policy,

FIGURE 4.13   The factors that affect the attractiveness of venture capital vary by country across the region

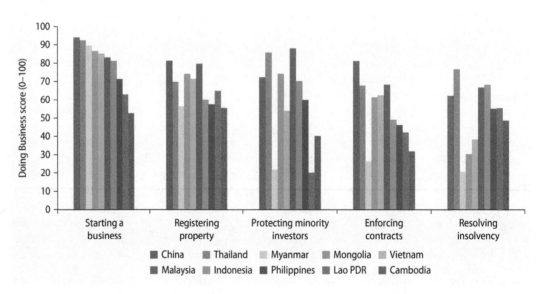

Source: World Bank elaboration from 2020 Doing Business data.
Note: For more detailed explanations of the variables, see the Doing Business website: https://www.doingbusiness.org/en/doingbusiness. A score of 100 indicates the best performance within a specific topic. Lao PDR lacks a "resolving insolvency" score because data on that variable were unavailable.

is critical to enabling innovation at the firm and country levels. Understanding the roles of these complementary factors is particularly important because the countries of developing East Asia face ongoing challenges in developing an adequate skills base as well as sufficiently deep and diverse financial sectors to foster innovation effectively. The specific skills and financing needs and challenges differ by country and depend on whether one is focusing on innovation defined as diffusion and adoption of existing technologies or as invention—the latter requiring more advanced skills and more sophisticated risk financing instruments.

Regarding skills development, several key messages emerge from the analysis in this chapter:

- *Higher-order cognitive, socioemotional, and technical skills* are critical enabling factors for all types of innovation— although these skills become increasingly important as firms move toward the technological frontier.
- *Inadequate provision of foundational skills* remains a fundamental challenge facing most developing East Asian countries. Their national education systems are not providing students with the basic reading, math, and science skills upon which more-advanced skills must be built.
- *A dual challenge for the region's policy makers,* consequently, is that of (a) ensuring that their education systems deliver the necessary foundational skills to their populations, while (b) strengthening the ability of education and training systems to support the types of advanced skills development needed to enable innovation-led growth.
- *Rapidly changing technologies* make confronting this dual challenge all the more urgent because they are quickly ratcheting up the skills needed to innovate, whether defined as diffusion and adoption or invention. The emerging economic and social challenges associated with climate change and the COVID-19 pandemic just add to this urgency.

As for financing innovation, several additional messages emerge:

- *Both the availability and the type of financing* matters for innovation at the firm level. In most of developing East Asia, however, financial sectors remain heavily bank based, having neither the depth nor the breadth to support innovation-led growth.
- *Firm-level financial constraints*—while not as severe in developing East Asia as in other developing regions—do affect firms' decision to innovate, the extent to which they innovate, and the quality of innovation.
- *Diverse sources of finance* can help to enable greater and higher-quality innovation by helping to reduce problems of asymmetric information between the financier and the borrower. Such information asymmetries are more severe for projects that are innovative than for those that are not. Information asymmetries are particularly severe in the context of invention.
- *Continued financial deepening* is needed in developing East Asia to support greater innovation in all its forms. This becomes particularly important as firms and countries move up the "capabilities escalator" from a focus on technological catch-up to innovation at the technological frontier.

Meeting the challenges associated with ensuring adequate skills and financing for innovation in developing East Asia will take concerted public action. Specific directions for policy to strengthen these critical complementary factors are discussed in chapter 6.

Notes

1. A study of the effects of research and development (R&D) expenditures and human capital on innovation behavior in Spain, for example, finds a positive relationship between the share of workers with university degrees and the number of patents that firms produce (Gumbau-Albert and Maudos 2009). Similarly, a study of French industrial firms finds a robust positive relationship between worker training and firm-level patenting activity (Gallié and Legros 2012). An analysis

of Finnish manufacturing firms finds, moreover, that innovative firms with more-educated employees, higher technical skills, and greater research skills are more profitable than non-innovative firms (Leiponen 2000).

2. As discussed in chapter 3, managerial quality is critical to enabling innovation among firms. It increases innovation directly as well as through more efficient use of R&D (Cirera, Maloney, and Sarrias 2020).

3. For a review of the literature on skills for innovation, see Kataoka and Alejo (2019).

4. In addition to the five categories listed in table 4.2, the Organisation for Economic Co-operation and Development (OECD) includes a separate domain of socioemotional skills called "compound skills," which represent a combination of two or more individual skills. One such compound skill is self-efficacy (strongly believing in one's own ability to execute tasks and achieve goals), which represents a combination of conscientiousness, emotional stability, and extraversion (OECD 2017). Bassi et al. (2012) find that greater self-efficacy is associated with better labor market outcomes among workers in South America.

5. Although China's CEES collected data only on manufacturing firms, the 2016 China Urban Labor Survey (CULS), collected in six large Chinese cities, includes many of the same individual-level variables as the CEES, which enables some comparison of how skills demands differ across the manufacturing and services sectors. As with more-innovative manufacturing firms in China, employees in high-skill services sectors tend to be relatively young and well educated. According to the 2016 CULS data, 72 percent of workers in high-skill services sectors are college educated, compared with 42 percent in manufacturing and 26 percent in low-skill services (Park and Xuan 2020). In addition, just over one-third of tertiary graduates in high-skill services firms have STEM degrees, comparable to the share among high-innovation firms surveyed in the CEES and slightly higher than the share in all manufacturing firms surveyed in the CULS.

6. The assessment of cognitive skills in the Vietnam ESIS provides a holistic perspective on literacy, capturing a person's "ability to understand, evaluate, use and engage with written texts to participate in society, to achieve one's goals, and to develop one's knowledge and potential" (OECD 2013, table 2.1). The literacy proficiency levels identified in the assessment, scaled from 0 to 5, characterize individuals' range of cognitive abilities from basic to advanced. Proficiency levels 1 and 2 capture individuals' capacity to retrieve information and apply it in routine and predictable ways, whereas proficiency levels 3 and above capture the capacity to analyze, evaluate, and create new information, which are precursors to fluid problem solving, critical thinking, and creativity. Proficiency level 3 can be considered the minimum proficiency level required for individuals to function autonomously in carrying out nonroutine tasks (Miyamoto and Sarzosa 2020).

7. Park and Xuan (2020) also find that open-mindedness ("openness to experience") is strongly positive and statistically significant at the 5 percent level when controlling for firm-level characteristics. It is no longer significant when controlling for individual characteristics, however. The authors find the same regarding a measure of "risk-seeking" orientation, which can be interpreted as a proxy for entrepreneurial spirit.

8. Analysis of data from Indonesia, Mongolia, the Philippines, and Vietnam further suggests that returns to nonroutine analytical tasks tend to be increasing over time (Macdonald 2018).

9. These findings are from World Bank calculations based on Enterprise Survey data.

10. Similar analysis was carried out for non-innovating firms. A significant share of non-innovating firms also reported skills-related challenges when hiring. In many but not all cases, the reported skills deficits were larger for innovating than for non-innovating firms. Differences in reported skills deficits between innovating and non-innovating firms reflect differences in skills demand across the firm types, which also appear to differ across countries.

11. For more information and the 2018 PISA data, see the PISA website: https://www.oecd.org/pisa/.

12. Data on learning outcomes comparable to PISA are not available outside China's major urban centers. Nevertheless, a recent study carried out jointly by China's Development Research Center and the World Bank highlights continuing learning challenges

faced by students in China's rural areas (World Bank and DRC 2019).

13. PISA data for 2018 are from the PISA website: https://www.oecd.org/pisa/. Although several lower-middle-income countries in the region have not participated in the PISA exams, Early Grade Reading Assessments (EGRAs) in Cambodia, Lao PDR, and Myanmar provide further evidence of the challenges that countries in the region face in building adequate foundational skills among their populations. Results from the 2012 EGRAs in Cambodia and Lao PDR showed, for example, that nearly one-third of second-grade students in those countries could not read a single word (World Bank 2018).

14. Asymmetric information arises when the parties involved in a transaction have different information sets (for example, one party has more accurate information than the other).

15. Stronger disclosure requirements may be beneficial for investors. For example, more stringent disclosure requirements on alternative investment funds (including venture capital and private equity firms) enable a higher supply of capital and business creation (Cumming and Knill 2012).

16. Moral hazard occurs after a contract is signed and a borrower changes behavior—for instance, by taking on more risk than a lender would have envisioned at the time of signing the contract.

17. For a theoretical and quantitative illustration on how financial frictions affect the quality of firm innovation, see Cole, Greenwood, and Sanchez (2016). For empirical evidence, see Ayyagari, Demirgüç-Kunt, and Maksimovic (2011); Gorodnichenko and Schnitzer (2013); and Cao (2020).

18. Financing and investment decisions are closely related, with the available mix of financing affecting a firm's choice of the source of finance.

19. Aghion, Howitt, and Mayer-Foulkes (2005) formulate a theory where the "advantage of backwardness" argued by Gerschenkron (1952)—that is, the advantage to technologically lagging countries of adopting frontier technology developed elsewhere—is not fully exploited because of financial constraints.

20. The statement applies to formal sources of finance. There is limited theory and evidence on the role of financing received from family, friends, and nonfinancial entities.

21. For a detailed explanation of how different sources of finance address diverse market frictions in different manners, see Mare, de Nicola, and Liriano (forthcoming) and the references therein.

22. Abraham, Cortina, and Schmukler (2019) document a growth in capital market financing in East Asia Pacific since the early 2000s. The authors note, however, that capital market access is still limited to a relatively small share of large corporations.

23. Fixed assets represent long-term investments of firms; such assets can proxy for investment in innovation, because innovative characteristics could be incorporated in new capital equipment, for example.

24. A key factor enabling risk finance for innovation projects is the possibility that investors can liquidate their investments when conditions are favorable. Such liquidation is possible where capital markets are well developed. In such settings, private equity investors can liquidate their investment in an innovative firm in one of several ways: (a) the firm can be acquired by another firm; (b) it can be sold to another investor or bought by those in the firm itself; (c) it can go public via an initial public offering (IPO); or (d) in the worst-case scenario, if the firm defaults, the private equity investor can file for bankruptcy.

25. See the Hurun Research Institute's Global Unicorn List 2019, which ranks the world's billion-dollar tech start-ups founded in the 2000s and not yet listed on a public exchange: http://www.hurun.net.

26. For more information on these indexes, including more detailed explanations of the variables, see the World Bank's Doing Business website: https://www.doingbusiness.org/en/doingbusiness.

References

Abraham, Facundo, Juan J. Cortina, and Sergio L. Schmukler. 2019. "The Rise of Domestic Capital Markets for Corporate Financing." Policy Research Working Paper 8844, World Bank, Washington, DC.

Acemoglu, Daron, Philippe Aghion, and Fabrizio Zilibotti. 2006. "Distance to Frontier, Selection, and Economic Growth." *Journal of the European Economic Association* 4 (1): 37–74.

Acemoglu, Daron, and Pascual Restrepo. 2017. "Robots and Jobs: Evidence from US Labor Markets." NBER Working Paper No. 23285, National Bureau of Economic Research, Cambridge, MA.

ADB (Asian Development Bank). 2020. *Asian Development Outlook 2020: What Drives Innovation in Asia?* Semiannual report, April 2020. Manila: ADB.

Aghion, Philippe, Antonin Bergeaud, Richard Blundell, and Rachel Griffith. 2019. "The Innovation Premium to Soft Skills in Low-Skilled Occupations." Discussion Paper No. 1665, Centre for Economic Performance, London School of Economics.

Aghion, Philippe, Peter Howitt, and David Mayer-Foulkes. 2005. "The Effect of Financial Development on Convergence: Theory and Evidence." *Quarterly Journal of Economics* 120 (1): 173–222.

Autor, David H., David Dorn, and Gordon H. Hanson. 2015. "Untangling Trade and Technology: Evidence from Local Labor Markets." *Economic Journal* 125 (584): 621–46.

Avvisati, Francesco, Gwenaël Jacotin, and Stéphan Vincent-Lancrin. 2013. "Educating Higher Education Students for Innovative Economies: What International Data Tell Us." *Tuning Journal for Higher Education* 1 (1): 223–40.

Ayyagari, Meghana, Asli Demirgüç-Kunt, and Vojislav Maksimovic. 2011. "Firm Innovation in Emerging Markets: The Role of Finance, Governance, and Competition." *Journal of Financial and Quantitative Analysis* 46 (6): 1545–80. doi:10.1017/S0022109011000378.

Bassi, Marina, Matías Busso, Sergio Urzúa, and Jaime Vargas. 2012. *Disconnected: Skills, Education and Employment in Latin America.* Washington, DC: Inter-American Development Bank.

Beck, Thorsten, Ross Levine, and Norman Loayza. 2000. "Finance and the Sources of Growth." *Journal of Financial Economics* 58 (1–2): 261–300.

Berger, Allen N., Phil Molyneux, and John O. S. Wilson. 2020. "Banks and the Real Economy: An Assessment of the Research." *Journal of Corporate Finance* 62: 101513.

Bodewig, Christian, Reena Badiani-Magnusson, with Kevin Macdonald, David Newhouse, and Jan Rutkowski. 2014. *Skilling Up Vietnam: Preparing the Workforce for a Modern Market Economy.* Directions in Development Series. Washington, DC: World Bank.

Brown, James R., Steven M. Fazzari, and Bruce C. Petersen. 2009. "Financing Innovation and Growth: Cash Flow, External Equity, and the 1990s R&D Boom." *Journal of Finance* 64 (1): 151–85.

Bughin, Jacques, Eric Hazan, Susan Lund, Peter Dahlström, Anna Wiesinger, and Amresh Subramaniam. 2018. "Skill Shift: Automation and the Future of the Workforce." Discussion paper, McKinsey Global Institute, McKinsey & Co., New York.

Cao, Yu. 2020. "Financial Constraints, Innovation Quality, and Growth." Doctoral dissertation, University of Southern California, Los Angeles.

Chen, Su-Chang, Ming-Chung Wu, and Chun-Hung Chen. 2010. "Employee's Personality Traits, Work Motivation and Innovative Behavior in Marine Tourism Industry." *Journal of Service Science and Management* 3 (2): 198–205.

Cirera, Xavier, and William F. Maloney. 2017. *The Innovation Paradox: Developing-Country Capabilities and the Unrealized Promise of Technological Catch-Up.* Washington, DC: World Bank.

Cirera, Xavier, William F. Maloney, and Mauricio Sarrias. 2020. "Management Quality as an Input for Innovation." Unpublished, World Bank, Washington, DC.

Cirera, Xavier, and Leonard Sabetti. 2019. "The Effects of Innovation on Employment in Developing Countries: Evidence from Enterprise Surveys." *Industrial and Corporate Change* 28 (1): 1–16.

Cirera, Xavier, and Antonio Soares Martins-Neto. 2020. "Do Innovative Firms Pay Higher Wages? Micro-Level Evidence from Brazil." Policy Research Working Paper 9442, World Bank, Washington, DC.

Cole, Harold L., Jeremy Greenwood, and Juan M. Sanchez. 2016. "Why Doesn't Technology Flow from Rich to Poor Countries?" *Econometrica* 84 (4): 1477–1521.

Crespi, Gustavo, Ezequiel Tacsir, and Mariano Pereira. 2019. "Effects of Innovation on Employment in Latin America." *Industrial and Corporate Change* 28 (1): 139–59.

Cumming, Douglas, and April Knill. 2012. "Disclosure, Venture Capital and Entrepreneurial Spawning." *Journal of International Business Studies* 43 (6): 563–90.

Cusolito, Ana Paula, Daniel Lederman, and Jorge Peña. 2020. "The Effects of Digital-Technology Adoption on Productivity and Factor Demand: Firm-Level Evidence from Developing

Countries." Policy Research Working Paper 9333, World Bank, Washington, DC.

Czarnitzki, Dirk, and Hanna Hottenrott. 2011. "R&D Investment and Financing Constraints of Small and Medium-Sized Firms." *Small Business Economics* 36 (1): 65–83.

Das, Mitali, and Benjamin Hilgenstock. 2018. "The Exposure to Routinization: Labor Market Implications for Developed and Developing Economies." Working Paper No. 18/135, International Monetary Fund, Washington, DC.

Deming, David, and Lisa B. Khan. 2018. "Skill Requirements Across Firms and Labor Markets: Evidence from Job Postings for Professionals." *Journal of Labor Economics* 36 (S1): S337–S369.

de Nicola, Francesca. 2019. "Assessing How Returns to Innovation Vary Depending on the Business Environment and Firms' Characteristics." Background paper for this study, World Bank, Washington, DC.

Doran, Justin, and Geraldine Ryan. 2014. "Firms' Skills as Drivers of Radical and Incremental Innovation." *Economics Letters* 125 (1): 107–09.

Du, Yang, and Albert Park. 2017. "Changing Demand for Tasks and Skills in China." Unpublished manuscript, Chinese Academy of Social Science, Beijing, and Hong Kong University of Science and Technology.

Dutz, Mark A., Rita K. Almeida, and Truman G. Packard. 2018. *The Jobs of Tomorrow: Technology, Productivity, and Prosperity in Latin America and the Caribbean.* Directions in Development Series. Washington, DC: World Bank.

Engen, Marit, and Inger Elisabeth Holen. 2014. "Radical versus Incremental Innovation: The Importance of Key Competences in Service Firms." *Technology Innovation Management Review* 4 (4): 15–25.

Gallié, Emilie-Pauline, and Diègo Legros. 2012. "Firms' Human Capital, R&D and Innovation: A Study on French Firms." *Empirical Economics* 43 (2): 581–96.

Gerschenkron, Alexander. 1952. "Economic Backwardness in Historical Perspective." In *The Progress of Underdeveloped Areas*, edited by Bert F. Hoselitz. Chicago: University of Chicago Press.

Gorodnichenko, Yuriy, and Monika Schnitzer. 2013. "Financial Constraints and Innovation: Why Poor Countries Don't Catch Up." *Journal of the European Economic Association* 11 (5): 1115–52.

Graetz, Georg, and Guy Michaels. 2018. "Robots at Work." *Review of Economics and Statistics* 100 (5): 753–68.

Green, Lawrence, Barbara Jones, and Ian Miles. 2007. "Mini Study 02 – Skills for Innovation." Paper for the INNO-Grips (Global Review of Innovation Intelligence and Policy Studies) INNO-Views Policy Workshop, "Skills for Innovation: Fostering Skills to Improve European Innovation Performance," Glasgow, September 27–28.

Gumbau-Albert, Mercedes, and Joaquin Maudos. 2009. "Patents, Technological Inputs and Spillovers among Regions." *Applied Economics* 41 (12): 1473–86.

Hall, Bronwyn H., and Josh Lerner. 2010. "The Financing of R&D and Innovation." In *Handbook of the Economics of Innovation*, vol. 2, edited by Bronwyn H. Hall and Nathan Rosenberg, 609–39. Amsterdam: Elsevier.

Harrison, Rupert, Jordi Jaumandreu, Jacques Mairesse, and Bettina Peters. 2014. "Does Innovation Stimulate Employment? A Firm-Level Analysis Using Comparable Micro-Data from Four European Countries." *International Journal of Industrial Organization* 35: 29–43.

Hottenrott, Hanna, and Bettina Peters. 2012. "Innovative Capability and Financing Constraints for Innovation: More Money, More Innovation?" *Review of Economics and Statistics* 94 (4): 1126–42.

Hsieh, Hsiow-Ling, Jia-Ru Hsieh, and I-Ling Wang. 2011. "Linking Personality and Innovation: The Role of Knowledge Management." *World Transactions on Engineering and Technology Education* 9 (1): 38–44.

Hsu, Po-Hsuan, Xuan Tian, and Yan Xu. 2014. "Financial Development and Innovation: Cross-Country Evidence." *Journal of Financial Economics* 112 (1): 116–35.

Kataoka, Sachiko, and Ana Alejo. 2019. "Skills for Innovation." Background paper for this report, World Bank, Manila, Philippines.

Kato, Masatoshi, Hiroyuki Okamuro, and Yuji Honjo. 2015. "Does Founders' Human Capital Matter for Innovation? Evidence from Japanese Start-Ups." *Journal of Small Business Management* 53 (1): 114–28.

Lachenmaier, Stefan, and Horst Rottmann. 2011. "Effects of Innovation on Employment: A Dynamic Panel Analysis." *International Journal of Industrial Organization* 29 (2): 210–20.

Leiponen, Ada. 2000. "Competencies, Innovation and Profitability of Firms." *Economics of Innovation and New Technology* 9 (1): 1–24.

Levine, Ross. 2005. "Finance and Growth: Theory and Evidence." In *Handbook of Economic Growth*, vol. 1A, edited by Philippe Aghion and Steven N. Durlauf, 865–934. Amsterdam: North-Holland Elsevier.

Lopez, Elyssa. 2019. "No Country for Unicorns: Why Philippine Start-Ups Are Struggling." *South China Morning Post*, September 16. https://www.scmp.com/week-asia/economics/article/3027171/no-country-unicorns-why-philippine-start-ups-are-struggling.

Macdonald, Kevin. 2018. "Task Composition Globally and their Returns in Select East Asian Countries." Background paper for *A Resurgent East Asia: Navigating a Changing World*. Washington, DC: World Bank.

Macdonald. 2019. "How Do Innovating Employers' Value and Use of Skills Differ from Non-Innovating Employers in Vietnam?" Background paper for this study, World Bank, Washington, DC.

Maloney, William F., and Carlos Molina. 2016. "Are Automation and Trade Polarizing Developing Country Labor Markets, Too?" Policy Research Working Paper 7922, World Bank, Washington, DC.

Maloney, William F., and Mauricio Sarrias. 2017. "Convergence to the Managerial Frontier." *Journal of Economic Behavior & Organization* 134: 284–306.

Mare, Davide S., Francesca de Nicola, and Faruk Miguel Liriano. Forthcoming. "Financial Structure and Firm Innovation: Cross-Country Evidence." Policy Research Working Paper, World Bank, Washington, DC.

Mason, Andrew D., Vera Kehayova, and Judy Yang. 2018. "Trade, Technology, Skills and Jobs: Exploring the Road Ahead for Developing East Asia." Background paper for *A Resurgent East Asia: Navigating a Changing World*. Washington, DC: World Bank.

Mason, Andrew D., and Sudhir Shetty. 2019. *A Resurgent East Asia: Navigating a Changing World*. East Asia and Pacific Regional Report. Washington, DC: World Bank.

Miyamoto, Koji, and Miguel Sarzosa. 2020. "Workforce Skills and Firm Innovation: Evidence from an Employer-Employee Linked Survey Data in Vietnam." Unpublished manuscript, World Bank, Washington, D.C.

Nor, Eliza. 2015. "Venture Capitalists in Malaysia: Challenges and Future Directions." *Journal of Business and Management Sciences* 3 (4):124–29.

OECD (Organisation for Economic Co-operation and Development). 2011. *Skills for Innovation and Research*. Paris: OECD Publishing.

OECD (Organisation for Economic Co-operation and Development). 2013. *OECD Skills Outlook 2013: First Results from the Survey of Adult Skills*. Paris: OECD Publishing.

OECD (Organisation for Economic Co-operation and Development). 2016. *Innovating Education and Educating for Innovation: The Power of Digital Technologies and Skills*. Paris: OECD Publishing. doi:10.1787/9789264265097.

OECD (Organisation for Economic Co-operation and Development). 2017. "Social and Emotional Skills: Well-Being, Connectedness and Success." Report on the Study on Social and Emotional Skills, OECD, Paris.

OECD and Eurostat (Organisation for Economic Co-operation and Development and the statistical office of the European Union). 2005. *Oslo Manual: Guidelines for Collecting and Interpreting Innovation*. 3rd ed. Paris: OECD; Luxembourg: Eurostat.

Park, Albert, and Wenshi Xuan. 2020. "Skills for Innovation in China." Background paper for this report, Hong Kong University of Science and Technology, Hong Kong SAR, China.

Piva, Mariacristina, and Marco Vivarelli. 2005. "Innovation and Employment: Evidence from Italian Microdata." *Journal of Economics* 86 (1): 65–83.

Poole, Jennifer P., Amelia U. Santos-Paulino, Maria V. Sokolova, and Alisa DiCaprio. 2017. "The Impact of Trade and Technology on Skills in Viet Nam." Working Paper No. 770, Asian Development Bank Institute, Tokyo.

Scheela, William, Edmundo Isidro, Thawatchai Jittrapanun, and Nguyen Thi Thu Trang. 2015. "Formal and Informal Venture Capital Investing in Emerging Economies in Southeast Asia." *Asia Pacific Journal of Management* 32 (3): 597–617.

Toner, Phillip. 2011. "Workforce Skills and Innovation: An Overview of Major Themes in the Literature." Science, Technology and Industry (STI) Working Paper, Organisation for Economic Co-operation and Development, Paris.

Vivekarajah, Sivapalan. 2018. "What Ails Venture Capital in Malaysia and Why Consolidation Is Not the Answer." Digital News Asia, October 9. https://www.digitalnewsasia.com/insights/what-ails-venture-capital-malaysia-and-why-consolidation-not-answer.

World Bank. 2012. *Putting Higher Education to Work: Skills and Research for Growth in East Asia.* East Asia and Pacific Regional Report. Washington, DC: World Bank.

World Bank. 2016. *World Development Report 2016: Digital Dividends.* Washington, DC: World Bank.

World Bank. 2018. *Growing Smarter: Learning and Equitable Development in East Asia and Pacific.* East Asia and Pacific Regional Report. Washington, DC: World Bank.

World Bank. 2020. "PISA 2018: East Asia and Pacific Regional Brief." Unpublished manuscript, Education Global Practice, World Bank, Washington, DC.

World Bank and DRC (Development Research Center of the State Council, The People's Republic of China). 2019. *Innovative China: New Drivers of Growth.* Washington, DC: World Bank.

Innovation Policies and Institutions in the Region: An Assessment | 5

Introduction

This chapter assesses the adequacy of policies and institutions in addressing the constraints firms face regarding diffusion, technology adoption, and invention in developing East Asia. It pays special attention to the effectiveness of knowledge creation and its transfer to firms as well as the adequacy of countries' institutions and policies in facilitating this transfer and generating innovation. The chapter first identifies the gaps in the policy mix that support innovation in the region and highlights the key principles to improve the efficiency and effectiveness of implementing agencies. It then evaluates the public research institutions that aim to facilitate innovation and knowledge transfer.

As described in chapter 2, innovation policy must use multiple policy instruments simultaneously to address the market failures that discourage innovation (Cirera et al. 2020). This introduces some complexity in its design because of complementarities that exist across policy instruments. It also raises the premium associated with identifying and prioritizing those policies that are most effective in enabling innovation and facilitating diffusion. For firms to reach the technological frontier, policies and institutions must focus on building the capabilities of the private sector and forging effective linkages between different actors in the innovation system. This requires adequate capacity on the part of public agencies to implement such policies—capacity that is often limited due to scarce human and financial resources.

Policy makers should follow several steps when thinking about innovation and technology policies. First, the policy mix should effectively address the constraints on the private sector's ability to build innovation capabilities. Second, it is essential to implement robust policy-making processes, using good practices in public management. Just as for firms, good quality management practices also matter for public policy (Rasul and Rogger 2017). Third, innovation agencies should have the incentives and governance structures to perform good diagnostics of the main market failures that constrain innovation and diffusion, as well as the resources to deliver effective policies. And policy makers need to understand not only the market failures but also the risks of government failure when innovation policies are not well designed and implemented, or when institutional fragmentation and lack of coordination result in undesired program overlaps, inefficiencies, or mistargeting of beneficiaries. This chapter examines each of these elements.

The central actors of the national innovation system (NIS) include institutions such as universities and public research organizations (PROs), whose main role is to generate knowledge that can become an innovation when brought to the market or implemented in society. In more mature innovation systems, the flow or transfer of knowledge from these knowledge-creating institutions to firms is fluid. However, in many low- and middle-income economies, the diffusion of knowledge to firms is often limited by the lack of adequate policies to support commercial research as well as the lack of well-functioning industry-research linkages, resulting in low innovative activity and little technology transfer. Often, these knowledge institutions neither facilitate diffusion nor perform their mission of finding the technological solutions needed to address key societal challenges, such as COVID-19 or climate change.

Understanding the quality and strengths of these knowledge institutions, along with their governance structures, is critical to maximizing their contributions to innovation. The chapter discusses these issues using the results of new surveys implemented to assess the quality of these institutions in three countries in developing East Asia: Malaysia, the Philippines, and Vietnam (Cirera, Kuriakose, and Zuñiga 2021).

Are policies coherent with the objective of supporting diffusion as well as invention?

A key characteristic of innovation policies in many low- and middle-income countries is fragmentation, with little coordination, resulting in unnecessary overlaps in interventions. Also, paradoxically, the use of public resources is often determined by research and development (R&D) considerations, focusing on instruments that do not necessarily support more basic innovation projects (such as quality upgrading or the adoption of new technologies) that would benefit most firms. Rather, large amounts of resources are focused on supporting R&D projects carried out by PROs or through tax incentives benefiting firms already doing R&D.

Therefore, a key question is whether the combination of policies supporting innovation is adequate to building the basic innovation capabilities that most firms require. Or, rather, are policies biased toward higher-end R&D projects that benefit a much narrower set of enterprises? As discussed in chapters 2 and 3, given innovation capabilities, policies and public resources in developing East Asia should focus more on diffusion and adoption than on invention.

Importance of good practices in policy design and implementation

Another key issue for innovation policy, in addition to policy mix, is the quality of policy design and implementation. Cirera and Maloney (2017) describe the need for innovation policies to respond to clearly identified innovation problems and market failures. Doing so requires the adoption of good practices in public management, monitoring, and evaluation. When governments lack the capacities to design and implement sound innovation policies, the risks of policy capture, inefficiency, and ineffectiveness escalate—potentially creating policy distortions that can undermine innovation. As a result, it is important that countries in developing East Asia invest in the adoption of these good practices to maximize the impact of their policies.

This section discusses the policy mixes used to support innovation and technology adoption in three countries in the region based on novel data collected by World Bank policy effectiveness reviews (PERs) in Indonesia, the Philippines, and Vietnam. PERs collect data at the national level on policy instruments, including information on objectives, beneficiary types, and budgets.[1] These data enable a granular characterization of countries' policy mixes, and although the ultimate effectiveness of individual policy instruments can only be determined via rigorous impact evaluations, these reviews facilitate a detailed qualitative assessment of the extent to which resources are being directed toward areas where previous analysis suggests they can have the greatest impact. (See box 5.1 for a detailed description of the methodology.)

BOX 5.1   Policy effectiveness reviews in developing East Asia

The World Bank has implemented policy effectiveness reviews (PERs) on science, technology, and innovation (STI) in several countries in Latin America (Argentina, Brazil, Chile, and Colombia) and developing East Asia (Indonesia, the Philippines, and Vietnam, and currently in Malaysia). The goals of the PERs are (a) to assess whether the government's allocation of resources has an impact on STI outcomes, and (b) to support policy makers in increasing their capacity for, and the quality of, their STI policies.

PERs include an analysis of the quality of the policy mix and a functional review (assessment of the quality of design, implementation, and governance of the different innovation policy instruments). Specifically, they answer the following questions:

- How much is being spent on STI policy? For what? And by whom?
- How coherent is the policy mix with the country's greatest innovation challenges?
- How well does this spending align with the country's strategic aspirations?
- What are the opportunities to improve the capacity and coordination of implementing agencies?

Quality of the policy mix

The analysis of the policy mix relies on examining the patterns of public spending on STI and the way resources get allocated. This component provides the basis for analysis of policy coherence and consistency. PERs focus on the policy "instrument" as the unit of analysis. An instrument is a mechanism or intervention by which the government uses public expenditures, laws, or regulations to achieve specific objectives. Examples of an innovation policy instrument include credit guarantees for innovation projects or tax incentives for R&D.

PERs start with a policy mapping exercise, collecting data to map the portfolio of innovation-supporting policy instruments. This provides the basis for generating descriptive analytics and for profiling the portfolio of interventions that provides support to firms for innovation.

Functional review

A functional review is the second part of a PER, which assesses specific policy instruments for the use of good practices in design, implementation, and coordination. The functional review provides the analytical foundation to make recommendations to strengthen the design, delivery, and effectiveness of policy instruments under implementation as well as to inform the design of new instruments. Based on models of good public management, the analysis assesses whether good practices are implemented in key elements of policy making, such as the following:

- The market failure is identified, and it justifies design and intervention.
- The policy instrument is originated by a sound identification of a problem, and it is not ad hoc.
- The policy instrument features clearly identified objectives that are measurable.
- The policy instrument has an explicit and realistic logical framework.
- The selection of beneficiaries is appropriate.
- The policy instrument builds upon sufficient human, financial, and organizational resources, and it features good managerial practices.
- The choice of instrument is evidence based, and consideration of costs and alternatives is well documented.
- The policy instrument employs monitoring and evaluation (M&E) frameworks, with sound indicators and good measurement. Consideration of impact evaluation is well documented.
- There is a formal system to adopt lessons and learning to make the policy instrument more efficient over time.

The methodology of the functional review involves using semistructured interviews for a sample of policy instruments previously identified to evaluate the quality of design, implementation, coordination among instruments and among institutions, and their relation to international best practices. A scoring matrix assigns values to instruments from 1 to 5 based on best practices, with 1 being the lowest score and 5 the highest. Scores are based on a previously developed matrix of good practices.

Assessing the innovation policy mix

A first step in analyzing the quality of the different policy mixes in Indonesia, the Philippines, and Vietnam involves mapping all of the relevant policy instruments (as described in box 5.1). This requires combining data from secondary sources, including budget reports and specialized documents from key government agencies. Expenditure data used in the mapping exercise include both budget expenses and forgone revenue from tax incentives. The data on public spending underestimate total expenditure on innovation, as they exclude block funding to PROs and other institutions. The data also exclude regulatory instruments that support innovation but do not receive budgetary funding, such as regulatory measures for equity investments for start-ups.

The scope of the analysis includes policy instruments that use public expenditure and whose resources are usually competitively allocated—covering instruments that extend credit to firms; offer tax incentives to firms that invest in innovation; and deliver direct support in the form of grants, technical assistance, and other services.

Innovation policies in developing East Asia tend to be fragmented, with budget allocations concentrated on a few instruments, some of which focus on large R&D projects

The policy portfolio analyzed in Indonesia, the Philippines, and Vietnam includes 146, 70, and 127 policy instruments, respectively, with corresponding total expenditures of approximately US$1.12 billion, US$455 million, and US$1.16 billion (table 5.1).

The relatively small number of instruments and total expenditures for the Philippines is partly due to the government's interest in instruments that support small and medium enterprises (SMEs), which may drive some of the differences with the other two countries discussed below. Vietnam's median expenditure on policy instruments is significantly lower than in the other two countries, but its total portfolio is the largest because of the high value of its top two tax incentive programs.

Analyzing the policy mixes in Indonesia, the Philippines, and Vietnam reveals a lack of coherence in how resources are allocated, especially relative to the objectives outlined in the countries' innovation strategies. These strategies emphasize outcomes such as greater innovation activity and faster productivity and employment growth. However, the resources to support innovation are highly concentrated in a few programs that largely support research, as follows (figure 5.1):[2]

- *Vietnam's strategy* emphasizes innovation activity and productivity growth, but resources are highly concentrated in programs dedicated to supporting R&D-based innovation in firms via foreign direct investment (FDI) spillovers. The 10 largest policy instruments in terms of spending account

TABLE 5.1 **Policy effectiveness reviews in Indonesia, the Philippines, and Vietnam assess the portfolio of innovation policy instruments and related spending**

Country	Policy instruments (number)	Total portfolio (US$, millions)	Policy instrument level of expenditure (US$, thousands)			
			Minimum	Average	Median	Maximum
Indonesia	146	1,129	12	7,735	289	959,476
Indonesia (excluding top policy instrument)	145	170	12	1,172	287	52,473
Philippines	70	456	8	6,507	788	72,257
Vietnam	127	1,155	1	9,097	52	939,605
Vietnam (excluding top two policy instruments)	125	71	1	567	52	11,384

Source: World Bank elaboration based on country-level policy effectiveness reviews.
Note: Expenditure data are from 2018 for Indonesia and from 2017 for the Philippines and Vietnam.

FIGURE 5.1 **Despite numerous innovation policy instruments in Indonesia, the Philippines, and Vietnam, public spending concentrates on only a few**

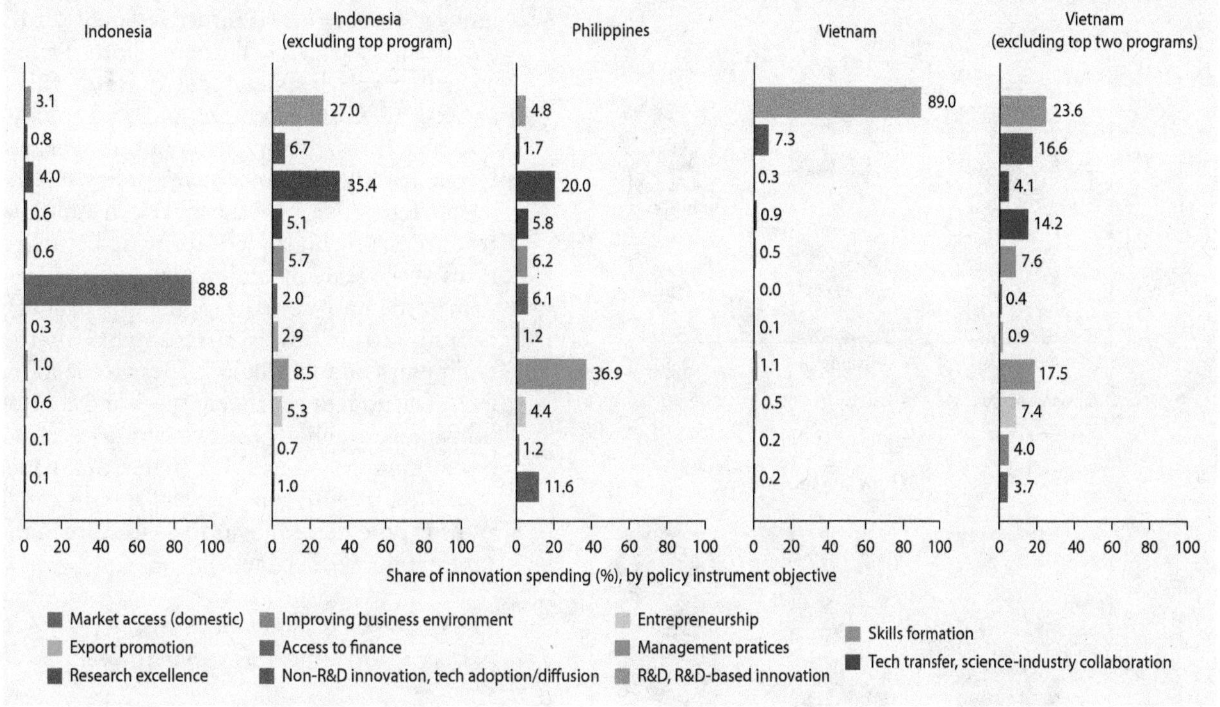

Indonesia: 3.1, 0.8, 4.0, 0.6, 0.6, 88.8, 0.3, 1.0, 0.6, 0.1, 0.1

Indonesia (excluding top program): 27.0, 6.7, 35.4, 5.1, 5.7, 2.0, 2.9, 8.5, 5.3, 0.7, 1.0

Philippines: 4.8, 1.7, 20.0, 5.8, 6.2, 6.1, 1.2, 36.9, 4.4, 1.2, 11.6

Vietnam: 89.0, 7.3, 0.3, 0.9, 0.5, 0.0, 0.1, 1.1, 0.5, 0.2, 0.2

Vietnam (excluding top two programs): 23.6, 16.6, 4.1, 14.2, 7.6, 0.4, 0.9, 17.5, 7.4, 4.0, 3.7

Share of innovation spending (%), by policy instrument objective

Legend:
- Market access (domestic)
- Improving business environment
- Entrepreneurship
- Skills formation
- Export promotion
- Access to finance
- Management pratices
- Research excellence
- Non-R&D innovation, tech adoption/diffusion
- R&D, R&D-based innovation
- Tech transfer, science-industry collaboration

Source: World Bank elaboration based on country-level policy effectiveness reviews.
Note: Spending percentages refer to the allocation of resources either directly (via subsidies or technical assistance) or indirectly (via forgone revenue to beneficiaries that can be firms, research organizations, or entrepreneurs). The percentages exclude direct funding to public research organizations (PROs) and universities. R&D = research and development.

for 97 percent of the total portfolio; and if two large policy instruments that provide tax exemptions for high-tech enterprises are excluded, R&D still accounts for 24 percent of total spending and the largest single share of all instruments.
- *The Philippines' strategy* emphasizes the growth of micro, small, and medium enterprises (MSMEs) and employment, but a large share of policy resources is devoted to skills formation and research excellence.
- *Indonesia's strategy* emphasizes a mix of the two other countries' objectives, but the top 10 policy instruments, which account for 93 percent of the total portfolio, are largely devoted to an interest subsidy for MSMEs (whose total expenditure is

almost six times that of the rest of the policy instruments combined) and research excellence.

Importantly, few resources are allocated in any of the three countries to technology diffusion, adoption, or non-R&D-related efforts to build firms' capabilities (figure 5.1). Similarly, relatively little funding is allocated toward technology transfer, entrepreneurship or improving market access, especially for export promotion. As discussed in chapter 3, most firms in these countries are a significant distance from the technology frontier and could most efficiently increase innovation by adopting existing technology from more advanced countries.

FIGURE 5.2 **The distribution of public resources for innovation, by firm type, varies considerably across Indonesia, the Philippines, and Vietnam**

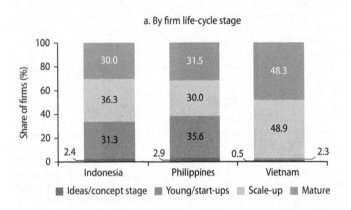

a. By firm life-cycle stage

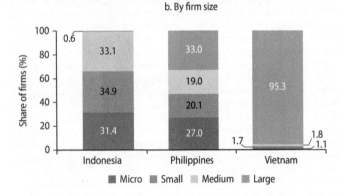

b. By firm size

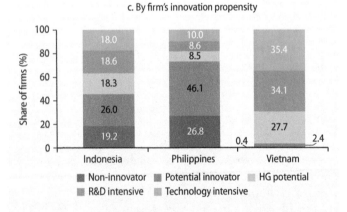

c. By firm's innovation propensity

Source: World Bank elaboration based on country-level policy effectiveness reviews.
Note: Graphs show the percentage of innovation policy instruments that target each category in the three countries. HG = high growth; R&D = research and development.

The three selected countries target innovative firms and beneficiaries very differently

The distribution of resources by firm size and innovation potential is rather different across countries (figure 5.2). Vietnam's portfolio has a distinctively heavier focus on large firms as well as R&D-intensive and technology-intensive firms, driven partly but not entirely by the top two tax incentives policy instruments (figure 5.2, panels b and c). In addition, resources are highly concentrated toward firms at the scale-up and mature stages rather than at the start-up stage (figure 5.2, panel a).

Innovation policy instruments in the Philippines and Indonesia appear to be more inclusive, targeting different types and sizes of firms more evenly. These two countries spend more resources on MSMEs (figure 5.2, panel b) and on incentivizing the less-sophisticated firms ("potential innovators") to start innovating (figure 5.2, panel c).

The countries also exhibit a strong policy bias against supporting innovation in services

One interesting element is the bias against firm beneficiaries in the services sectors. Figure 5.3 shows the allocation of resources between policy instruments that target ex ante (as objectives of the program) firms in services sectors and those that do not include firms in services as potential beneficiaries. The results are striking, showing a large bias of innovation policies toward manufacturing firms. This strong bias ignores the innovation activities among firms in the services sector and that innovation in services (including "servicification," as discussed in chapter 2) is an increasingly important part of innovation and adoption of technologies in manufacturing.

Analyzing innovation policy coherence

The coherence of a particular *policy mix* can be analyzed along two dimensions: internal and external coherence. Internal coherence refers to avoiding overlaps and ensuring that the scale of policy instruments is sufficient to achieve the expected results.

External coherence refers to the extent to which the main policy instruments aim to address the key challenges and market failures faced by the private sector with a view to minimizing gaps in key areas of support. Assessing the coherence of existing policy instruments provides important information about the alignment (or lack thereof) of existing policies, highlighting some potential risks to their effectiveness.

Fragmentation of policy instruments often results in the lack of scale for large impact
One problem related to excessive fragmentation is the lack of meaningful scale of policy instruments to achieve significant impact. For example, a policy instrument in one of the countries analyzed aimed to increase productivity in a sector by 6 percent, but it was supporting only small innovative projects in seven firms in that sector. There was clearly a mismatch between the objective and the instrument: because the instrument supported less than 1 percent of all firms in the sector, extremely large productivity gains would have been needed to diffuse across the majority of supported firms to have a measurable impact on sector productivity. In addition, resources allocated to the instrument were too small in scale to achieve any meaningful impact.

Overall, policy instruments are relatively larger in the Philippines and thus present less of a scale problem. Nevertheless, the lack of scale appears to be an issue for at least some policy instruments in all three countries. In the Philippines, there are 10 policy instruments (around 14 percent of instruments) and in Indonesia, 27 policy instruments (about 19 percent), with annual budgetary resources of less than US$100,000—an amount that could support very few beneficiaries (figure 5.4). In Vietnam, there are 70 such policy instruments, representing more than half of all policy instruments in the portfolio. At face value, these policy instruments operate at a very low scale, raising questions about whether they have a viable minimum scale and, if not, whether they should either be merged with similar programs or discontinued.

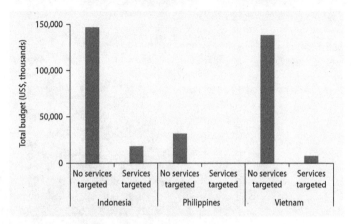

FIGURE 5.3 **Indonesia, the Philippines, and Vietnam allocate few, if any, public resources to innovation policy instruments whose potential beneficiaries include firms in services sectors**

Source: World Bank elaboration based on country-level policy effectiveness reviews.
Note: The budget allocations shown include those made directly (through grants, subsidies, or technical assistance) or indirectly (through tax incentives) for innovation policy instruments targeting two beneficiary groups: those instruments that exclude services firms as potential beneficiaries ("No services targeted") and those that include services firms ("Services targeted").

There are important overlaps in policy instruments across agencies in the region
Duplication of innovation instruments across agencies can lead to further inefficiencies in countries' national innovation systems. Table 5.2 shows the incidence of innovation policy instruments that overlap in scope in each country—with respect to objectives, target beneficiaries, and support mechanisms.

In all countries, a nonnegligible share of policy instruments have an identical scope with at least one other policy instrument. The incidence of overlap appears particularly high in Indonesia, with 80 such policy instruments (more than half of the current portfolio) having similar objectives. In one instance, 14 policy instruments run by a single agency pursue the same objective of improving research quality through provision of research infrastructure to researchers and other government agencies.

Assessing the quality of policy design and implementation

For innovation policies to be effective, the quality of policy design and implementation is critical. Although empirical evidence on the impact of policy design and implementation is scarce, the literature is starting to evaluate how

FIGURE 5.4 **In all three studied countries, numerous innovation policy instruments have expenditures below US$100,000, indicating a potential lack of scale for significant impact**

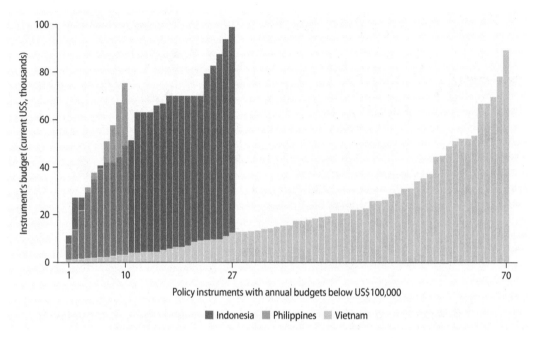

Source: World Bank elaboration based on country-level policy effectiveness reviews.
Note: The figure ranks each country's innovation policy instruments with budgets below US$100,000, from lowest to highest budget.

TABLE 5.2 **In all three countries, a significant share of innovation policy instruments have overlapping scope**

Country	Policy instruments for which at least one other instrument has an identical objective (number)	Share of policy instruments for which at least one other instrument has an identical objective (%)
Indonesia	80	55
Philippines	13	19
Vietnam	43	34

Source: World Bank elaboration based on country-level policy effectiveness reviews.
Note: Scope is defined as the combination of policy instrument objectives, supporting mechanisms, and target beneficiaries.

robust public management processes affect policy outcomes. In the case of Nigeria, for example, good project management practices affect the quality of the outcomes achieved in infrastructure projects (Rasul and Rogger 2017). However, to date, discussions of innovation and technology policies have commonly ignored these critical issues. This section summarizes the results from an evaluation of the design, implementation, and interinstitutional coordination for selected policy instruments in the Philippines and Vietnam.

This functional review examined key features of functionality for a sample of policy instruments (15 instruments in the Philippines and 13 in Vietnam) based on the quality of design and implementation processes as well as complementarities between instruments within and across government institutions. Scores were assigned to 31 key processes related to policy instrument design, implementation, and governance or coordination. Scores range from 1 (poor practice) to 5 (best practice).

In design, implementation, and governance, innovation policies in the region are far from the public management frontier

The analysis reveals major weaknesses in design and implementation that are prevalent across policy instruments in both countries. Figure 5.5 shows each country's average score for each metric under the three dimensions—design, implementation, and governance or coordination. The average scores for the two countries, across agencies and across dimensions of public policy, are 3.0 and 2.8 for the Philippines and Vietnam, respectively, implying that there is room for substantial improvement in practices and that the implementation

of innovation support policy instruments is still a significant distance from the frontier.

The analysis reveals ample scope to improve policy design and implementation

The most important design shortcomings relate to the lack of adequate economic justification, the absence of a logical framework used to develop the intervention, and a lack of M&E mechanisms for most policy instruments. Often, the origin of policy instruments is not based on well-identified market failures, and the process of introducing new instruments is in some cases ad hoc. The lack of economic justification for the policy

FIGURE 5.5 **Innovation policy instruments in the Philippines and Vietnam remain far from the design, implementation, and governance frontiers**

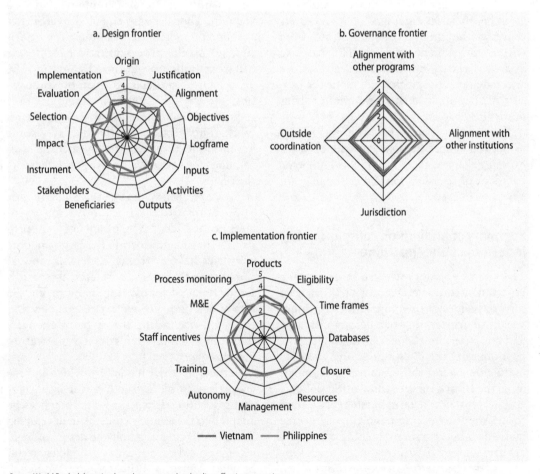

Source: World Bank elaboration based on country-level policy effectiveness reviews.
Note: The radar diagrams show the average score for each dimension between 1 (poor practice) and 5 (best practice). The sample includes 15 and 13 policy instruments in the Philippines and Vietnam, respectively. M&E = monitoring and evaluation.

instruments may result in design problems (poor quality of entry) and, more importantly, in inefficiencies in the choice of instruments to address an identified problem.

In general, the design of most policy instruments is also not based on a logical framework. The objectives tend to be unrealistic—with no clear theory of change from inputs to activities to outputs to impacts—and without due consideration of external conditions that affect impact.

As for implementation, M&E frameworks are generally absent, and lax reporting requirements with discretionary formats prevent systematic collection of information that could provide real-time feedback to improve policy instruments and decisions on future resource allocation. Moreover, data on applications for support and program beneficiaries are fragmented and rarely shared within and across institutions, even within government agencies. There is also a lack of clarity on how beneficiaries are selected in practice, which can make the capture of support by a small number of firms more likely.

Beyond the issues of design and implementation of specific policy instruments, the overall quality of the policy mix is hampered by a lack of coordination across the relevant government agencies.

Summary of findings on coherence of innovation policy instruments

The mix of policies reviewed in developing East Asian countries are not well oriented toward building firms' capabilities for innovation or accelerating technology diffusion and adoption. Assessment of the policy mix in Indonesia, the Philippines, and Vietnam highlights several shortcomings that undermine the effectiveness of innovation policy.

The most important bottlenecks relate to (a) significant fragmentation of policy instruments, with many lacking minimum viable scale; (b) unnecessary overlaps across instruments in some countries; and (c) an allocation of resources that is inadequate to support the building of

innovation capabilities and the diffusion of technology—objectives that are especially important to countries that are placed low on the capabilities escalator (see chapter 2, figure 2.8). Countries in the region need to reduce this fragmentation and existing overlaps by better clarifying the objectives of innovation policy and developing stronger coordinating mechanisms.

Moreover, it is critical for these countries to adopt good practices in public management. This will require better mechanisms to recruit qualified staff as well as training to strengthen staff knowledge and capacity.

Agencies to support innovation

As discussed in the previous section, innovation policies are not implemented in a vacuum. They are implemented by agencies and line ministries that establish the priorities, set up the processes, and execute the different policy programs. Evaluating the adequacy of policies to promote innovation and the diffusion of technologies thus requires understanding how these agencies work. This section briefly discusses some important features required by such agencies to implement effective innovation policies in the region.

Governments have taken various approaches to creating innovation agencies; no one ideal type of agency is appropriate in all circumstances. High-income countries have different models of innovation agencies, generally related to the different types of innovation being promoted (see annex 5A). For example, agencies that focus on upgrading differ from agencies that aim at more sophisticated innovation and discovery.

Although agency models from high-income countries can be instructive, it is important that institutional structures and practices be adapted to the country contexts in developing East Asia. Trying to mimic the design of high-income countries' agencies would likely result in what Andrews, Pritchett, and Woolcock (2012) call "isomorphic mimicry"—that is, when copying other countries' successful designs and practices may not address the local context and hence result in a failure of functionality. Determining which kind of innovation agency is best for a given context is difficult given a scarcity of relevant data, but recent experience in the region provides some guidance.

Some innovation agencies in the region have overlapping mandates and are not aligned with the country's key innovation challenges

Although most developing East Asian countries have acknowledged the importance of innovation and have taken laudable steps to improve their NISs and establish a related innovation agency, most efforts to create a dedicated agency charged with promoting innovation are rather nascent (OECD 2013). In general, the sophistication and efficiency of NISs in developing East Asian countries, while uneven, broadly correlate with countries' levels of economic development. Nonetheless, Indonesia, Malaysia, Thailand, and Vietnam all have innovation institutions that appear fairly ad hoc in nature, characterized by multiple layers of decision and policy making and, often, redundant or overlapping interventions.

A dedicated innovation agency should design and execute instruments that respond to the country's economic profile and innovation needs. With the exception perhaps of China, developing East Asian countries are not at the innovation frontier and are still net importers of technology. FDI is also critical for these countries not only in terms of capital but also for knowledge inflows. Innovation agencies in the region should thus focus on instruments that would bring the following results:

- Greater commercialization of public research
- Greater innovation by the private sector
- Better links between SMEs and multinational enterprises (MNEs)
- Higher FDI and associated knowledge transfer
- Stronger entrepreneurial culture with greater focus on business models.

There are different possible models for innovation agencies, but existence of an implementing agency is not sufficient to address institutional and coordination weaknesses

Innovation agencies operate within a given NIS, and their role is mostly focused on the execution of innovation policy instruments. They do not play a significant role in formulating innovation policies, because national strategies are usually designed by ministries. Some good practices in the region can be found in Malaysia and Singapore, where the Agensi Inovasi Malaysia (AIM, the Malaysian Innovation Agency) and the National Research Foundation (NRF), respectively, are under the authority of the prime minister's office to coordinate innovation policy across ministries and agencies.

Having a dedicated innovation agency, however, will not fix the inherent weaknesses in the innovation policy framework in developing East Asian countries. The success of the Malaysian and Singaporean agencies relies on their professional management and sufficient convening power to coordinate innovation-related initiatives across the range of relevant actors. Without a strong mandate and competent, professional management, the establishment of agencies with similar functions in other East Asian countries could potentially result in greater fragmentation of innovation policy.

Innovation agencies ought to help bring about greater industry orientation to science, technology, and human resources in the country. Furthermore, where possible, they should steer public research to align more closely with industry needs. Although countries often aspire toward more radical, cutting-edge types of innovation (as the next section will discuss), given weak public R&D systems and PROs, many countries should prioritize more incremental improvements—including through greater diffusion and technology adoption. Among the categories of innovation agencies described in annex 5A, the "directed upgraders" and "productivity facilitators" are perhaps most apt for developing East Asian countries. These agency models focus primarily on supporting small-scale, incremental product and process innovations. Such an approach would help steer public sector research toward industry needs.

Of the various governance models for an innovation agency, a government agency with high autonomy is perhaps the most appropriate and feasible in the region. Although a public-private partnership might be ideal, such an approach does not appear feasible given the political economy of many developing East Asian countries. More importantly, by staying within the government ambit, the agency would have a greater chance of informing science, technology, and innovation (STI) policies.

Assessing public research institution performance in facilitating innovation and technology transfer

Knowledge-creating public institutions—namely public research organizations (PROs) and universities—are critical actors in the NIS, central to innovation and technology adoption. This section first discusses research performance in the region. It then describes the results of a survey of PROs and university research centers in Malaysia, the Philippines, and Vietnam with the objective of assessing the effectiveness of these institutions and identifying performance bottlenecks. A key message from these surveys is that these institutions must adopt changes if they are to support governments' expressed goals of promoting the successful adoption and diffusion of existing technologies in local contexts and strengthening firms' capabilities.

Research capabilities and national strategies

Research effort in the region has increased in recent years

Over the past 10 years, the number of researchers in PROs and higher education institutions (HEIs) has grown by 8–9 times in Malaysia, by about 10 times in Indonesia, and has more than doubled in Thailand, while China and the Republic of Korea have continued to expand their base of researchers in both the public and

private sectors (Cirera, Kuriakose, and Zuñiga 2021). Today, Malaysia has about as many researchers as Korea (more than 60,000), although the number of researchers per person in the labor force in Malaysia is still lower than the average in high-income countries.

A common trend in national policy agendas has been the increasing recognition of the importance of STI policies as potential engines of growth and development. Differences in levels of income and institutional development across the region result in different levels of R&D spending relative to gross domestic product (GDP), sometimes referred to as R&D intensity. China and Singapore spend about 2 percent of GDP on R&D, for example, while Malaysia spends 1.4 percent and Indonesia, 0.2 percent. Countries with the lowest rates of R&D intensity also report the highest participation of the public sector in the funding of R&D (figure 5.6).

As countries' levels of development rise, the share of R&D financed by the private business sector also increases, which, combined with high rates of public investment, pulls total R&D intensity upward. Thus, China, Korea, Malaysia, Singapore, and Thailand have high rates of overall R&D intensity, with the business sector performing a high share of R&D (near or exceeding 60 percent of total spending).

The enhanced resources invested in public research, along with a growing supply of human resources in several countries, has enabled scientific output to increase dramatically since the mid-1990s (figure 5.7, panel a). According to 2020 bibliometric data from the SCImago Journal & Country Rank portal, between 2008 and 2018, the number of peer-reviewed publications in Indonesia increased 20 times and quadrupled in Malaysia. Peer-reviewed publications in the Philippines, Singapore, and Thailand doubled, or nearly doubled, over the period.[3]

Research efficiency remains low in the region, however

Despite improvements in some countries, the quality of research—as reflected in the citation impact index of scientific publications (the H-index)[4]—remains low in most of developing East Asia compared with that of high-income

FIGURE 5.6   The distribution of R&D spending in East Asia, by sector, reflects variations in R&D intensity related to countries' levels of income and institutional development

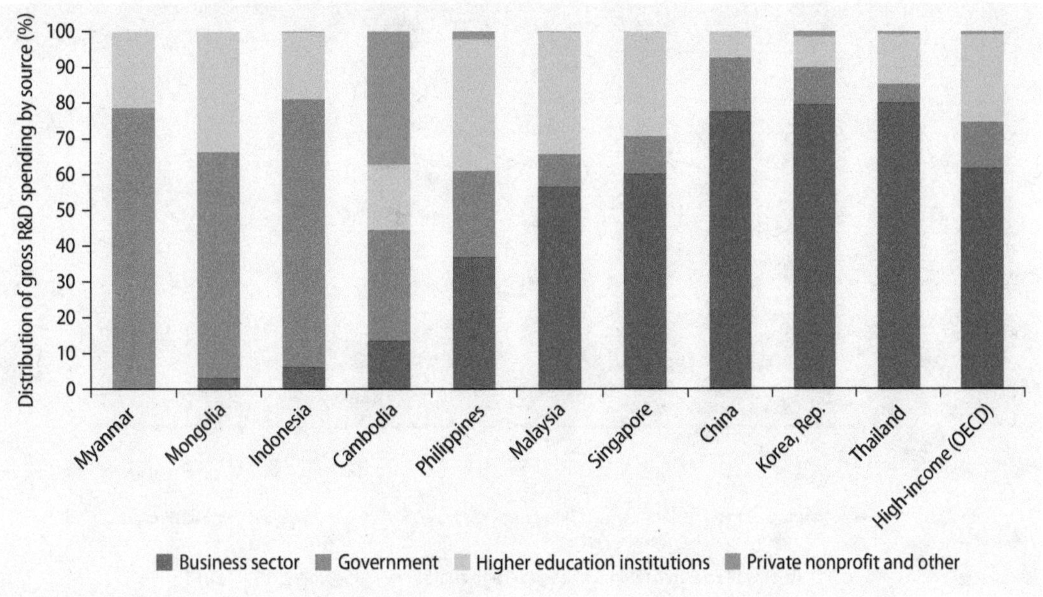

Source: Cirera, Kuriakose, and Zuñiga 2021.
Note: Gross research and development (R&D) spending data are from 2017 or the latest year available. OECD = Organisation for Economic Co-operation and Development.

economies (figure 5.7, panel b). Furthermore, as in most low- and middle-income countries, the use of domestic scientific knowledge (reflected in the citation intensity of domestically authored publications) also remains low. This highlights the continuing importance of learning from foreign sources of scientific knowledge in most countries; it also likely reflects a limited impact of domestic research that is building on local knowledge.

Measuring technology transfer activities

Surveys of PROs and university research centers (RCs) in Malaysia, the Philippines, and Vietnam, developed specifically for this report, were implemented between November 2019 and February 2020. The purpose of the surveys is to deepen policy makers' understanding of how knowledge institutions in the region function and to gauge their ability to transfer knowledge to industry and society. The surveys collected information about institutions' research capacity; the prevailing types of institutional governance; the use of public policies for research and technology

transfer; and the state of technology transfer links between scientific institutions, industry, and government.[5]

The combined sample from the three countries includes 80 institutions, covering a range of institutions by scientific field.[6] All the institutions surveyed are involved in R&D. The RCs in the sample allocate roughly 46 percent of their R&D expenditures to applied research and 43 percent to basic research. This greatly contrasts with the PROs, whose main R&D activities are in applied research (52 percent of R&D expenditure) and experimental development and preproduction activities (34 percent of R&D expenditure).

Assessing governance and performance monitoring

Good governance of RCs and PROs is key to making public research systems more accountable, more mission oriented, and more impact driven, with connections to productive systems and to society more broadly. The governance issues explored by the survey include institutions' level of autonomy; links

FIGURE 5.7   **Across several East Asian countries, scientific output has increased dramatically, but scientific productivity trails that of high-income countries**

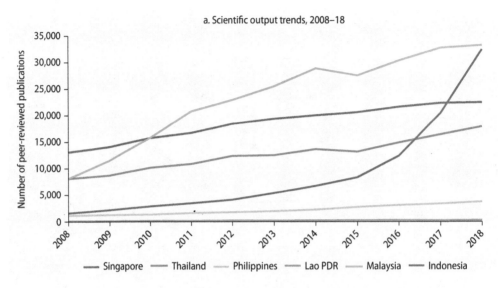

a. Scientific output trends, 2008–18

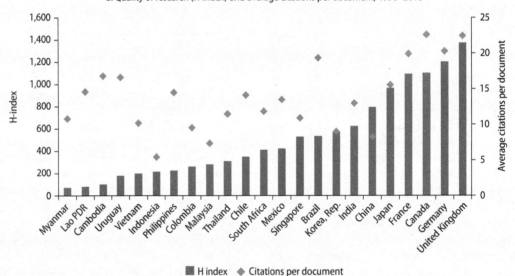

b. Quality of research (H-index) and average citations per document, 1996–2018

■ H index   ◆ Citations per document

Source: SCImago Journal & Country Rank bibliometric indicators (https://www.scimagojr.com).
a. Scientific output is measured by the number of peer-reviewed publications per country per year.
b. Scientific productivity is measured by the average number of citations per document of national authors (right axis) and by the H-index (left axis). The H-index measures how many national researchers' publications have at least *h* number of citations each. For example, an H-index of 5 indicates that the average scientist has five articles with five citations each. As such, the H-index is a measure of the number of highly impactful papers that a country's researchers have published.

between funding and performance; and management practices, including M&E.

Limited autonomy can impair the effectiveness of national research institutions
Institutional autonomy and governing structures that engage external stakeholders are

key features of high-performing PROs and universities (Cruz-Castro and Sanz-Menéndez 2018). These governance structures include recruitment procedures, criteria for career promotion, rules regarding the creation of intellectual property rights (IPRs) and technology commercialization, and support programs for knowledge transfer and commercialization. Autonomy should not lead to strategies or rules that are disconnected from national policies for research and innovation, however. Compliance with national strategies, while preserving autonomy, can be promoted through funding mechanisms (at both institutional and project levels) and through institutional performance assessments.

Only 24 out of the 80 institutions in the sample are legally autonomous. Moreover, the level of autonomy of PROs varies across institutions depending on their legal status and their relationship with the corresponding ministries or departments. In Malaysia, for example, a group of research organizations have private company status and enjoy a high level of autonomy and independence. For most PROs, however, autonomy is limited by statute and by their financial dependence on sectoral ministries or departments.

Within PROs, the weakest areas of autonomy relate to institutional policies and salary setting because these are often defined by broader laws governing the employment of civil servants. The areas where PROs enjoy the strongest decision-making powers are in day-to-day operational management and revenue generation strategies, with half of all PROs in the sample reporting they have full autonomy in these areas.

RCs report having less autonomy than PROs. This is not surprising, because RCs are generally subordinated to the university management and rectorates and must comply with institutional directives regarding budget allocation, infrastructure management, commercialization, and IPRs. Consequently, the only area where RCs report having full autonomy is in the setting of research objectives, with about 70 percent of them declaring autonomous decision making in this area.

Autonomy is positively associated with the intensity of collaborative links between PROs and RCs and industry, including the intensity of technology contracting with SMEs (figure 5.8, panel a). On average, autonomous institutions (both PROs and RCs combined) demonstrate a larger number of collaborative links (per researcher) than

FIGURE 5.8   **Research institutions in Malaysia, the Philippines, and Vietnam that were autonomous and included industry stakeholders on their boards engaged in greater collaboration with industry in 2017–18**

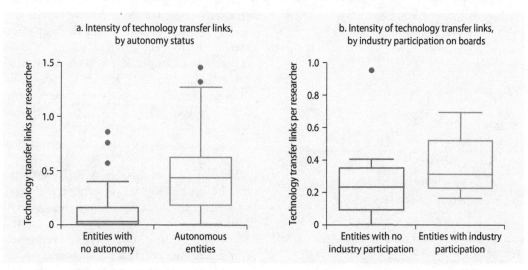

Source: Cirera, Kuriakose, and Zuñiga 2021.
Note: In both panels, "technology transfer links" refers to all collaborative agreements and contracts with industry, including personal exchanges and training services, collaborative research, contract research, technology services contracts, and licensing of intellectual property rights. The average reported number of collaborative links (per researcher) covers all contracting activity over the period 2017–18 for all researchers in 2018. The combined sample from the three countries included 80 institutions, covering a range of public research organizations and university research centers by scientific field.

institutions that are not autonomous, with a median value of 0.4 links (agreements and contracts) per researcher. This compares with a median value of close to zero for nonautonomous research institutions. The variance in outcomes is also higher among the group of autonomous institutions, however. In addition, institutions whose boards of trustees include industry stakeholders tend to have a greater number of collaborative links with industry per researcher than those institutions without industry participation on their boards of trustees (figure 5.8, panel b).

Overall, institutions having more *good governance* practices in place—for example, boards of trustees, autonomy, industry representation on steering committees or boards of trustees, performance evaluations, and performance-based funding

systems—demonstrate greater collaboration with industry and better technology transfer performance (figure 5.9). Despite some evidence of outliers in the data, a positive correlation exists between the extent of good governance, as measured by an index of governance indicators, and the extent of collaboration between national research institutions and industry.

Private sector funding of R&D increases commercialization

Another way to incentivize greater technology transfer from research organizations to industry is through performance-based funding schemes. Performance-based agreements (PAs) are a growing mechanism for funding among HEIs in high-income countries.[7] These contracts set performance goals and, in most cases, bind a share of their block funding allocation to reaching those targets.

Such contracts can stimulate knowledge transfer by including not only traditional targets related to teaching and research but also targets associated with the level of engagement with firms or the commercialization of research results. Indeed, the share of research funding coming from the private sector could be indicative of how much research institutions work with industry and other innovation actors through commercialization activities. The survey data reveal, for example, that PROs with more private sector funding engage in more technology transfer and collaborative projects (figure 5.10).

Institutions need to continually strengthen research management practices and M&E

Monitoring and evaluation (M&E) is essential to measure the impact of resources invested as well as to guide future policies.[8] Across Malaysia, the Philippines, and Vietnam, 65 percent of the institutions surveyed report that authorities conduct performance evaluation of their research and technology transfer activities. However, most entities lack implementation plans to achieve evaluation and technology transfer goals. Only Malaysia implements performance-based mechanisms

FIGURE 5.9   **Research institutions with good governance exhibit a greater intensity of technology transfer**

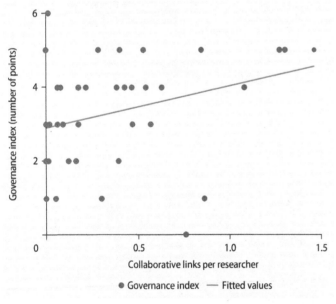

● Governance index   — Fitted values

Source: Cirera, Kuriakose, and Zuñiga 2021.
Note: The figure displays the number of technology transfer links (average per researcher over 2017–18) in relation to an index of good governance. This index is the sum of points (one point per feature) attributed to each of the following features of governance: (a) having autonomy; (b) having a board of trustees or steering committee; (c) having industry representation on boards of trustees; (d) receiving funding through performance-based funding systems; and (e) being subject to institutional performance evaluation for research and technology transfer activities. Outliers were excluded (entities with more than 100 collaborative links and more than 1.5 agreements per researcher on average over 2017–18). The combined sample included 80 institutions from Malaysia, the Philippines, and Vietnam, covering a range of public research organizations and university research centers by scientific field.

and has steps to link institutional funding to performance and governance reforms (OECD 2016). Even there, performance-based funding is not the main budget source. So, questions remain as to how significantly that approach affects research institutions' activities.

The survey results show that some important research management practices and use of performance evaluation (PE) systems (periodical evaluations, internal rewards, and so on) are well-established practices in Malaysian and Philippine institutions. However, Vietnamese entities (both PROs and RCs) appear significantly behind in most managerial and good governance practices. Despite the increased use in Vietnam of good managerial and policy frameworks, their effects on technology transfer performance and researchers' engagement on innovation projects with the private sector remain unclear.

In all three countries, publications remain the major determinant in research evaluations, while technology transfer activity is not considered adequately in performance frameworks or decisions about researchers' career advancement. This absence of institutional incentives could, in turn, be a major deterrent to researchers engaging in technology transfer activities.

Strategies for applied research and technology transfer

Commercialization of innovations and transfer of technology in developing East Asia is limited by a lack of mission-oriented institutional planning, limited services to support commercialization and technology transfer, little emphasis given to technology extension services, and weak technology transfer offices.

The surveyed public research organizations lack mission orientation

The use of mission-oriented research or innovation policies can bring enormous benefits by accelerating research and innovation solutions and breaking up institutional silos and barriers to knowledge and technology transfer

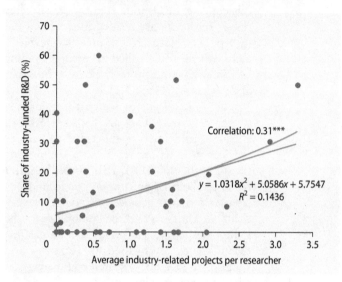

FIGURE 5.10 **Research organizations with higher shares of industry-funded R&D undertake more research collaboration**

$$y = 1.0318x^2 + 5.0586x + 5.7547$$
$$R^2 = 0.1436$$

Correlation: 0.31***

Source: World Bank calculations from survey data on public research organizations and university research centers.
Note: The intensity in collaborative research with industry is the average number of collaborative research projects with firms per scientist (in 2017–18) including joint and contract research, doctoral projects, and technology services with small and medium enterprises (SMEs). The combined sample included 80 institutions from Malaysia, the Philippines, and Vietnam, covering a range of public research organizations and university research centers by scientific field. The figure excludes entities reporting a share of industry-funded research and development (R&D) exceeding 60 percent as well as outliers. *** designates a 99 percent confidence level.

activities across the NIS (Mazzucato 2015). Malaysia and the Philippines have recently increased their emphasis on mission-oriented research, and their national research strategies have also defined research priorities for innovation and competitiveness to improve alignment with industry and societal needs and challenges. Nevertheless, the survey shows that despite having a legal mandate to serve private sector needs, half of the PROs in those two countries have neither strategic plans for technology transfer activities nor permanent consultation mechanisms with industry. Except for a few star performers (in agriculture mostly), PROs remain weak in deploying strategies and implementing efforts to achieve their mission-oriented commitments.

Services to support commercialization and technology transfer are limited

The survey also measures how much of a priority PROs and RCs give to commercialization and technology transfer activities, as well as whether PROs and RCs are currently beneficiaries of public programs in those areas. In this context, PROs indicated that far greater public resources are needed in translational (or applied) research and product development, whereas RCs called for greater funding for proof of concept, technology validation, and packaging (figure 5.11).

The policy areas in which these institutions participate least are those related to start-ups and nurturing services, business services support programs, and technology transfer offices (TTOs). To address the latter issue, public funding support for technology transfer activities has been expanded considerably in Malaysia and the Philippines. In the Philippines, a stronger policy agenda has just recently been established for start-ups and spin-offs to facilitate research commercialization and entrepreneurship.[9]

In line with these findings, programs for start-ups (including incubation services) and

funding for entrepreneurial support services are considered the least important priorities for RCs, while start-up support as well as TTOs and science and technology parks appear the least important for PROs. This is not surprising given that regulations restrict public servants working at PROs from engaging in entrepreneurial activities—which, in practice, critically limit PROs' technology transfer to industry as well as the creation of spin-off enterprises.

The region lacks technology extension services to support last-mile transfer of technology to industry

The provision of technology extension services (TES) is an important channel for technology transfer, and in high-income countries. TES represents a core area of PROs' missions. However, in developing East Asia, survey respondents from both PROs and RCs report that this type of policy

FIGURE 5.11   **The survey showed which technology transfer activities are most important and attract the most participation from research organizations**

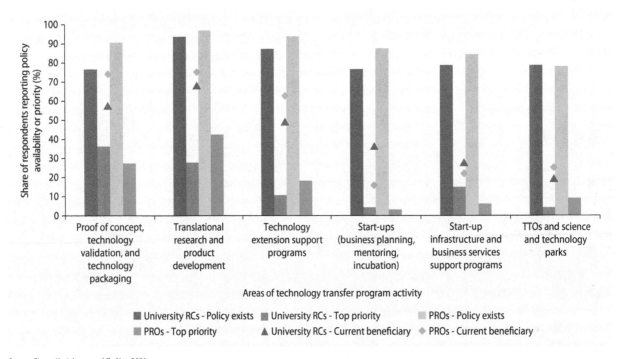

Source: Cirera, Kuriakose, and Zuñiga 2021.
Note: The figure displays percentages of public research organizations (PROs) and university research centers (RCs) for which the specified areas are a priority as well as the percentages of PROs and RCs that participate in some government program in those areas. The combined sample included 80 institutions from Malaysia, the Philippines, and Vietnam, covering a range of public research organizations and university research centers by scientific field. TTOs = technology transfer offices.

intervention is only considered of moderate importance (figure 5.11)—with the possible exception of support for agriculture and electronics in Malaysia. Moreover, the survey results indicate that TES for manufacturing systems and industrial upgrading are mostly weak or missing in countries' NISs.

There is an ongoing need for clear strategies for technology transfer and intellectual property revenue sharing
Institutional policies for IPR ownership and commercialization of intellectual assets are expected to provide certainty and clarity in the legal framework (especially if no national policy or law on IPRs exists), thereby reducing transaction costs related to asymmetric information and agency problems (Macho-Stadler, Martinez-Giralt, and Perez-Castrillo 1996; Siegel, Veugelers, and Wright 2007). It is now common practice to vest the rights of intellectual property ownership to the research institutions themselves (instead of to inventors or national councils) and to provide revenue participation rights for stakeholders (such as researchers and university faculties as well as TTOs).

In Malaysia and the Philippines, IPR and technology transfer laws have been enacted to promote the management and commercialization of research output at PROs and public universities. Although institutions are the main owners of IPRs, there is some degree of flexibility, and other university stakeholders can also be entitled with ownership rights. As for revenue-sharing incentives and the rights of researchers to profit from the revenues derived from IPR commercialization, there is a great deal of heterogeneity across the countries. Vietnam lacks a clear policy framework at the national level, whereas national laws in Malaysia and the Philippines provide inventors with equity participation rights in addition to other financial incentives (for example, for invention disclosures and patenting in Malaysia).[10]

Research entities also lack sufficient technology transfer services
Most of the entities surveyed report the presence of a TTO or an industry liaison unit.

However, TTOs cannot provide all the services needed to support technology transfer and commercialization processes. Seventy percent or more of the surveyed RCs report that most technology transfer services are available internally, but the surveys also indicate that many of these services (for example, assistance with searching for partners, networking, and assessing the value of new technologies) are inadequate to address current needs.

Among PROs, access to funding for technology transfer activities and assistance in intellectual property protection and management, as well as in the creation of spin-offs and start-ups, are provided in only about half of the institutions surveyed. Assessing the value of new technologies also remains a critical task, not easily accessed or insufficiently provided by the TTOs.

Industry links and technology transfer activities

There are few links between public research institutions and industry
There are still relatively few links for knowledge transfer between PROs or RCs and industry. Only a handful of institutions are engaged in a large variety of such links, with most of them undertaking only two or three types of knowledge transfer or collaborative activities. Traditional means of knowledge transfer—such as human capital exchanges (for example, research staff taking on temporary assignments in industry) or doctoral projects in industry—appear underdeveloped.

The most frequent technology transfer activities are collaborative research projects with industry and with government (figure 5.12). University RCs are more active than PROs in these projects, reporting a higher average number of collaborative projects (per researcher) with both industry and government as well as a greater number (albeit still low) of human capital exchanges.

Institutions' engagement in commercialization activities and technology services remains weak
Engagement by both RCs and PROs in commercialization activities involving technology

FIGURE 5.12   **PROs are more likely than RCs to report collaboration and knowledge transfer links with industry**

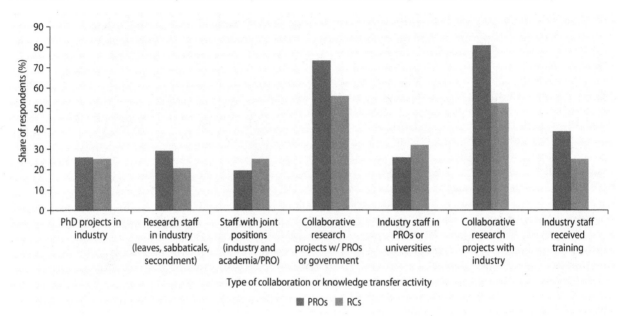

Source: Cirera, Kuriakose, and Zuñiga 2021.
Note: The figure shows the percentages of surveyed research entities that reported undertaking activities in 2017–18. The combined sample included 80 institutions from Malaysia, the Philippines, and Vietnam, covering a range of public research organizations and university research centers by scientific field. PROs = public research organizations; RCs = university research centers.

services (not involving IPRs), licensing of IPRs, and entrepreneurship also remains weak. As in other low- and middle-income countries—despite a significant increase in patenting in universities (and in some PROs) and other forms of IPRs—technology commercialization through licensing of IPRs and start-up creation remains embryonic in Malaysia, the Philippines, and Vietnam.

PROs are significantly more involved than RCs (in terms of both participation and intensity) in technology services and training because of PROs' institutional mandates to provide technical expertise and training to industry, especially to MSMEs. University RCs appear less inclined than PROs to engage in collaborative research with industry. This pattern illustrates the lack of common interest and difficulties on the part of academia in engaging with the business sector to conduct joint research projects.

Except for research contract and technology services (not involving IPRs) such as technical assistance, engineering, and product

testing services, technology commercialization activities are absent or marginal in both PROs and RCs. Entrepreneurial activities by start-ups using new technologies (licensing to start-ups) and spin-off ventures are also marginal in both PROs and RCs.

The role of academic incentives

Both international experience and academic research underscore the importance of providing appropriate incentives to those who participate in and manage the technology transfer process (Siegel, Waldman, and Link 2003; Siegel, Veugelers, and Wright 2007). An appropriate policy framework should recognize the role of researchers and encourage them to engage in technology transfer activities. Incentives may include (a) inventor royalty compensation and economic participation in revenues from technology services; (b) awards; (c) recognition in curricula (for example, credits for tenure); and (d) equity participation in spin-offs, among others.

The use of incentives is widespread, and on average, 72–90 percent of survey respondents reported having individual performance evaluation and career incentives for technology transfer as well as public recognition rewards and assistance in IPR protection and management (figure 5.13, panel a). However, while more than half of the institutions surveyed report having performance evaluation criteria that take technology transfer activities into account, universities still generally consider publication activity as the main indicator of scientific performance (figure 5.13, panel b) and thus the key requirement for career advancement. Most institutions have some type of financial incentives in place, but the survey indicates that only a few institutions implement them. In practice, financial rewards from commercialization are weak or insufficiently implemented.

Equity participation and funding for start-ups and spin-offs are the least developed types of incentives employed by the institutions surveyed. Only a few large organizations are able to launch entrepreneurial funding and assistance support through specialized units

such as incubators and accelerators, and these types of services are still uncommon at public institutions (figure 5.13, panel a). Further, researchers consider launching start-ups or spin-offs to be a difficult process, with complex procedures. In many cases, PROs are less inclined than RCs to undertake start-up or spin-off development because of regulatory constraints that prevail for civil servants and public institutions under ministerial authority.

Summary of findings on the role of research institutions in facilitating technology transfer

The findings presented in this chapter suggest that national research policies still support a model of innovation and technology that is heavily supply driven. With little industry participation, the relevance of PROs' and RCs' outputs to firms and the broader society remains weak. Government mandates for technology commercialization through start-ups and licensing have had little impact to date.

FIGURE 5.13   **Research institutions report a variety of financial and nonfinancial incentives for technology transfer**

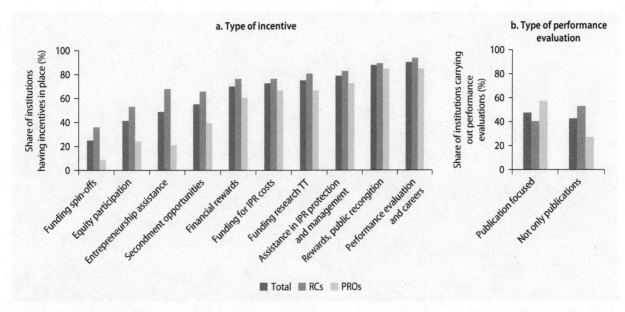

Source: Cirera, Kuriakose, and Zuñiga 2021.
Note: The combined sample included 80 institutions from Malaysia, the Philippines, and Vietnam, covering a range of public research organizations and university research centers by scientific field. IPR = intellectual property right; PROs = public research organizations; RCs = research centers; TT = technology transfer.

Key conclusions from the surveys include the following:

- Efforts to strengthen research and education systems have lacked (except in Malaysia) a link between institutional funding policies and performance measurement, including with respect to promoting technology transfer.
- The lack of autonomy in many universities and PROs and the lack of good management practices in many public research institutions in the region further impede the effectiveness of these institutions in generating and transferring technologies that promote private sector innovation.
- The use of monitoring and performance evaluation practices is limited, impeding the ability to assess what has worked well, what has not, and how to enhance institutions' impacts on innovation and technology adoption and diffusion.
- There remains considerable scope for strengthening incentives for researchers to engage in technology transfer from public research institutions to private sector enterprises. University-industry partnerships, technology transfer initiatives, and other entrepreneurial activities are inadequately rewarded in the performance evaluations and careers of scientists, with a much heavier weight placed on scientific publications. This, again, inhibits the impact that research institutions could have in supporting innovation-led growth in the region.

Annex 5A What is the role for innovation agencies?

Innovation depends on the availability of national and sectoral factors, such as capital availability, knowledge, entrepreneurial culture, a well-educated workforce, and a well-functioning intellectual property regime. The efficacy of these factors relies on institutions' interconnectivity to collectively promote innovation and on government's role to create conditions for innovation to flourish.

Innovation agencies help governments to design and implement innovation policy. Many countries have established dedicated agencies to develop and implement strategies to address challenges within their NISs. Some of these, in addition to executing innovation interventions, are also responsible for formulating government innovation policy. However, agencies vary in purpose and structure along with the array of policy interventions reflecting each country's unique set of NIS needs. In low- and middle-income countries, innovation agencies play a specific and limited role, providing more narrowly defined interventions than do innovation agencies operating at a subnational level in high-income nations. For instance, the United

States has several mission-oriented innovation agencies, such as the National Institute of Standards and Technology (NIST), the Defense Advanced Research Projects Agency (DARPA), and the Small Business Innovation Research (SBIR) program.

Despite differences in structure and economic and political context, innovation agencies have many similarities in the way they operate and the challenges they face. Table 5A.1 provides an overview of the main support methods provided by some of the best-known agencies globally.

Key elements in designing an effective innovation agency

The small number of studies analyzing innovation agencies have drawn only a few conclusions about how successful innovation agencies are designed and managed. The challenge of this literature is the lack of well-defined performance indicators that allow one to assess success across different models and agencies. Nevertheless, these studies suggest a few design features that some of the agencies in the most innovative countries possess that could be correlated with effectiveness (Glennie and Bound 2016):

TABLE 5A.1 Overview of main support mechanisms used by leading innovation agencies

Agency	Direct financial support[a]			Nonfinancial assistance[b]	Support for intermediaries[c]	Connecting and institution building[d]	In-house R&D projects[e]
	Grants	Loans	Other				
FFG, Austria	x	x	x	x	x	x	
Finep, Brazil	x	x	x		x	x	
Corfo, Chile	x	x	x		x	x	
Tekes, Finland	x	x	x	x	x	x	
OCS, Israel	x	x		x	x	x	
VINNOVA, Sweden	x			x	x	x	
CTI, Switzerland	x			x	x	x	
ITRI, Taiwan, China				x	x	x	x
Innovate UK, United Kingdom	x			x		x	
DARPA, United States	x		x	x		x	x

Source: Glennie and Bound 2016.
Note: Corfo = Production Development Corporation; CTI = Swiss Commission for Technology and Innovation; DARPA = Defense Advanced Research Projects Agency; FFG = Austrian Research Promotion Agency; Finep = Funding Authority for Studies and Projects; ITRI = Industrial Technology Research Institute; OCS = Israel Innovation Authority (formerly Office of the Chief Scientist); Tekes = Finnish Funding Agency for Technology and Innovation; VINNOVA = Sweden's innovation agency.
a. The type of financial support the agency provides for innovation.
b. Whether the agency provides nonfinancial assistance such as technical assistance and expertise.
c. Whether the agency supports intermediary institutions for innovation such as accelerators or technology centers.
d. Whether the agency provides support by connecting institutions.
e. Whether the agency and its staff implement research and development (R&D) projects.

- Innovation agencies should operate with considerable autonomy to be effective.
- Innovation agencies cannot be entirely separate from political processes.
- Measuring and evidencing the long-term or systemic impact of their portfolio is challenging for innovation agencies.
- It is hard to identify a single model of a "successful" innovation agency.

Despite a wide range of innovation agencies in low- and middle-income countries, certain parameters have emerged from studying different agencies. The four observed key steps involved in the design and management of an effective innovation agency are as follows (Glennie and Bound 2016):

- Identifying the right organizational *mission* depending on markets and identified challenges
- Choosing effective *management* structures and staffs with relevant skills and experience
- Selecting the most appropriate set of *methods* and tools, such as diagnostic-based interventions to address NIS gaps (Aridi and Kapil 2019)
- Establishing a set of *metrics* and measurements that will help the agency to understand and achieve impact through internal or external capabilities.

Almost all parameters relate to an organization's strategic and operational capabilities, complement each other, and adjust to the evolving needs of the NIS. Strategic capabilities clearly define and adjust the agency's mission according to market needs to enhance their relevance and impact (Aridi and Kapil 2019). Managerial capabilities allow staff and teams to grow, learn, and establish conducive partnerships.

Governance of innovation agencies

Effective governance and management structures involve balancing two competing goals: (a) autonomy to make decisions based on their professional judgment given the strategic positioning of the agency within the NIS (Aridi and Kapil 2019); and (b) necessary oversight and accountability for a public or quasi-public organization.

Innovation agencies commonly have one of four types of governance structures: ministerial unit, government agency, government agency with a high degree of autonomy, and nonprofit public-private partnership.

A ministerial unit is an office within a ministry that reports to the minister and receives allocations from the ministry's budget. Although it is controlled by and aligned with the ministry's strategy (therefore making it more accountable), it may be hampered by bureaucracy and political pressures constraining resources as well as by weak firm or entrepreneurial know-how.

A government agency, being a formal governmental bureaucracy under direct political control, generally has stronger long-term planning ability but is resource dependent, prone to political pressure, and has less flexibility to hire and retain talent. However, *a government agency with high autonomy* is an agency owned by the government but with a degree of independence and flexibility to derive its funding from multiple sources, such as from donors or the private sector. However, its decision making is still prone to political influence.

Finally, *a nonprofit public-private partnership* is a separate legal entity, often a nonprofit organization or a foundation. It combines resources from public and private sources and is led by the private sector to establish credibility in the market and to develop relevant services to firms. Nevertheless, this governance structure may drift from public sector priorities as activities are adapted to "follow the money."

Funding of innovation agencies

Sustainable funding is essential to avoiding funding fluctuations that jeopardize programs and agencies. Reliable funding, often from government sources, is critical for hiring and training staff, designing policies, and establishing M&E protocols. Relying too heavily on government funding, however, may mean fluctuations in funding, which in turn can jeopardize the program and even the agency's existence.

Proactive agencies cultivate multiple funding sources to enhance program offerings and diversify their portfolios, which is critical to ensure the sustainability of financing. Alternative funding sources include (a) international partners from high-income countries offering economic and social assistance; (b) multinational or international organizations as part of their overall economic development program; (c) charitable foundations that contribute to social goals within low- and middle-income countries; (d) fee-based services; and (e) investment income from direct equity investments.

Innovation agencies and public sector R&D

Rapid technological and economic changes place a premium on the effective design of innovation agencies as it relates to public sector R&D. In this context, four different agency categories have been defined in more developed-country contexts: "directed upgraders," "productivity facilitators," "state-led disruptors," and "transformation enablers" (Breznitz, Ornston, and Samford 2018). These categories differ in (a) the level of public sector R&D involvement, (b) the agencies' positioning within the public sector, and (c) the degree of embedding within private industry. Table 5A.2 shows the four innovation agency categories with examples from around the world that vary in the specificity and structure of their missions.

Productivity facilitators. The Danish GTS institutes (Research and Technology Organizations) represent almost ideal examples of "productivity facilitators" (Breznitz, Ornston, and Samford 2018). These institutions vary in size and specialization, but all work closely with private sector partners to identify and solve technological challenges. Even though the government views them as an important policy instrument and funds roughly 10 percent of their activities, they operate at the periphery of the public service, with almost all their budget coming from private industry.

Like the GTS institutes in Denmark, Canada's Industrial Research Assistance Program (IRAP) is another example of a productivity facilitator. Its mission is to assist SMEs with technological innovation and diffusion to promote firm growth. IRAP's embeddedness enables it to effectively address barriers to innovation. Moreover, rather than solving particular issues by developing technological solutions themselves, the organization's industrial technology advisers (ITAs) use their networks to locate other organizations that can assist with the necessary R&D. In doing so, they construct a framework for technological diffusion and continuous, incremental innovation.

Directed upgraders. Another way to organize an innovation agency is through reliance on the public sector, rather than the private sector, to steer technological development. Singapore's Agency for Science, Technology and Research (A*STAR) and Chile's Production Development Corporation (Corfo) are examples of "directed upgraders" (Breznitz, Ornston, and Samford 2018). Singapore's A*STAR is a centrally situated, classic developmental agency that is connected to private industry while also having close ties to other public sector actors. Corfo, another example of a directed upgrader, maintains close relationships to the private sector—both individual firms and industry organizations—as a means of understanding the kinds of market failures that prevent Chilean firms from upgrading and what technologies might be imported from abroad to assist the local economy.

State-led disrupters. "State-led disruptors" (Breznitz, Ornston, and Samford 2018) also take a primary role in the performance of research and technology development; however, their position at the periphery of the public sector and autonomy from established industries enable them to develop radical, novel innovations. The Industrial Technology Research Institute (ITRI) of Taiwan, China, and DARPA of the United States are state-led disruptors and sit at the periphery of the public sector. Further, both are actively involved in network creation

TABLE 5A.2   **Examples of innovation agencies, by type**

Category	Definition	Organizational features	Examples
Productivity facilitator	Introduces small-scale, incremental product and process innovations across a wide range of established industries	Locus of R&D: Private Position in public sector: Peripheral Relation to established industry: Embedded	GTS institutes (Denmark) IRAP (Canada)
Directed upgrader	Specializes in incremental innovation but mobilizes resources around a relatively narrow range of industries and activities, facilitating large-scale change	Locus of R&D: Public Position in public sector: Core Relation to established industry: Embedded	A*STAR (Singapore) Corfo (Chile)
State-led disruptor	Excels at radically innovative technological breakthroughs	Locus of R&D: Public Position in public sector: Peripheral Relation to established industry: Autonomous	ITRI (Taiwan, China) DARPA (United States)
Transformation enabler	Radically innovative but characterized by many small-scale experiments rather than a narrow, focused approach	Locus of R&D: Private Position in public sector: Peripheral Relation to established industry: Autonomous	Sitra (Finland) OCS (Israel)

Source: Breznitz, Ornston, and Samford 2018.
Note: A*STAR = Agency for Science, Technology and Research; Corfo = Production Development Corporation; DARPA = Defense Advanced Research Projects Agency; GTS = Research and Technology Organizations; IRAP = Industrial Research Assistance Program; ITRI = Industrial Technology Research Institute; OCS = Israel Innovation Authority (formerly Office of the Chief Scientist); R&D = research and development; Sitra = Finnish Innovation Fund.

with an ever-changing set of private firms where the agency sits at the nodal point charting out technology trajectories up to the level of specific early-stage products. The main difference between these two agencies is that while ITRI is actively engaged in R&D, DARPA contracts out the R&D to external researchers, private firms, and universities.

Transformation enablers. While DARPA and ITRI actively shape and steer technological change, "transformation enablers" (Breznitz, Ornston, and Samford 2018) such as the Finnish Innovation Fund (Sitra) and Israel's Israel Innovation Authority (OCS, formerly Office of the Chief Scientist) operate more indirectly. DARPA, for example, is a classic mission-oriented agency intended to identify and develop cutting-edge technologies for defense. Sitra, on the other hand, was established in the 1960s to promote private industry during a period that was dominated by state-owned enterprises and heavily regulated industries. It did so by prioritizing technological innovation.

Annex 5B Sampling and implementation of the World Bank survey of public research institutions

A proportional-stratified random sampling was implemented in three countries—Malaysia, the Philippines, and Vietnam—based on the type of institution and location, and with the aim of capturing research engagement and sufficient heterogeneity in research capabilities across institutions. In the case of universities, the focus was research-engaged institutions. Institutions involved in the social sciences, management, and arts and humanities were excluded. The surveys were implemented from November 2019 to February 2020 through face-to-face interviews with directors of PROs and university RCs. Interviewees received questionnaires one to two weeks in advance. In most cases, half of the survey was covered during the interview, while the rest of the questionnaire was completed and submitted after the meetings.

In Malaysia, the survey was administered to 10 PROs and 16 university RCs across four public research universities. Both PROs and RCs were randomly selected. The PROs surveyed are under different ministerial bodies covering different technical fields and industries. The list of public research institutes compiled by the Malaysia Science and Technology Information Centre (MASTIC) under the Ministry of Science, Technology and Innovation (MOSTI) was used as a sampling frame, supplemented by a list of PROs compiled by World Bank staff. Random samples were drawn from this list, with PROs representing various ministries in Malaysia. For universities, the team used the national listing of "research universities" officially defined by the government. Before a random sample was drawn, the research centers were classified into three categories: (a) Higher Institution Centers of Excellence (HICoEs), which are specified by the Ministry of Education; (b) Centers of Excellence (CoEs), classified by the universities; and (c) research centers that are neither HICoEs nor CoEs. Each university has at least one of each type of research center within the sample to ensure accurate and robust representation. RCs were randomly selected, but an effort was made to ensure that the team surveyed at least one HICoE, one CoE, and one research center per university.

For the Philippines, an initial stratified sample of 14 RCs out of a total of 47 research centers (engaged and producing STI outputs) and 14 out of 17 PROs was defined. Roughly 59 percent of the 17 PROs are under the Department of Science and Technology (DoST), followed by 29 percent under the Department of Agriculture (DA), while the others belong to other line agencies. To identify RCs, the Commission on Higher Education (CHED) provided the team with a list of HEIs, which identified 882 universities conducting R&D in the Philippines. Out of these, 243 conduct research activities associated with science, technology, and innovation—42 percent of which are in the National Capital Region (Manila), Region III, and Region IVA. The final sample contained 15 RCs and 8 PROs.

For Vietnam, which has more than 1,000 universities, the list of research universities was produced based on the top 20 universities whose publication activity in 2016 and 2017 is recorded in the Web of Science citation indexing database (of the Institute for Scientific Information, or ISI). From this list, the selection focused only on two cities: Hanoi and Ho Chi Minh City (HCMC). Next, for each university, a comprehensive list of RCs was produced and analyzed by accessing the university websites and selecting RCs using the following criteria: an RC unit must (a) conduct research, (b) have a research director, and (c) have equipment or a laboratory for doing research. In Vietnam, for both PROs and RCs, the target sample for PROs was 20. The final sample contained 16 RCs and 16 PROs.

Notes

1. Policy instruments usually have a defined set of objectives, group of beneficiaries, and logical framework. They often involve one mechanism of intervention—for example, a grant, scholarship, or tax incentive. They differ from government programs in that government programs often include several policy instruments and much broader objectives. For example, a national program to support start-ups can include a range of instruments, such as incubators, accelerators, hackathons, and equity finance policy instruments.

2. Although there is no blueprint for how expenditure for innovation should be distributed, the concentration of resources for innovation in just a few programs in these countries is higher than what is observed in most Organisation for Economic Co-operation and Development (OECD) countries.

3. The region's lower-middle-income countries (for example, Lao PDR) have also increased their publication activity, but their total numbers remain low relative to other countries in the region.

4. The H-index is a measure of the number of highly impactful papers that researchers have published in the country. The more influential are publications, as measured by citations, the higher the H-index.

5. For additional details on the implementation of the survey, see annex 5B.

6. For 35 percent of the entities, their main research field is engineering (environmental engineering, chemical engineering, transport engineering, and so on); 21 percent specialize in electronics and telecommunications research; 14 percent in medical sciences; 7.5 percent in life sciences and biotechnology; and the remainder in other fields including agricultural research.

7. The OECD (2016) estimates that about 60 percent of universities in OECD countries have adopted this funding mechanism.

8. In several OECD countries, evaluation is mandatory for the renewal of research funding agreements through the use of multiannual performance-based contract-agreements, which require specific results to be accomplished. M&E systems are also being adopted to assess the progress of national research and innovation plans (OECD 2016).

9. In the Philippines, the Startup Innovation Act (passed in 2019) provides incentives for innovative start-up creation and growth, including subsidies for firm creation, use of facilities, training on entrepreneurship and intellectual property, and financial assistance to start-ups. The act solidifies mechanisms in providing financial assistance through the creation of the Startup Grant Fund and the Startup Venture Fund.

10. Invention disclosures take the form of a report that represents the first recording of the invention. The disclosure describes the invention's novelty and establishes the date and scope. Such disclosures are needed to ensure that inventors do not lose patent rights associated with their inventions.

References

Andrews, Matt, Lant Pritchett, and Michael Woolcock. 2012. "Escaping Capability Traps through Problem-Driven Iterative Adaptation (PDIA)." Working Paper No. 299, Center for Global Development, Washington, DC.

Aridi, Anwar, and Natasha Kapil. 2019. "Innovation Agencies: Cases from Developing Economies." Report, World Bank, Washington, DC.

Breznitz, Dan, Darius Ornston, and Steven Samford. 2018. "Mission Critical: The Ends, Means, and Design of Innovation Agencies." *Industrial and Corporate Change* 27 (5): 883–96.

Cirera, Xavier, Jaime Frias, Justin Hill, and Yanchao Li. 2020. *A Practitioner's Guide to Innovation Policy: Instruments to Build Firm Capabilities and Accelerate Technological Catch-Up in Developing Countries.* Washington, DC: World Bank.

Cirera, Xavier, Smita Kuriakose, and Pluvia Zuñiga. 2021. "Assessing the Effectiveness of Public Research Institutions in the Transfer of Knowledge and Technology to Industry and Society: Evidence from a New Survey in Three Developing East Asia Countries." Unpublished, World Bank, Washington, DC.

Cirera, Xavier, and William F. Maloney. 2017. *The Innovation Paradox: Developing-Country Capabilities and the Unrealized Promise of Technological Catch-Up.* Washington, DC: World Bank.

Cruz-Castro, Laura, and Luis Sanz-Menéndez. 2018. "Autonomy and Authority in Public Research Organisations: Structure and Funding Factors." *Minerva* 56 (2): 135–60. doi:10.1007/s11024-018-9349-1.

Glennie, Alex, and Kirsten Bound. 2016. "How Innovation Agencies Work: International Lessons to Inspire and Inform National Strategies." Report, Nesta, London.

Macho-Stadler, Ines, Xavier Martinez-Giralt, and David Perez-Castrillo Jr. 1996. "The Role of Information in Licensing Contract Design." *Research Policy* 25 (1): 43–57.

Mazzucato, Mariana. 2015. "Beyond Market Failures: Shaping and Creating Markets for Innovation-Led Growth." In *Mission-Oriented Finance for Innovation: New Ideas for Investment-Led Growth*, edited by Mariana Mazzucato, and Caetano C. R. Penna, 147–59. London: Rowman & Littlefield.

OECD (Organisation for Economic Co-operation and Development). 2013. *Innovation in Southeast Asia.* OECD Reviews of Innovation Policy Series. Paris: OECD Publishing.

OECD (Organisation for Economic Co-operation and Development). 2016. "Enhancing Research Performance through Evaluation, Impact Assessment and Priority Setting." Report, Directorate for Science, Technology and Innovation, OECD, Paris.

Rasul, Imran, and Daniel Rogger. 2017. "Management of Bureaucrats and Public Service Delivery: Evidence from the Nigerian Civil Service." *Economic Journal* 128 (608): 413–46. doi:10.1111/ecoj.12418.

Siegel, Donald S., Reinhilde Veugelers, and Mike Wright. 2007. "Technology Transfer Offices and Commercialization of University Intellectual Property: Performance and Policy Implications." *Oxford Review of Economic Policy* 23 (4): 640–60.

Siegel, Donald S., David Waldman, and Albert Link. 2003. "Assessing the Impact of Organizational Practices on the Relative Productivity of University Technology Transfer Offices: An Exploratory Study." *Research Policy* 32 (1): 27–48.

Action for Innovation: A Policy Agenda | 6

Introduction

This report started by making the case for a change in the growth model for developing East Asia. The productivity growth slowdown, exacerbated by the numerous challenges ahead—ongoing trade tensions, rapid technological advances that threaten existing production methods and trade patterns, large economic shocks from the COVID-19 pandemic, and increasing climate change challenges—demand swift policy actions to accelerate innovation and the adoption of new technologies. Such actions are critical if the region's countries are to transition successfully to high-income status with rapid poverty reduction and increased shared prosperity.

Chapter 3 provided a diagnostic of some of the main bottlenecks limiting innovation in the region. It highlighted the need for more firms to adopt new technologies and engage in innovation, while those firms already undertaking innovation activities should focus on building their capacities to implement more sophisticated innovation projects and invent new technologies. Chapter 4 highlighted additional bottlenecks to innovation in the region, specifically the lack of adequate skills and finance, which are important complementary factors for innovation.

Chapter 5 argued that the region's policies and agencies are not well positioned to promote increased innovation and technological catch-up. The main factors that undermine the impact of policies on innovation include a mismatch between policy objectives, innovation capabilities, and resource allocation, as well as weak governance and institutional capacity among innovation agencies and public research organizations (PROs).

This final chapter discusses several sets of policy actions that can help policy makers address these three key bottlenecks—policies, complementary factors, and institutions—to facilitate technological catch-up and promote greater innovation-led growth in the region.

Addressing the innovation policy mismatch and building firms' capabilities

To spur innovation more effectively—both diffusion of existing technologies and invention at the frontier—and to better keep pace with the wave of new technologies, the region's policy makers must better align country policies, innovation capabilities, and resources. They must also work to build firms' capacities to innovate. But what does this look like in practice? How should policy makers deal with the substantial heterogeneity in firms' innovation capabilities?

Several sets of policy actions are critical to strengthening national innovation policies: (a) reorienting policy objectives in a graduated manner—guided by the capabilities escalator—to build innovation capabilities; (b) eliminating biases against diffusion and adoption relative to invention and against services sector innovation relative to manufacturing; and (c) choosing the most appropriate policy instruments to support countries' objectives.

Adjusting the innovation policy mix to enable diffusion and adoption

The capabilities escalator can guide innovation policy choices

Innovation policy requires clear objectives and sustained commitment. At the same time, the appropriate combination of policies, emphasizing specific instruments, is likely to change as innovation capabilities evolve.

Chapter 2 presented the idea of the "capabilities escalator" to help guide the choice of innovation policy instruments. As the chapter illustrated (in figure 2.8), different types of policies are required at different stages of development of countries' national innovation systems. An approximation of where the countries in the region are located with respect to innovation capabilities was presented in figure 2.7, which shows three clusters of countries that largely correspond to the capability levels shown in figure 2.8.

At the lower levels of innovation capability, where most countries in the region (except China) can be found, the emphasis should be on supporting more firms to initiate innovation projects and adopt new technologies. For firms that are already carrying out research and development (R&D), however, the emphasis should be on enabling them to perform more complex R&D projects, patenting, and invention. Thus, given the region's current innovation capabilities, one should expect more public resources to be allocated to policy instruments that encourage more-basic innovation activities—that is, to diffusion and adoption.

But which policy instruments can most effectively promote innovation in the region? The answer depends on the specific innovation-related objective as well as where countries, sectors, and firms are situated on the capabilities escalator. Cirera et al. (2020) provide a detailed description of the main policy instruments available to support innovation, the conditions needed for their successful implementation, and the existing evidence on impact. Table 6.1 summarizes some of the key innovation policy objectives (column 1), the minimum state of capabilities needed (column 2), the challenges firms face and the types of firms that should be targeted (column 3), and the policy instruments that can support each objective (column 4).

Objectives 1 and 2 in table 6.1—"build basic innovation capabilities" and "accelerate technology diffusion and adoption"—are critical to building the foundation for greater innovation, specifically adoption and diffusion. These objectives, and the related policy instruments, are broadly relevant in developing East Asia but are particularly important in countries that have relatively undeveloped ("incipient") national innovation systems (NISs) and where most firms do not engage in innovative activities and use outdated technologies. The main objectives in these contexts should be in building basic innovation capabilities and supporting more firms in undertaking more innovation activities, especially adopting new technologies. Although these objectives should be at the center of innovation policies in relatively low-capability, lower-middle-income countries such as Cambodia, the Lao People's Democratic Republic, and Myanmar, they continue to apply broadly to countries and firms across the region.

As countries' and firms' innovation capabilities increase, other objectives begin to take greater precedence. These include (a) taking advantage of the positive spillovers from collaborating with multinational enterprises (MNEs) and participating in global value

TABLE 6.1   The most appropriate mix of policy instruments to facilitate innovation and diffusion depends on countries', sectors', and firms' innovation capabilities

Innovation policy objective (1)	Minimum state of innovation capabilities (2)	Challenges firms face and types of firms to be targeted (3)	Key policy instruments to support innovation objective (4)
1. Build basic innovation capabilities	• Usually low- and lower-middle-income countries • Low production capabilities • Very low technological capabilities	• Low general innovation activity due to low capabilities; many firms not engaged in innovation or adoption • Most firms in all countries in the region • Firms operating in traditional manufacturing and services, nonexport sectors	• Business advisory services to improve managerial capabilities • Technology extension services to provide information and know-how for adopting new technologies • National quality infrastructure (NQI) services to support quality standards and upgrading • Cluster- or network-based policies to facilitate diffusion of technologies within sectors • Vouchers for innovation to incentivize collaboration between knowledge providers and institutions and firms
2. Accelerate technology diffusion and adoption	• Usually low- and lower-middle-income countries • Low production capabilities • Very low technological capabilities	• Use of old, outdated technology; very low technology adoption • Most firms in all countries in the region • Firms operating in traditional manufacturing and services, nonexport sectors	• Business advisory services to improve management processes and support organizational changes required to implement new technologies. • Technology extension services to provide information and know-how for adopting new technologies • Technology centers for sector-specific technical assistance and support in adapting existing technologies • Loans to purchase new equipment and finance technology adoption
3. Maximize spillovers from MNEs and GVCs	• Usually middle-income countries • Medium production capabilities • Low and medium technological capabilities	• Few technological and innovation spillovers from MNEs • Firms operating in · Export manufacturing and other sectors integrated into GVCs · Services sectors that provide services to GVCs	• Supplier development programs to build suppliers' capabilities to absorb technology and innovate • Open innovation programs[a] to find innovative solutions for MNEs and large firms • Science and technology parks to attract MNEs to establish R&D centers and collaborate with local universities and industry
4. Increase the number of innovative start-ups	• Usually middle-income countries • Medium production capabilities • Low and medium technological capabilities • Some research and technology transfer capabilities	• Few young innovative ventures • Potential for enterprise spin-offs from universities • Firms operating in the digital space and in services sectors	• Incubators to provide business advisory services for transforming innovative ideas into ventures • Accelerators to help initiate and scale up start-ups • Equity finance and angel investment

table continues next page

TABLE 6.1 The most appropriate mix of policy instruments to facilitate innovation and diffusion depends on countries', sectors', and firms' innovation capabilities *(continued)*

Innovation policy objective (1)	Minimum state of innovation capabilities (2)	Challenges firms face and types of firms to be targeted (3)	Key policy instruments to support innovation objective (4)
5. Strengthen collaboration for technology generation, transfer, and commercialization	• Usually middle-income countries • Medium production capabilities • Low and medium technological capabilities • Medium research and technology transfer capabilities	• Weak technology generation and commercialization • Potential for enterprise spin-offs from universities • Few effective technology transfer channels and limited collaboration between universities/PROs and industry • Firms operating in lead sectors and/or connected to GVCs	• Governance reforms at universities and PROs to incentivize collaboration with industry, technology generation, and commercialization • Technology transfer offices to enable transfer of new technologies from universities and PROs to industry • Technology centers to facilitate the diffusion of new technologies to industry and to provide links to PROs and universities • Technology extension services to support diffusion to industry • Collaboration grants to support university-industry collaboration
6. Increase quantity and quality of R&D investments	• Usually middle- and high-income countries • Medium and high production capabilities • Medium and high technological capabilities • Medium and high research and technology transfer capabilities	• Suboptimal investment in R&D • A mass of medium and large firms conducting R&D in different sectors, including technology sectors • A base of technological start-ups	• Tax incentives for R&D projects • Grants for individual and collaborative R&D projects between firms and between firms and knowledge providers • Loans to purchase R&D equipment and finance technology adoption • Science and technology parks to attract MNEs to establish R&D centers and collaborate with local universities and industry
7. Support frontier innovation via high-risk and complex R&D projects	• Usually high-income countries • Medium and high production capabilities • Medium and high technological capabilities • Medium and high research and technology transfer capabilities	• High-risk, long-term R&D and technological projects taking place • High R&D capabilities and strong collaborative projects R&D • Large and leading firms	• Tax incentives for R&D projects • Long-term grants for R&D projects and collaboration to perform joint and complex R&D projects • Long-term finance for innovation projects • Precommercial innovation procurement[b]

Source: World Bank elaboration, adapted from Cirera et al. 2020.

Note: GVC = global value chain; MNE = multinational enterprise; PRO = public research organization; R&D = research and development.

a. In open innovation programs, firms typically identify problems in their production and management processes and search for solutions, often working with other firms, universities, and knowledge providers. For further details, see Cirera et al. (2020).

b. Precommercial innovation procurement refers to support to firms' innovation through the purchase of R&D services that include the delivery of a "product prototype" or some innovation project before it is commercialized. For further details, see Cirera et al. (2020).

chains (GVCs) (table 6.1, objective 3); and (b) expanding the base of innovative start-ups in the country (table 6.1, objective 4). Strengthening the foundations for technology generation, transfer, and commercialization—by promoting greater collaboration between research entities and industry—also becomes a priority as countries move up the capabilities escalator (table 6.1, objective 5). Promoting the generation and effective transfer of new technologies requires more advanced techno-logical capabilities, as are generally found in upper-middle-income countries such as China and Malaysia.

While countries often strive to do more and better R&D (table 6.1, objective 6), effective R&D projects require that countries and firms have adequate capabilities to carry out such initiatives. These capabilities tend to be more common in more-developed economies and, within them, among larger firms and firms in more technology-intensive sectors. Finally, suc-cessfully supporting frontier innovation proj-ects (invention) through high-risk and complex R&D projects (table 6.1, objective 7) requires high innovation capabilities (along with sig-nificant coordination between research enti-ties, universities, and firms) that are difficult to find in countries with less-mature NISs. China is an exception in the region—with a number of firms already engaged in frontier R&D—as are Malaysia and Thailand, to a lesser extent.

Building on the policy objectives, innova-tion challenges, and policy instruments out-lined in table 6.1 as well as the concept of the capabilities escalator illustrated in chapter 2 (figure 2.8), table 6.2 illustrates a set of policy priorities for the countries in developing East Asia. Country priorities shown in the table reflect the analysis in this report along with other World Bank country studies on innova-tion (Garcia et al. 2020 [on the Philippines]; Kuriakose and Tiew 2020 [on Malaysia]; World Bank 2020 [on Vietnam]; World Bank and DRC 2019 [on China]). The darker cells indicate higher levels of priority considering countries' and firms' innovation capabilities.

A few aspects of the table are noteworthy: First, although countries in the region have different levels of innovation capabilities, it is still important for all of them to focus on

encouraging non-innovating firms to innovate by building basic innovation capabilities (policy objective 1) and on accelerating technology adoption and diffusion (policy objective 2). As discussed throughout this report, most firms in the region are not innovating and continue to use old or outdated technologies.

Second, most countries in the region should also focus on realizing positive spill-overs from MNE investments and GVC participation (policy objective 3). Especially for countries with relatively low to moder-ate innovation capabilities, scarce public resources in these countries are better spent on adoption of existing technologies embod-ied in foreign direct investment (FDI) and par-ticipation in GVCs than on efforts to generate cutting-edge technologies directly.

Third, as countries' innovation capabilities increase, they will benefit from progressively adjusting their policy focus to include support to innovative start-ups (policy objective 4); improving collaboration between research entities and industry to increase technology generation, transfer, and commercializa-tion (policy objective 5); strengthening of domestic R&D (policy objective 6); and, ulti-mately, pursuing complex and high-risk R&D projects at the frontier (policy objective 7).

Countries should adjust their policy priorities as they develop their innovation capabilities

Climbing the capabilities escalator is a dynamic process and hence requires adjustment of inno-vation policy priorities over time. This can be seen in the experience of highly innovative countries in the region, such as the Republic of Korea and Singapore, that have periodically updated their policy mixes to achieve conver-gence with the technological frontier.

Table 6.3 summarizes Korea's innovation policy journey since the 1960s. While the journey reflects the country's specific charac-teristics—for example, the presence of large business conglomerates ("chaebols")—it has also two important lessons for develop-ing East Asia: First, the country has pursued a consistent and overarching objective of developing technological capabilities over the entire period. Second, Korea has regularly

TABLE 6.2 Developing East Asian countries have varying innovation policy priorities, based on the capabilities escalator

Innovation policy objective	Lao PDR	Myanmar	Cambodia	Indonesia	Philippines	Mongolia	Vietnam	Thailand	Malaysia	China
1. Build basic innovation capabilities										
2. Accelerate technology diffusion and encourage adoption										
3. Maximize spillovers from MNEs and GVCs										
4. Increase the number of innovative start-ups										
5. Strengthen collaboration for technology generation, transfer, and commercialization										
6. Increase quantity and quality of R&D investments										
7. Support frontier innovation via high-risk, complex R&D projects										

Source: Original table for this publication.

Note: Darker cells denote higher policy priorities. The order of the countries presented in this table reflects their location on the capabilities escalator as shown in chapter 2, figure 2.8 (ranging from lower capabilities on the left to higher capabilities on the right). GVCs = global value chains; MNEs = multinational enterprises; R&D = research and development.

TABLE 6.3   Republic of Korea's innovation policies continually evolved to reflect its accumulation of capabilities

Policy aspect	Innovation capabilities, objectives, and priorities
1960s–1970s: An incipient national innovation system (NIS)	
Innovation capacity and enabling conditions	In the early 1960s, Korea was largely a closed agrarian economy with limited natural resources, a small domestic market, and cheap labor.
	Firms: Low awareness and lack of technological literacy and managerial capabilities to assimilate foreign technologies or conduct R&D
	Markets and institutions: Low export orientation, FDI intensity, and associated knowledge flow; state-owned commercial banks that provided policy loans; weak intellectual property rights (IPR) framework
	Research: Newly established PROs and low R&D capacity in universities; incipient innovation infrastructure with low availability of laboratories and testing facilities
	Skills: Basic STEM education and postsecondary technical programs
Policy objectives	• Build institutions and human resources to strengthen the country's science and technology (S&T) capabilities
	• Develop domestic technologies as well as adopt, absorb, and assimilate imported technologies
	• Promote the growth of heavy and chemical industries led by large firms (chaebols) to increase exports and promote import substitution
Policy mix	• Management extension programs
	• Grants and loans for business innovation and productivity improvements in strategic industries
	• Loan guarantees and accompanying TA
	• Tax incentives for technology adoption and R&D
	• Technology licensing
	• Standards and basic NQI infrastructure
	• Export promotion policies
	• Shared R&D facilities within industrial parks and cooperatives
	• Specialized PROs in strategic industries
	• Expanded domestic STEM education, overseas training scholarships, and repatriation of experts
1980s: A maturing NIS	
Innovation capacity and enabling conditions	By the 1980s, the economy had grown rapidly, led by chaebols in strategic industries and supported by interventionist policies.
	Firms: Links to GVCs and export markets; growing investment in in-house R&D (surpassing the government's R&D expenditure); improvements in large firms' product standards
	Markets and institutions: Increasing export orientation and FDI intensity, leading to some knowledge spillovers; expanded access to finance from rapidly growing nonbanking financial institutions owned by chaebols; improved IPR framework
	Research: Emerging clusters of applied research in PROs and universities; strong links and collaboration with strategic industries but not with other sectors; availability of competitive scientific research funding
	Skills: Increased availability of STEM-skilled workers

table continues next page

TABLE 6.3 **Republic of Korea's innovation policies continually evolved to reflect its accumulation of capabilities** *(continued)*

Policy aspect	Innovation capabilities, objectives, and priorities
Policy objectives	• Obtain and supply advanced technologies and improve productivity of industries to secure competitiveness internationally
	• Enhance productivity, managerial capabilities, and technological literacy of SMEs
	• Strengthen R&D capacity of large firms and SMEs
	• Promote research cooperation among PROs, industry, and academia
Changes in policy mix	• Reduced policy loans for chaebols in strategic industries
	• Expanded and/or adjusted innovation policy instruments to better target SMEs and start-ups (such as tax incentives, grants, matching grants, loans, loan guarantees, business advisory services, and technology extension programs)
	• Accelerated import and FDI liberalization policies to introduce foreign competition and pressure domestic firms to enhance productivity
	• Public procurement for innovation (during commercial stages)[a]
	• Restructured PROs and competitively distributed R&D grants

1990s: A mature NIS

Innovation capacity and enabling conditions	With increasing globalization, Korea deregulated and opened its economy during the 1990s. *Firms:* Significant R&D activities at three to four times the level of government R&D expenditure; focus on increased competencies, especially for SMEs *Markets and institutions:* High export orientation, FDI intensity, and knowledge spillover; strong consumer protection mechanisms in place *Research:* Improved research quality in academia; modern R&D infrastructure; well-developed quality and standards infrastructure *Skills:* Readily available STEM- and other high-skilled workers
Policy objectives	• Catch up with high-income economies by developing high-tech industries
	• Shift government policies to support basic research and R&D activities in long-term projects and emerging technologies
Changes in policy mix	• National R&D projects targeting long-term public R&D needs
	• Creation of centers of excellence
	• Government funding to establish and operate corporate-affiliated research institutes
	• Deepening of export and investment promotion, including through promotion of outward FDI for firms seeking improved market access abroad

2000s–2010s: A mature NIS

Innovation capacity and enabling conditions	Korea pursued a knowledge-based economy and equitable growth, recognizing availability of advanced technologies as well as rising income disparities. *Firms:* Enhanced R&D capacity across firm size; emerging innovation clusters and increased collaboration in innovation projects across firms *Markets and institutions:* Increased access to early-stage finance; improvements needed in IPRs and developing standards for advanced technology companies *Research:* Weak links and cooperation among PROs, industry, academia, and international research institutes and firms *Skills:* Creativity and socioemotional skills desired among STEM- and other high-skilled workers
Policy objectives	• Transition from catch-up model to generation of domestic technological innovation through development of basic and original technologies
	• Expand support for SMEs, promote entrepreneurship, and create good-quality jobs

table continues next page

TABLE 6.3   Republic of Korea's innovation policies continually evolved to reflect its accumulation of capabilities *(continued)*

Policy aspect	Innovation capabilities, objectives, and priorities
Changes in policy mix	Increased focus on
	• Targeted support for firms with high growth potential, such as technology-extensive firms, start-ups, and medium-size enterprises
	• Government-backed venture capital (VC) to provide equity finance and early-stage capital
	• Business incubators and accelerators
	• Precommercial public procurement of R&D
	• Clusters and networking for R&D cooperation
	• Open innovation

Source: Frias, Lee, and Shin 2020.
Note: FDI = foreign direct investment; GVC = global value chain; IPRs = intellectual property rights; NIS = national innovation system; NQI = national quality infrastructure; PROs = public research organizations; R&D = research and development; S&T = science and technology; Skills = skills and human resources; SMEs = small and medium enterprises; STEM = science, technology, engineering, and mathematics; TA = technical assistance; VC = venture capital.
a. Public procurement for innovation involves support to innovation through the purchase of R&D services and innovative products that have already reached the commercialization stage. For further details, see Cirera et al. (2020).

revised its policies as its innovation and technological capabilities evolved. It updated its policy priorities to reflect changing challenges—from focusing on the building of basic innovation capabilities in the 1960s and 1970s; to maximizing links to GVCs, FDI, and entry into export markets in the 1980s; to a significant focus on R&D and patenting in the 2000s; and to technological leadership in some sectors in the 2000s.

These policy choices have paid off, as Korea has converged to the technological frontier in many sectors. Significant technological catch-up—proxied by patents and R&D spending—is observed from 1990, which is then consolidated in the 2000s (figure 6.1). Investment in R&D, especially in the private sector, accelerated in the early 1990s (figure 6.1, panel a) and then again in the 2000s, at which point Korea, like Israel, became one of the most R&D-intensive countries in the world. A similar picture is seen with patents (figure 6.1, panel b), which accelerated in 1995 and then converged with the intensity of the United States in the 2000s, as Korea surpassed the Organisation for Economic Co-operation and Development (OECD) average.

In developing East Asia, however, there is a mismatch between overarching policy objectives and capabilities. As highlighted in chapter 5, this is especially the case in

the allocation of public resources, which do not align well with the need to support greater adoption and diffusion among firms in Indonesia, the Philippines, and Vietnam. Although all three countries have set a de jure objective of promoting innovation and developing new technologies, the de facto reality—expressed through resource allocation and the implementation of policy instruments—does not match some of the key objectives (1 to 4) discussed in table 6.1. For example, none of these countries has well-developed management and technology extension services that can assist firms in adopting new technologies. Moreover, PROs are performing their role poorly—often more focused on bringing their own-developed technologies to industry than on addressing firms' specific technology needs.[1]

A more careful but long-term commitment to fostering innovation and technology adoption is needed in the region, one that provides services to build the needed innovation capabilities and, as discussed in chapter 2, to create a business environment for innovation.

Eliminating policy biases against innovation in services

The analysis in previous chapters showed that although services are becoming increasingly important in the wave of new technologies, a

FIGURE 6.1 **Republic of Korea's policy choices have enabled significant technological catch-up**

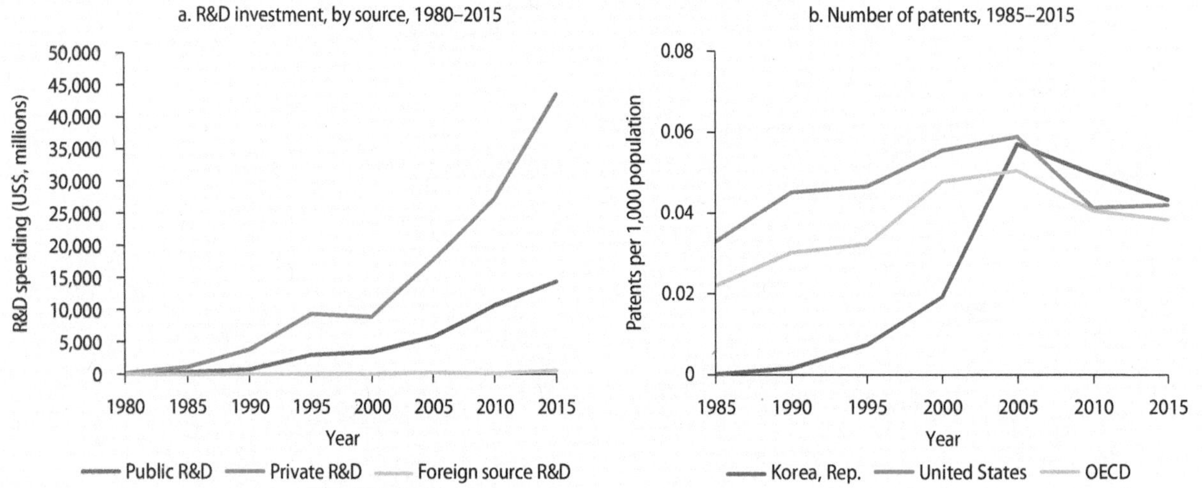

a. R&D investment, by source, 1980–2015

b. Number of patents, 1985–2015

Public R&D — Private R&D — Foreign source R&D

Korea, Rep. — United States — OECD

Source: Organisation for Economic Co-operation and Development (OECD) Innovation and Technology database (https://data.oecd.org/innovation-and-technology.htm).
Note: R&D = research and development.

strong bias persists against services in innovation policy support. Traditionally, innovation and technology development have been seen as primarily processes driven by the manufacturing and agriculture sectors. Networks of PROs performing R&D activities have been set up throughout the region as well as globally in narrowly defined areas of manufacturing and agriculture. The reality, however, is that innovation in services is increasingly important for competitiveness in manufacturing and for the strengthening of GVCs as well as for services themselves, which employ the largest share of people in all the countries.

For example, international business transactions depend on transport, logistics, and communication networks. Innovations in these services are thus key to facilitating integration of local firms into global networks. Moreover, improvements in digital infrastructure and digital networks and platforms are enabling the proliferation of innovative services firms. Yet innovation policy is still not focusing enough on promoting innovation in services.

Eliminating this bias requires actions on two fronts: First, it is important to reach out to services and retail firms with more traditional innovation policy instruments (for example, matching grants) that can finance

the implementation of innovation projects such as the digitization of management and delivery processes or the introduction of new services. Second, it is necessary to expand the scope of innovation activities that are financed to include activities such as design—a significant component of R&D (Cox 1990) in manufacturing but also in services—and to strengthen firms' digital capabilities.

Services sectors are extremely diverse, and innovation takes different forms across services subsectors. For example, digital and artificial intelligence (AI) elements are more important in routine services, whereas design, business models, and delivery are more important in knowledge-intensive services (Salter and Tether 2006). Recognizing these differences and designing policies that are aligned with different capabilities and needs will be critical to enabling innovation in this increasingly important sector of the economy.

Choosing the right policy instruments to accelerate technology adoption and diffusion

To support the choice of appropriate policy instruments to accelerate technology adoption and diffusion, this section provides a brief overview of five policy areas that are critical for countries in the region: (a) enabling technology adoption and diffusion; (b) maximizing spillovers from MNE and trade; (c) developing appropriate intellectual property (IP) policies; (d) strengthening the enabling environment by increasing market competition; and (e) building the infrastructure for innovation and technology adoption.

Enabling technology adoption and diffusion

A range of instruments can promote adoption and diffusion (left side of figure 6.2) as well as the generation, commercialization, and transfer of technology (right side of figure 6.2). Several instruments focus more directly on equipping firms with the capabilities to use technologies (technology adoption

and transfer), and others focus more on firms' capability to generate technologies, as follows (Cirera et al. 2020):

- *Business advisory services* focus on building firms' absorptive capacity for technology adoption.
- *Technology extension services* focus on helping small and medium enterprises (SMEs) adopt technologies and develop related capabilities. These policy instruments are critical to supporting the diffusion of technologies among firms.
- *Technology centers* support both the adoption and the generation of new technologies.
- *Technology transfer offices* support the generation and commercialization of technologies developed at universities and PROs. In some cases, these offices also

FIGURE 6.2 **A range of policy instruments can be used to promote technology adoption, diffusion, and invention**

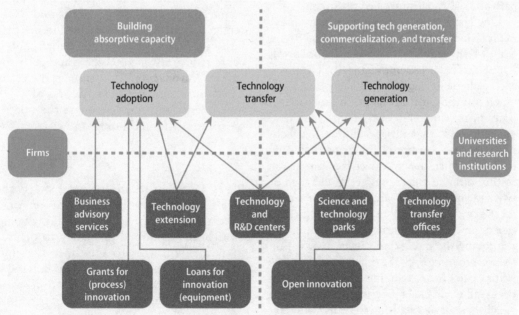

Source: Cirera et al. 2020. ©World Bank. Further permission required for reuse.
Note: The vertical dotted line separates the policy instruments supporting the demand (from firms) and supply (by universities and research institutions) of technologies and knowledge. Green boxes designate overarching objectives of technology policy, while the yellow boxes represent the three aspects of technology that the policy instruments (in dark blue boxes) support. R&D = research and development.

support researchers and entrepreneurs in addressing knowledge gaps in the commercialization process.

Other instruments that can facilitate adoption and diffusion include science and technology (S&T) parks and government support for innovation finance. In some cases, S&T parks can attract technology-intensive firms with the objective of generating spillovers with local universities and industries. As for government-supported finance, external finance for equipment can greatly facilitate the purchase of technology, especially in places where there are significant financial market inefficiencies.

A critical element of the model shown in figure 6.2 is the set of complementarities across different policy instruments. The effective transfer of technologies requires that firms have enough absorptive capacity to adopt new technologies. Similarly, the ability to discover and transfer new technologies depends on the capacity of some firms to implement complex R&D projects as well as on the quality and incentives in universities to perform high-quality applied research.

One challenge in the region is a frequent expectation that the transfer of technologies from MNEs and PROs to domestic firms will happen more or less automatically. However, such technology transfer is unlikely to happen when insufficient instruments are in place to build firms' capabilities. Another widespread expectation is that PROs will develop technologies that are useful for firms or industries even when the incentives facing research institutions and enterprises are not aligned or when the quality of research is not sufficient to meet firms' technology needs. Building capabilities among private firms, on one hand, and improving the quality and incentives within the research sector, on the other, must therefore be priorities for developing East Asian countries—all while facilitating invention among a small share of more-advanced firms with their own research capabilities.

Maximizing spillovers from MNEs and trade
FDI and trade have been critical channels for the region's growth and development.

However, it is unclear whether countries in developing East Asia have been able to maximize the absorption of technology and capabilities from MNEs and GVCs. The evidence indicates that technology and knowledge have not diffused widely across sectors and firms—suggesting that FDI and trade still remain large untapped sources of technological capabilities in the region. An important barrier to capturing the positive spillovers associated with MNEs and GVCs is local firms' continued lack of capacity to adopt new technologies and knowledge.

Most countries in the region have opted for "soft" or "friendly" policies to support the transfer of technologies from FDI and GVCs. These have focused primarily on incentives to MNEs to establish R&D centers and, more generally, to attract companies to locate in host countries through tax incentives and establishment of S&T parks. Some countries may also be tempted to adopt more-stringent forced technology transfer (FTT) measures, as China has done.[2] But the reality of developing East Asia is that countries are competing for the location of MNEs and R&D centers, and this competition could increase further if rapid technological change continues to reduce low labor cost advantages in the region.[3] Introducing FTT measures, therefore, could undermine the attractiveness of MNE investments and thus eliminate the related opportunities for technology transfer.

Developing appropriate intellectual property policies
A key factor in technology transfer is the intellectual property (IP) framework. Historically, however, patent frameworks have been developed primarily to protect inventors and not to facilitate technology transfer (although, clearly, having a functional IP system can facilitate transfer through FDI and trade). A recent literature review finds that FDI and trade are both positively correlated with the strength of intellectual property rights (IPR) enforcement (Hall 2014). Less clear is the impact of a strong IP system on domestic innovation (Branstetter 2004).

An older literature, which examined the successful cases of Japan and Korea, suggested that weak IP protection supported the accumulation of technological capabilities as countries pursued technological catch-up (Kim 2003; Kumar 2003). This is also reflected in the so-called "patent puzzle": the lack of correlation between patent activity and productivity (Boldrin and Levine 2013). Indeed, a recent review of innovation policies concludes that the impact of IP policies on technology generation in high-income economies is unclear (Bloom, Van Reenen, and Williams 2019).

In short, patents and the IP framework appear to be of relatively low importance for inducing invention in middle-income countries (Hall 2020), including in developing East Asian countries. An IP framework that facilitates FDI and complies with the World Trade Organization (WTO) Agreement on Trade-Related Aspects of Intellectual Property Rights (TRIPS Agreement) is needed for any hope of some transfer of technology (Branstetter, Fisman, and Foley 2006). To be effective, however, this framework needs to be implemented jointly with the complementary technology transfer policies discussed above.

Strengthening the enabling environment by increasing market competition

Market competition is a key driver of innovation. Firms are driven to be more efficient and productive and to offer new and improved products and services to customers in more open and competitive markets. Thus, there is a role for competition policies to encourage innovation. In some developing East Asia countries, this implies that the state should move away from engaging directly in productive activities via state-owned enterprises (SOEs) and focus on playing a more market-supportive role. A study by Brahmbhatt and Hu (2010) shows a strong negative association between state ownership and innovation. The study also finds a positive association between innovation and the extent of competition faced by firms. FDI, as well as domestic competition, may enhance productivity in the rest of the economy by increasing firms'

efficiency or through spillovers of technology and expertise.

Evidence from OECD countries on the relationship between market competition and innovation paints a more nuanced picture, however. Aghion et al. (2005) observe, for example, that greater product market competition between incumbent firms could have different effects that both discourage and promote innovation. Their study finds strong evidence of an "inverted-U curve" in multi-industry panel data for UK firms. In industries where competition is low and firms have similar technological capability, more competition may promote innovation by giving the innovating firm a competitive advantage—although in industries where there is already high product market competition and one firm has a large technological lead over others, greater competition may discourage innovation among lagging firms. A study using firm-level data from Chile finds a positive relationship between markups and innovation in lagging firms, although this relationship is not significant in more-advanced firms (Cusolito, Garcia-Marin, and Maloney 2018). The authors find, moreover, that the precise relationship between competition and innovation depends on the sector and type of firm.

On balance, the literature suggests that greater market competition can help enable innovation, especially in cases where competition is low to start with. Increasing competition could be particularly beneficial for the services sector in developing East Asia, where market restrictions are greater than in OECD countries (Constantinescu, Mattoo, and Ruta 2018). Without competitive pressure, firms have little incentive to innovate. Reducing restrictions in the services sector would help to promote greater competition and growth of services.

More importantly, opening up the services sector to both foreign and domestic private investment would also facilitate the "servicification" of manufacturing (that is, the integration of services and manufacturing), which is currently lower in developing East Asia than in higher-income countries. In doing so, opening up the services sector would also serve to strengthen countries' manufacturing competitiveness.

Building the infrastructure for innovation and technology adoption

A final important element is the need to develop adequate infrastructure to enable innovation. This includes infrastructure to support universal digitization (for example, through broadly available, affordable fixed and mobile broadband) as well as infrastructure to ensure quality standards, such as a national quality infrastructure (NQI) for metrology and testing. Although countries in the region have made progress in building both digital and quality infrastructure, further investments are needed. If digital infrastructure is poor, achieving universal digitization will not be possible; similarly, if firms lack access to testing labs and quality certification, quality upgrading will be impeded.

Strengthening key complementary factors: Skills and finance

The ability of firms to innovate depends on multiple factors that often fall outside the realm of innovation policy, strictly defined. These factors include the availability of a sufficiently skilled workforce and adequate financing to support firms'—often risky— innovation activities. This section focuses on policy approaches to help build these complementary factors to promote greater innovation, whether defined as diffusion and technology adoption or as invention.

Developing skills for innovation

Policy makers in much of the region face a dual challenge of strengthening basic learning outcomes and fostering advanced skills to support innovation

Evidence from the region and from high-income economies highlights the importance of advanced cognitive, socio-emotional, and technical skills in enabling innovation (as discussed in chapter 4). Such advanced skills become increasingly important as firms move from diffusion and technology adoption toward the technological frontier. However, most education systems in the region still face important challenges in generating adequate learning outcomes, even at the basic education level. The region's policy makers thus face a *dual challenge* of providing the necessary foundational skills to their populations while also developing the types of advanced workforce skills needed to enable innovation-led growth.

Successfully building skills for innovation will require action on several fronts, including strengthening basic educational quality; updating national curricula to increase focus on such innovation skills as creative problem solving and socioemotional skills; enhancing the quality and relevance of technical training and tertiary education; and increasing opportunities for continuous skills upgrading among adult workers.

Building foundational skills will require improvements in basic education

For most countries in the region, building the advanced skills needed to enable innovation-led growth will require sustained efforts to strengthen people's foundational skills. Building those skills will require raising education quality, starting at the basic level.

The experience of high-performing education systems in East Asia (for example, in Japan, Korea, and Singapore) and beyond suggests that building stronger foundational skills requires that school systems (a) strengthen the conditions for learning, including availability of educational materials; (b) improve teacher preparation and the quality of teaching; (c) ensure adequate public spending for basic education; (d) increase children's readiness to learn, including through early childhood education and development services; and (e) undertake regular learning assessments to diagnose challenges and inform improvements (World Bank 2018).

Development of advanced cognitive and socioemotional skills needs to start early

Recent studies on skills formation emphasize that building strong cognitive and socioemotional skills is best begun early (Arias, Evans, and Santos 2019; Cunningham and Villaseñor 2016). Efforts to build such skills are still underdeveloped in much of the region, however. Even where developing East Asian countries have recognized the importance of better cultivating critical thinking, creativity, problem solving, and the ability to work effectively in teams, there remains a need to institutionalize the development of advanced cognitive and socioemotional skills into standard school curricula and extracurricular programs.

Several high-income innovators in the region—Japan, Korea, and Singapore—have already done this, revising their curricula to include emphasis on higher-order cognitive and socioemotional skills development. These adaptations to school curricula are part of a broader set of cross-cutting measures in these countries to foster innovation skills among their workforces (table 6.4).

Developing advanced technical skills for innovation will require addressing both access and quality issues

Developing increasingly advanced technical skills in the labor force is also a critical part of strengthening workers' skills for innovation. This is exemplified by the importance that highly innovative firms in the region assign to hiring employees with science, technology, engineering, and mathematics (STEM) education (chapter 4). Technical skills are often sector or discipline specific, and require knowledge of specific tools or processes. And the focus on technical skills development typically begins later, around the secondary school level.

Given the region's significant heterogeneity in firm capabilities and technology adoption, the needs for technical skills across firms are also quite diverse. For firms focused on diffusion and adoption of existing technologies, basic digital literacy and the capacity to use general purpose technologies and existing software applications may be sufficient. As firms move toward the technical frontier, however, more sophisticated technical skills are required.

TABLE 6.4   **Japan, Republic of Korea, and Singapore have integrated innovation skills into their curricula**

Country	Strategies for building innovation skills
Japan	• Revision of national curriculum to focus on active learning strategies to strengthen problem solving, creativity, and critical thinking and to strengthen motivation to learn • Provision of online learning opportunities for tertiary education (for example, Cyber University, accredited by the Ministry of Education, Culture, Sports, Science and Technology) • Provision of technical and vocational education and training (TVET) through TVET institutions, upper secondary schools, and higher education institutions
Korea, Rep.	• Revision of national curriculum to focus on higher-order cognitive skills (such as information processing skills and creative thinking) • Creation of a mid- and long-term Master Plan for Vocational Education to address Industry 4.0-related challenges • Establishment of employment-oriented high schools and the Meister Vocational High School Program • Provision of online learning opportunities for tertiary education (for example, Open Cyber University, authorized by the Ministry of Education) and vocational training (for example, the Online Lifelong Education Institute, funded by the Korean Ministry of Employment and Labor)
Singapore	• Shift from traditional focus on academic performance to emphasis on socioemotional skills through "positive education" model • Provision of TVET through polytechnic schools offering work immersions (often incentivizing on-the-job training in small and medium enterprises) • Establishment of an independent training authority, the Institute of Technical Education, with close links to industry and a recognized certification system

Sources: Kataoka and Alejo 2019, drawing from Banerji et al. 2010; Moore and Kearsley 2012; OECD 2018; World Bank 2015; and Yian and Park 2017.

In developing the technical skills needed for innovation, most countries in the region still face challenges related to both educational access and quality. Tertiary enrollment rates are relatively low in much of the region (chapter 4, figure 4.8), and the quality of technical education remains highly variable among tertiary institutions. Efforts to broaden access to and raise the quality of TVET and tertiary education will thus be increasingly important as countries seek to build the technical skills necessary to innovate and as firms seek to move progressively toward the technical frontier.

Japan, Korea, and Singapore have all been working to strengthen their TVET systems as part of their strategies to build innovation skills (as summarized in table 6.3). In Japan, TVET is provided by upper secondary and higher education institutions as well as TVET institutions, and it commonly includes both on-the-job and off-the-job training conducted within private enterprises (World Bank 2015). In Korea, the government has developed a Master Plan for Vocational Education to address lifelong learning challenges arising from Industry 4.0. The plan emphasizes skills like creativity, problem solving, and learning agility that are essential in the 21st-century workplace (Chung 2019). Korea has also established the Meister Vocational High School Program, which offers training in specialized skills needed by local industries, with curricula developed in collaboration with industry partners (Yian and Park 2017). And in Singapore, polytechnic schools offer a variety of courses as well as "work attachments" with firms to equip learners with practical skills (Yian and Park 2017). To support TVET's role in lifelong learning, independent training authorities have been established with close links to the private sector (Banerji et al. 2010).

Lifelong learning systems will be important to build innovation skills in the current workforce
To strengthen firms' abilities to innovate, it is also important to regularly upgrade the skills of the current workforce, especially in the face of rapid technological change. To do so, the region's policy makers should focus on developing continuous skills development—or lifelong learning—systems for adult workers.

TVET can play an important role as part of countries' broader skills development and lifelong learning strategies. To be effective, however, programs should be designed and implemented in close coordination with the private sector, including via partnerships in which leaders from private sector firms help design the curricula as well as deliver training. Indeed, studies show that returns to TVET and related trainings are higher when they are demand driven and well adapted to labor market needs (Kluve 2016).

Several recent studies also show that on-the-job training can contribute to greater firm-level innovation activity (ADB 2020; Iootty 2019; Miyamoto and Sarzosa 2020). Although on-the-job training appears to be relatively rare among firms in the region, there may be scope for governments to incentivize training as a way to build greater skills innovation. One promising approach to incentivizing skills development can be seen in Singapore, where the government has created the SkillsFuture Council to promote lifelong learning. Under this initiative, Singaporeans aged 25 and above receive an opening SkillsFuture Credit of US$500 that they can use to take training courses. The credit does not expire, is periodically topped up by the government, and can be accumulated over time.

Strengthening finance for innovation

Financing firm innovation requires that countries have vibrant, well-diversified financial markets that offer a broad range of financial instruments to enterprises
As discussed in chapter 4, both access to external finance and to a suitable range of financial instruments are important to enable the financing of firm innovation. However, most developing East Asian countries still rely heavily on the banking system for external finance. In addition, in countries with relatively

well-developed financial markets, such as China and Malaysia, it appears to be mostly large firms that have benefited from the deepening of domestic capital markets (Abraham, Cortina, and Schmukler 2019).

To ensure that their financial sectors can better support innovation, the region's countries will need to implement policies in three important areas: developing a well-functioning capital market; promoting venture capital (VC) markets; and improving and broadening the range of available financial instruments through the banking sector.

Well-developed capital markets provide firms with access to a diverse set of financial instruments, eventually increasing the quantity and quality of firm innovation
The development of deep capital markets is paramount to offering alternative sources of external capital to innovative firms at different stages of a firm's life cycle. Some countries in the region have already made progress in this area by introducing capital market reforms targeted to increasing the investor base; improving financial market infrastructure (for example, introducing a capital market data warehouse system); and enhancing investor protections (Abraham, Cortina, and Schmukler 2019). Nonetheless, access to these markets is still mostly available to relatively large firms. In many countries, financial markets still lack the necessary depth to cover the financial needs of a wide range of firms. Continued efforts to develop and deepen countries' financial markets are thus necessary.

Financial policies can enable firm innovation by promoting VC funding
There are three broad and complementary dimensions for the development of successful VC markets: (a) *enhancing the VC supply* by enabling domestic investment and attracting foreign capital; (b) *stimulating demand* by building an active entrepreneurial and innovative ecosystem; and (c) *supporting all market players* by strengthening the institutional and regulatory framework (Owen and Mason 2019). Whether the development of these conditions happens simultaneously, or occurs

in gradual steps, will depend on the level of development of a country's financial sector.

Deep private markets require the creation of an ecosystem of investors (both private and public) and of fledgling businesses with viable projects (Lerner 2010). Stimulating cooperation between industry and universities helps to build a more robust stream of innovative ideas that attract private investors. Moreover, it is important to attract experienced international fund managers, as seen in the development of the VC market in Israel (box 6.1). In East Asia, Singapore has fostered innovation by encouraging research and entrepreneurial activity in universities, courting global venture capital funds to establish connections, and welcoming foreign entrepreneurs. Entrepreneurial efforts have also been rewarded and recognized through national competitions and awards. China's multipronged policy approach has also been successful in spurring development of the country's VC market (box 6.1).

The success of private capital market development depends heavily on policy design. Governments can play an important role by investing directly or by participating in public-private partnerships. Successful examples of cooperation between the public and private sectors are the Yozma program in Israel (which, among other things, established limited partnership companies with a 40 percent investment from the government)[4] and the Small Business Innovation Research (SBIR) program in the United States, which involves partnership between SMEs and nonprofit research institutions (Audretsch, Link, and Scott 2019). There are less successful examples, however, such as Canada's creation in the 1980s of labor-sponsored venture capital corporations (LSVCCs) to invest primarily in SMEs; in later decades, public funding crowded out private investment (Cumming and MacIntosh 2006).

A successful design is one in which public support empowers private investors in channeling resources to innovative ventures. Hence, a hybrid model where governments play the role of arm's-length investor, while allowing private fund managers to make

BOX 6.1   Innovation financing done right: Lessons from Israel and China

Israel's phased approach to building VC foundations

Israel has fostered venture capital (VC) funding over time. The background conditions phase (1970–89) and the preemergence phase (1989–92) demonstrate the importance of developing solid underlying structures that can support and facilitate the later stages.

During the background conditions phase, Israel tried to shift research and design (R&D) from the military sector toward the academic and business sectors. To achieve this goal, it relied heavily on links with American experts and researchers who had the most experience with the development of private capital markets to finance high-tech projects. The government undertook policies to ensure stabilization and liberalization of capital markets. To attract foreign investment, policies were put in place allowing full repatriation of earnings from financial investments. These policies created rife opportunities for innovation projects, generating demand for capital and a sprawling pipeline of projects for the nascent VC industry to invest in.

During the preemergence phase, policy was more directly aimed at the creation of a VC market to address financing and management failures. The first formal attempt, a government-backed insurance company for publicly traded funds called Inbal, was mired by bureaucracy and micromanagement, however, and was not successful.

The emergence phase (1993–2000) saw the introduction of Yozma, a government program that combined several important aspects of a successful VC market design. It served as a fund of funds—that is, it provided funds to VC firms, which in turn provided financing to domestic firms with a technological base. Program funds had to be matched by the entrepreneur, and local VC firms had to attract and pair with a foreign investor. Interactions with foreign capital investors were important sources of learning and expertise while also serving as a check on the performance of local VCs. The program was a great success: VC firms raised about US$10 billion in total capital, the number of foreign investment banks increased from 1 to 26, and the firms backed by VC funds totaled more than 2,000. Moreover, the program led to the growth of the VC market beyond its scope, as it attracted many follow-on funds that were not funded by the program itself.

China's three-dimensional approach to VC market development

China's gradual, three-dimensional approach exemplifies a successful VC market development policy from developing East Asia (Lin 2017). The government introduced policy reforms to attract capital, established a new investment vehicle (the limited partnership), and fostered entrepreneurship. In terms of capital, China has introduced market liberalization reforms that have allowed more institutional investors to enter the VC market. The government has also taken a market approach to public funding, implementing matching programs between government and private funds. And recognizing the importance of foreign capital and knowledge, it has introduced capital liberalization and foreign-investor-friendly business environment reforms.

On the fiscal side, China provided tax exemptions for limited partnerships and tax deductions to firms operating in science parks and incubators. Regarding financial markets, the government has invested in the development of stock markets (NEQ and Chinext) and lowered listing requirements to allow VC-backed firms to exit successfully. To build a strong ecosystem of VCs and innovative firms, it has introduced reforms to streamline business operations.

China's approach has been clearly policy led and is a good example of the balance that the government needs to strike—providing support but not overreaching its scope. Hence, there are lessons to be learned from its approach. In fact, other countries in developing East Asia are already introducing similar reforms. For example, Vietnam is introducing a company law reform to make business incorporation and operations easier (Lin 2017).

investment decisions, can be successful. This type of intervention need not be overly costly, because private investors provide a share of the funding. Government funds can identify and support market segments with financing gaps, while private sector participation ensures that funds are allocated to the most promising ventures. Regular impact evaluations and monitoring are important to making sure that programs are effectively and efficiently tackling the associated market failures.

Government interventions can leverage bank-firm relationships and enable firm innovation by targeting underserved or strategic segments

As noted earlier, bank loans remain the main source of external finance for innovative firms in the region. Governments can take advantage of this by channeling financing to innovative firms through the banking sector, thereby increasing availability and lowering the cost of risk financing. One benefit of this approach is that it can take advantage of existing bank-firm relationships.

An alternative to direct loans for innovation is credit guarantee schemes.[5] This instrument may be more efficient than direct subsidized loans because it makes use of existing lending products, allowing banks to select projects while maintaining the incentives to monitor borrowers' behavior. Loan guarantees also have less of an impact on government budgets because credit schemes are funded by the intermediaries. As with loans, however, guarantees should be targeted at credit-constrained firms in later innovation stages and should not be considered a substitute for private capital markets. Moreover, careful implementation is critical to ensuring that by providing guarantees, the government does not incentivize banks' moral hazard behavior or disincentivize rigorous screening and monitoring procedures (Cirera et al. 2020).

Reforming innovation institutions and agencies and building their capacity

As highlighted in chapter 5, innovation agencies and knowledge-creation institutions in the region experience important governance gaps and commonly lack incentives to perform their role in fostering firm-level innovation. Moreover, many of these institutions have large gaps in their capacity to design and implement innovation policies. It will therefore be important for countries to address critical governance challenges in these institutions and invest in their capacity to make policy if developing East Asian countries are to transition to more innovation-led growth models.

Investing in institutional capacity

To date, discussions of innovation and technology policies have commonly ignored the capacity of countries to effectively design and implement innovation policy, but this is critical for the effectiveness of interventions. Good project management also affects the quality of the outcomes. Nonetheless, several countries in developing East Asia still do not apply best practice in public management to innovation policy.

Some of the most significant shortcomings relate to the lack of an adequate economic justification, the absence of a logical framework to develop interventions, and a lack of monitoring and evaluation (M&E) mechanisms. Recall the example in chapter 5 of a program aiming at sectorwide productivity growth but supporting only a handful of firms with few resources. A clear logical framework would have helped policy makers see that the program was too small to achieve a meaningful impact. Weaknesses in the identification and selection of innovation policies are also often reinforced during their implementation. For most policy instruments analyzed for this report, no resources were allocated to evaluate whether programs' intended outcomes were achieved.

These capacity bottlenecks need to be addressed, and to do so it will be critical to invest in capacity for policy making. Agencies in the region need to recruit capable staff, as well as provide adequate training for staff working on innovation policy. In addition to on-site training in public management, it is important to ensure that managers have adequate digital infrastructure to perform necessary management tasks, such as monitoring beneficiaries and registering project outcomes.

Building more professionalized innovation agencies and increasing interagency coordination

Agencies supporting innovation policy in the region use outdated governance models and lack coordination across entities, which undermines policy alignment. Innovation policy, because of its cross-cutting nature, requires coordination among agencies or ministries. The current lack of coordination results in significantly fragmented efforts along with policies that are poorly designed and executed. Innovation agencies in the region need to (a) ensure better coordination across ministries and institutions responsible for innovation policy, and (b) adopt new agency models that enable recruitment of sufficient talent and professionalized services.

There are several models for coordination. Some coordination mechanisms have been elevated to prime ministers' offices to ensure mobilization of resources and actors. Other models have been integrated into or led by economics ministries that oversee all economic areas;[6] still others are located in education or science ministries. A weakness of the latter model is that education and science ministries tend to experience more difficulties in coordinating other ministries and agencies because they are less connected to the relevant budgetary processes. With this in mind, each country needs to assess which coordination model best fits its institutional realities. Even if carried out by ad hoc coordination working groups, effective coordination is a necessary condition for more integrated, focused, and effective innovation policy.

Increasing the private sector's contribution to innovation policy making

Innovation policy aims to foster innovation and the diffusion of technology mainly in the private sector. However, private sector stakeholders are severely underrepresented in the identification, design, governance, and monitoring of such policies in the region. This often results in a misalignment between policies and private sector needs, as shown in the earlier discussion of PROs (chapter 5).

Innovation support programs are often captured by a small number of firms—and often the same ones time and again. It is thus critical to have broad private sector representation in the formulation and implementation of innovation policies to avoid policy capture

by a small number of firms and to ensure the alignment of objectives and the use of efficient solutions. For example, private sector participation on boards of trustees of research institutions can help guide PROs toward greater industry collaboration. More importantly, some market failures in innovation are a function of coordination failures that can be addressed with broader mobilization of the private sector (rather than through more extensive use of public resources).

Strengthening the governance and incentive structures of PROs and research centers

The region's governments have been working to strengthen their national research capacity and have increased S&T investments in public research institutions to create new knowledge. The results of these efforts—and the impact of PROs on innovation—remain unclear, however.

As discussed in chapter 5, survey findings for three countries in the region (Indonesia, the Philippines, and Vietnam) suggest that PROs and university research departments have few links with industry (including knowledge links and human capital interactions). Moreover, technology transfer activities are still embryonic and are largely concentrated among a small number of research organizations. National research policies, despite being continuously updated, still follow a model of innovation that is heavily supply oriented. This is reflected in limited interaction with industry—in both governance and research activities—and in few technology transfer activities.

To maximize the contributions of these research institutions to innovation, governments must undertake reforms in four critical areas:

- *Improving governance conditions, public management practices, and strategic planning capacity* (in education, research, and technology transfer), including through measures to increase the autonomy of research institutions, disseminate good practices in research management, create clear legal mandates to support technology transfer, and strengthen the links between institutional funding policies and the performance of institutions

- *Improving academic incentives as engines of change* by increasing the recognition of technology transfer activities in the performance evaluation and career development of researchers, and by clarifying policy incentive frameworks and IPR regulations to strengthen researchers' engagement in technology transfer
- *Adopting mission-oriented policies though budget allocations* to address key societal challenges, such as those associated with COVID-19 and climate change
- *Strengthening the impact of public research* by (a) incentivizing PROs to provide technology extension and upgrading support services to firms (such as by offering piloting and testing services for new technologies); and (b) enhancing the links between PROs and universities or research centers to support new technology-based entrepreneurship, licensing of new technologies to SMEs, and start-up creation.

Final remarks

Over the past several decades, developing East Asia has achieved unprecedented growth that has lifted millions of people out of poverty and created unprecedented levels of economic security. Nevertheless, this report has argued that the region now faces an array of pressing challenges and that its extraordinary development performance is under threat if countries do not transform their growth model to place innovation at the forefront.

The impact of the COVID-19 pandemic has been severe, and as the region's policy makers turn their attention to recovery, there is an extraordinary opportunity to move forward with pending reforms to accelerate the process of technological catch-up and move toward a more innovation-led growth model. Taking advantage of this opportunity is not without precedent in the East Asia region; Japan, Korea, and later Singapore have become technological leaders over the past

40 years, and China is now achieving technological leadership in some sectors.

To accomplish this transformation, developing East Asian countries must update their objectives, giving greater priority to innovation policies; focus on technological diffusion; and incentivize more firms to innovate. This effort requires conducive regulatory frameworks but also the right policies—those aligned with the innovation capabilities of their private sectors. The COVID-19 pandemic has highlighted more than ever the urgency of achieving this transformation.

Notes

1. Although Vietnam is dedicating significant fiscal resources to facilitate R&D spillovers from MNEs, there is no evidence that such spillovers are being realized (World Bank 2017).
2. FTT policies aim to increase foreign-to-domestic technology transfer from FDI firms that tend to weaken appropriability of foreign innovations and related intellectual property (Prud'homme et al. 2018). Such policies are often implemented through requirements directed to investors and can include transfer of patented technologies to local companies or the forced location of R&D centers.
3. Prud'homme et al. (2018) analyze more formally the conditions required for effective technology transfer under FTT policies. They establish seven preconditions based on complementary policies along with monitoring and enforcement abilities that countries in developing East Asia are unlikely to possess.
4. For a detailed explanation of Israel's Yozma program, see Avnimelech, Schwartz, and Bar-El (2007).
5. An example of a successful credit guarantee scheme is the Korea Technology Finance Corporation (KOTEC), which provides guarantees for small and young firms in high-tech sectors. An impact evaluation study found that the program had been effective in increasing R&D investment for participants, especially for young high-tech firms (Heshmati 2013). Moreover, it led to higher sales and productivity.
6. The best-known case is the Israel Innovation Authority (formerly Office of the Chief Scientist in Israel), which is part of the Ministry of Economy.

References

Abraham, Facundo, Juan J. Cortina, and Sergio L. Schmukler. 2019. "The Rise of Domestic Capital Markets for Corporate Financing." Policy Research Working Paper 8844, World Bank, Washington, DC.

ADB (Asian Development Bank). 2020. *Asian Development Outlook 2020: What Drives Innovation in Asia?* Semiannual report, April 2020. Manila: ADB.

Aghion, Philippe, Nick Bloom, Richard Blundell, Rachel Griffith, and Peter Howitt. 2005. "Competition and Innovation: An Inverted-U Relationship." *Quarterly Journal of Economics* 120 (2): 701–28.

Arias, Omar, David K. Evans, and Indhira Santos. 2019. *The Skills Balancing Act in Sub-Saharan Africa: Investing in Skills for Productivity, Inclusivity, and Adaptability.* Africa Development Forum Series. Washington, DC: World Bank.

Audretsch, David B., Albert N. Link, and John T. Scott. 2019. "Public/Private Technology Partnerships: Evaluating SBIR-Supported Research." In *The Social Value of New Technology*, edited by Albert N. Link and John T. Scott, 264–78. Cheltenham, UK: Edward Elgar.

Avnimelech, Gil, Dafna Schwartz, and Raphael Bar-El. 2007. "Entrepreneurial High-Tech Cluster Development: Israel's Experience with Venture Capital and Technological Incubators." *European Planning Studies* 15 (9): 1181–98.

Banerji, Arup, Wendy Cunningham, Ariel Fiszbein, Elizabeth King, Harry Patrinos, David Robalino, and Jee-Peng Tan. 2010. "Stepping Up Skills for More Jobs and Higher Productivity." Report No. 55566, World Bank, Washington, DC.

Bloom, Nicholas, John Van Reenen, and Heidi Williams. 2019. "A Toolkit of Policies to Promote Innovation." *Journal of Economic Perspectives* 33 (3): 163–84.

Boldrin, Michele, and David K. Levine. 2013. "The Case against Patents." *Journal of Economic Perspectives* 27 (1): 3–22.

Brahmbhatt, Milan, and Albert Hu. 2010. "Ideas and Innovation in East Asia." *The World Bank Research Observer* 25 (2): 177–207.

Branstetter, Lee G. 2004. "Do Stronger Patents Induce More Local Innovation?" *Journal of International Economic Law* 7 (2): 359–70.

Branstetter, Lee G., Raymond Fisman, and C. Fritz Foley. 2006. "Do Stronger Intellectual Property Rights Increase International Technology Transfer? Empirical Evidence from U.S. Firm-Level Panel Data." *Quarterly Journal of Economics* 121 (1): 321–49.

Chung, Jisun. 2019. "Lifelong Learning and Skills Development: South Korea's Response to the 4th Industrial Revolution." Presentation at the World Bank Group Korea Office's webinar and brown bag lunch (BBL), "Bridging Skills Gap by Lifelong Learning, Advanced Technology and Skills," September 10. https://olc .worldbank.org/content/5-korea-office -bbl-bridging-skills-gap-lifelong-learning -advanced-technology-and-skills.

Cirera, Xavier, Jaime Frias, Justin Hill, and Yanchao Li. 2020. *A Practitioner's Guide to Innovation Policy: Instruments to Build Firm Capabilities and Accelerate Technological Catch-Up in Developing Countries.* Washington, DC: World Bank.

Constantinescu, Ileana Cristina, Aaditya Mattoo, and Michele Ruta. 2018. "Trade in Developing East Asia: How It Has Changed and Why It Matters." *East Asian Economic Review* 22 (4): 427–65.

Cox, Peter J. 1990. "Research and Development—or Research Design and Development?" *International Journal of Project Management* 8 (3): 144–50.

Cumming, Douglas J., and Jeffrey G. MacIntosh. 2006. "Crowding Out Private Equity: Canadian Evidence." *Journal of Business Venturing* 21 (5): 569–609. doi:10.1016/j .jbusvent.2005.06.002.

Cunningham, Wendy V., and Paula Villaseñor. 2016. "Employer Voices, Employer Demands, and Implications for Public Skills Development Policy Connecting the Labor and Education Sectors." *World Bank Research Observer* 31 (1): 102–34.

Cusolito, Ana Paula, Alvaro Garcia-Marin, and William F. Maloney. 2018. "Competition, Innovation and Within-Plant Productivity: Evidence from Chilean Plants." Background paper for *Productivity Revisited: Shifting Paradigms in Analysis and Policy.* Washington, DC: World Bank.

Frias, Jaime, Jin Lee, and Kyeyoung Shin. 2020. "Innovation Policy Learning from Korea: Lessons for Design and Execution of Innovation Policies in Emerging Economies." World Bank, Washington, DC.

Garcia, Andres F., Asya Akhlaque, Xavier Cirera, Jaime Frias, Cha Crisostomo, Anne Lopez, Kalyah Alaina Ford, Reinaluz Ona, and Yvette Camba, and 2019. "Philippines: Assessing the Effectiveness of MSME and Entrepreneurship Support". Report, World Bank, Washington, DC.

Hall, Bronwyn H. 2014. "Does Patent Protection Help or Hinder Technology Transfer?" In *Intellectual Property for Economic Development*, edited by Sanghoon Ahn, Bronwyn H. Hall, and Keun Lee, 11–32. Cheltenham, UK: Edward Elgar.

Hall, Bronwyn H. 2020. "Patents, Innovation, and Development." NBER Working Paper No. 27203, National Bureau of Economic Research, Cambridge, MA.

Heshmati, Almas. 2013. "The Effect of Credit Guarantees on R&D Investment of SMEs in Korea." Discussion Papers 7851, Institute of Labor Economics (IZA), Bonn.

Iootty, Mariana. 2019. "Assessing Innovation Patterns and Constraints in Developing East Asia: An Introductory Analysis." Policy Research Working Paper 8706, World Bank, Washington, DC.

Kataoka, Sachiko, and Ana Alejo. 2019. "Skills for Innovation." Background paper for this report, World Bank, Manila, Philippines.

Kim, Linsu. 2003. "Technology Transfer and Intellectual Property Rights: The Korean Experience." UNCTAD-ICTSD Issue Paper No. 2, International Centre for Trade and Sustainable Development, Geneva.

Kluve, Jochen. 2016. "A Review of the Effectiveness of Active Labour Market Programmes with a Focus on Latin America and the Caribbean." Working Paper No. 9, Research Department, International Labour Office, Geneva.

Kumar, Nagesh. 2003. "Intellectual Property Rights, Technology and Economic Development: Experiences of Asian Countries." *Economic and Political Weekly* 38 (3): 209–26.

Kuriakose, Smita, and Haris Tiew. 2020. "Assessing the Effectiveness of Public Research Institutions in Fostering Knowledge Linkages and Transferring Technology in Malaysia." Report, Malaysian Development Experience Series, World Bank, Washington, DC.

Lerner, Josh. 2010. "The Future of Public Efforts to Boost Entrepreneurship and Venture Capital." *Small Business Economics* 35 (3): 255–64. doi:10.1007/s11187-010-9298-z.

Lin, Lin. 2017. "Engineering a Venture Capital Market: Lessons from China." *Columbia Journal of Asian Law* 30 (1): 160–220. doi:10.2139/ssrn.2643311.

Miyamoto, Koji, and Miguel Sarzosa. 2020. "Workforce Skills and Firm Innovation: Evidence from an Employer-Employee Linked Survey Data in Vietnam." Unpublished manuscript. World Bank, Washington, DC.

Moore, Michael, and Greg Kearsley. 2012. *Distance Education: A Systems View of Online Learning*. 3rd ed. Belmont, CA: Wadsworth Cengage Learning.

OECD (Organisation for Economic Co-operation and Development). 2018. *Education Policy in Japan: Building Bridges Towards 2030*. Reviews of National Policies for Education, Paris: OECD. https://www.oecd.org/education/education-policy-in-japan-9789264302402-en.htm.

Owen, Robyn, and Colin Mason. 2019. "Emerging Trends in Government Venture Capital Policies in Smaller Peripheral Economies: Lessons from Finland, New Zealand, and Estonia." *Strategic Change* 28 (1): 83–93.

Prud'homme, Dan, Max von Zedtwitz, Joachim Jan Thraen, and Martin Bader. 2018. "'Forced Technology Transfer' Policies: Workings in China and Strategic Implications." *Technological Forecasting and Social Change* 134: 150–68.

Salter, Ammon J., and Bruce S. Tether. 2006. "Innovation in Services: Through the Looking Glass of Innovation Studies." Background paper for the Advanced Institute of Management (AIM) Grand Challenge on Service Science, April 7, Oxford University.

World Bank. 2015. "Japan—National Qualifications Framework Summary." Working paper, Report No. 120585, World Bank, Washington, DC.

World Bank. 2017. "Vietnam: Enhancing Enterprise Competitiveness and SME Linkages: Lessons from International and National Experience." Working paper, World Bank, Washington, DC.

World Bank. 2018. *Growing Smarter: Learning & Equitable Development in East Asia Pacific*. East Asia and Pacific Regional Reports. Washington, DC: World Bank.

World Bank. 2020. "Vietnam: Science, Technology and Innovation Report: Embracing Development Opportunities through Innovation and Technology Diffusion." World Bank, Washington, DC.

World Bank and DRC (Development Research Center of the State Council, The People's Republic of China). 2019. *Innovative China: New Drivers of Growth*. Washington, DC: World Bank.

Yian, Theresa Thang Tze, and Jonghwi Park. 2017. *Beyond Access: ICT-Enhanced Innovative Pedagogy in TVET in the Asia-Pacific*. Paris: United Nations Educational, Scientific and Cultural Organization (UNESCO) and UNESCO Bangkok Office.